Dirty Money

By

Ramesh S Arunachalam

Dedication

This book is dedicated to the
Citizens of the United States of America.

First published in USA, 2016 by: Shruthikka Media World

 Contact: shruthika438@gmail.com

Publishing Facilitation: AuthorsUpFront
Cover Design: Leena Swamy
Editing: Jyotirmoy Chaudhuri
Research and Analysis: SP Pandyan and SP Narayanan

Copyright Information

Ramesh S Arunachalam claims copyright only with the original writings, ideas, interpretation, and analysis done by the author, Ramesh S Arunachalam. No copyright is claimed with regard to any material that is quoted. Furthermore, much of the material that is quoted is taken from Congressional reports, orders of the Securities and Exchange Commission, Internal Revenue Service, Department of Justice, Courts and Statutory Enquiry Commissions, and so on. All of these, to the best of my understanding and interpretation of the law, are free of copyright protection. In fact, as per the website of the Office of the Law Revision Counsel United States Code[1] and the website of the United States Copyright office,[2] as per Section, 105. (Subject matter of copyright: United States Government works), copyright protection (under this title) is not available for any work of the United States Government.

---

[1]Office of the Law Revision Counsel United States Code, 17 USC: Subject Matter of Copyright: United States Government works, http://uscode.house.gov/view.xhtml?req=%28title:17%20section:105%20edition:prelim%29

[2] Copyright Law of the United States of America and Related Laws Contained in Title 17 of the *United States Code*, Section 105, Subject Matter of Copyright: United States Government works, http://www.copyright.gov/title17/92chap1.html#105

That said, every document that has been quoted has been thoroughly checked for copyright information and none of the documents from which quotes have been taken contain copyright notice either as a symbol © (the letter C in a circle), or the word "Copyright," or the abbreviation "Copr." There is no name of the owner, no abbreviation by which the name can be recognized, no generally known alternative designation of the owner, nor any indication of an owner of any copyright in these government works. Therefore, in the absence of the copyright notice and copyright owner information and as per Sections 105 and 403 of the Copyright Laws of the United States, it can only be inferred that these government reports, orders, releases etc. (representing work of the United States federal government), are not protected by copyright.

Likewise, the concerned websites have either stated that "information on State Department websites is in the public domain and may be copied and distributed without permission,"[3] or they have stated that "all of the content of the website constitutes a work of the United States federal government under sections 105[4] and 403[5] of title 17 of the U.S. Code,"[6] which again frees the information from copyright protection.

---

[3] U.S. Department of State, Copyright Information, http://www.state.gov/misc/87529.htm#copyright

[4] Subject Matter of Copyright: United States Government works, U.S Code 105.

[5] Copyright Law of the United States of America and Related Laws Contained in Title 17 of the *United States Code,* Section 403, Notice of copyright: Publications incorporating United States Government works, http://www.copyright.gov/title17/92chap4.html

[6] The Select Committee on Benghazi, Copyright, https://benghazi.house.gov/copyright.

Contents

Foreword

In *Dirty Money,* the author speaks little; he lets the facts, data, numbers, statistics, quotes from the Inquiry Commissions and extracts from official websites do the talking. And they speak clearly and loudly. With about one-third of the near 300-page book devoted to facts and figures, there is no place for skeptics to go into a "denial mode".

The book is like a developed X-Ray film—penetrating into the dark recesses of the U.S. political economic system, unseen by the normal human eyes. One need not be a radiologist to see the rottenness reaching up to the bones of the system. The book acts like a mirror held in front of the American presidential system, showing the real nature of the U.S. government: a government purported to be for *all* the people, but in practice being run by a *handful* of people and for a *handful* of people.

The book is not about corruption alone. It is about something much more serious. It is a chilling fact-finding narration of how an institutional wherewithal, which anchors stability of the U.S. economy in general and the financial sector in particular, is being undermined by a handful of people. If this institutional wherewithal, built painstakingly by well-intentioned, committed generations over decades, is expected to serve the *future* generations, then the onus lies on the *present* generation of adult citizens to be more vigilant. This book not only impresses upon the citizen-reader to be vigilant in this regard, but also cajoles them to act.

It is a wake-up call for all democracy-loving citizens, not from the U.S. alone, but from any democratic country, including India.

Prof. Sanjeev Chandorkar,
Tata Institute of Social Sciences,
Mumbai, India October 1, 2016.

Democracy and Campaign Finance: A Contextual Note

Vishakhapatnam
October 2, 2016.

Ramesh S Arunachalam's book, *Dirty Money: U.S. Presidential Elections 2016* provides a highly incisive critique of the evils of corporate financing of elections in the USA. What happens in the USA is of great relevance to the rest of the world, as the practices adopted in that country, whether good or bad, invariably influence the electoral systems elsewhere.

Abraham Lincoln, the 16th President of the USA, visualised a democratically elected government to be founded on the basic principle that "all men are created equal" and that it should represent a "government of the people, by the people, for the people". More than a century and a half later, one wonders whether his ideals are anywhere near being fulfilled!

In the guise of funding the ever increasing cost of election campaigning, the money power of individuals and corporate bodies seems to influence, like never before, government policies to the detriment of public interest.

Through a painstaking study of several prominent cases of corporate financing over the last three presidential campaign cycles in the USA, the author has credibly demonstrated how corporate funding of elections has often created a conflict of interest, once the candidate benefitting from it is elected to lead the government. The donors have often succeeded in influencing government policies to facilitate increasing laxity in regulation leading to greater tax avoidance and fraud; all at the expense of the American tax payer. The more disturbing aspect of this is that the cost burden of the scams arising from diluted regulation has ultimately hurt the national economy and the interests of the tax payer.

I hope that this insightful book will be read widely in the USA so that the people in that great democracy may appreciate how extravagance in election campaigning, necessitating dependence of political parties on corporate funding, can hurt their interests. The evil of corporate funding of elections has assumed global importance and all those interested in promoting the true spirit of democracy will, I hope, go through this excellent book and perceive the need to find alternate ways to conduct and fund election campaigning.

EAS Sarma (IAS, 1965 – 2000)
Former Secretary
(Ministries of Finance and Power)
Government of India

Dirty Money

Chapter 1

Introduction

If there is one issue that has dominated the U.S. presidential elections in 2016, it is the aspect of how the campaigns are financed.

In March 2016, Bernie Sanders—who is running[7] against Hillary Clinton for the Democratic presidential nomination—made a very strong statement against the campaign finance system.

The *Independent* reported in an article[8] that Sanders was critical about the $353,400-a-ticket fundraising dinner that was organized by the Hillary Clinton campaign, and featured George and Amal Clooney, going so far as to call it "corrupt and obscene."[9] According to the *Independent*, Bernie Sanders called

---

[7] Bernie Sanders endorsed Hillary Clinton prior to the Democratic Convention in Philadelphia (July 25-28, 2016).

[8] Matt Broomfield, Bernie Sanders says Hillary Clinton's $353,400-a-ticket fundraiser with George and Amal Clooney is "obscene", *Independent* (UK), March 28, 2016, http://www.independent.co.uk/news/world/americas/us-elections/bernie-sanders-hillary-clintons-353400-a-ticket-fundraiser-is-part-of-a-corrupt-obscene-system-a6956341.html

[9] In fact George Clooney agreed with the Sanders statement calling such fundraising "obscene," in a subsequent article: Reena Flores, George Clooney talks 'obscene' money in politics, *CBS News*, April 17, 2016, http://www.cbsnews.com/news/george-clooney-political-fundraisers-cost-an-obscene-amount-of-money/ and, Melissa Chan, George Clooney Admits Money He Raised for Hillary Clinton Is

out Hillary Clinton for seeking the help of big-money folks to finance her presidential campaign. The article also reports that Bernie recognized this as a problem in American politics when a corrupt finance system with "big money interests" had strong influence on the electoral and political processes.

While obscene may seem a harsh word, I would, however, like to state that the issue of campaign finance is an extremely critical one that needs close consideration, because it creates potentially huge possibilities for conflicts of interest. For example, while the short-term gain is the pleasure and prestige derived from being seen in such company, what would be the long-term expectations of someone willing to cough up a large sum of money (almost a third of a million dollars) to share a table with Hillary Clinton, and George and Amal Clooney?[10] The short-term gain, of course, being the pleasure and prestige derived from being seen in their company.

What do we mean by "conflict of interest" here? A conflict of interest is a conflict between the private interests and the duty, roles, and responsibilities of any official that could improperly and unfairly influence the performance of his/her official roles and responsibilities. Private interests would include financial, pecuniary and other interests that generate a direct personal benefit to the public official as well as personal affiliations, associations, and family ties, that could or would likely improperly and unfairly influence the official's performance of his/her roles, duties, and responsibilities.

Defined in this way, conflicts of interest include the potential to undermine the proper functioning of institutions (public, private, and not-for-profit), governments, and the like by:

"Obscene", *Time,* April 17, 2016, http://time.com/4297055/george-clooney-obscene-hillary-clinton/.

[10] I like George Clooney as an actor and hugely respect the kind of work he has done for the UN and the like. I also admire Amal Clooney's track record of wonderful human rights work.

a) Weakening adherence by officials to the ideals of impartiality, objectivity, fairness, and legitimacy in decision-making; and
b) Distorting the rule of law, the development and application of policy, the functioning of organizations and markets, as well as the allocation of resources.

Therefore, it is correct to assume that someone contributing significantly to the campaign funds of a presidential candidate could well expect to be granted special favors in the event of the said candidate assuming office as the President of the United States.

Please note that the operative word here is "could," which indicates a possibility, rather than a certainty, of a situation or event occurring that may give rise to a conflict of interest where there is a need to compromise power or position. I quote from the Final Report[11] of the Financial Crisis Inquiry Commission (FCIC), which talks about campaign funding, lobbying, and the 2008 financial crisis. This enlightening report drives home the above conflict of interest argument in a clear and decisive manner.

Talking about the mortgage finance companies Fannie Mae and Freddie Mac, the FCIC final report notes,

> Fannie and Freddie … reported spending more than $164 million on lobbying, and their employees and political action committees contributed $15 million to federal election campaigns. [12] (FCIC Report)[13]

---

[11] Financial Crisis Inquiry Report, Final Report Of The National Commission On The Causes Of The Financial And Economic Crisis In The United States, The Financial Crisis Inquiry Commission, 2011, http://fcic-static.law.stanford.edu/cdn_media/fcic-reports/fcic_final_report_full.pdf

[12] United States Senate, Senate Lobbying Disclosure Act Database, figures on employees and Political Action Committees compiled by the Center for Responsive Politics from Federal Elections Commission data, www.senate.gov/legislative/Public_Disclosure/LDA_reports.htm.

Take a look at the amounts that Fannie and Freddie spent on lobbying and the amounts contributed by their employees and political action committees (PACs) to the federal election process. They run into millions!

That is indeed sad because what Fannie Mae and Freddie Mac did was akin to cutting a big branch off the tree while sitting on that same branch. They had to fall and there was no other way out. Ironically, their political clout (acquired through lobbying and election support to candidates) meant that they resisted the very legislation that could have saved them.

Sadly, the "invisible hand" that was to regulate them remained invisible when something went wrong. Conflicts of interest in this case were indeed powerful.

The FCIC report further argues,

> In 1999, the financial sector spent $187 million lobbying at the federal level, and individuals and political action committees (PACs) in the sector donated $202 million to federal election campaigns in the 2000 election cycle. From 1999 through 2008, federal lobbying by the financial sector reached $2.7 billion; campaign donations from individuals and PACs topped $1 billion.[14]
>
> In November 1999, Congress passed and President Clinton signed the Gramm-Leach-Bliley Act (GLBA), which lifted most of the remaining Glass-Steagall-era restrictions. The new law embodied many of the measures Treasury had previously

---

[13] Financial Crisis Inquiry Report, The Financial Crisis Inquiry Commission, http://fcic-static.law.stanford.edu/cdn_media/fcic-reports/fcic_final_report_full.pdf

[14] FCIC Report (2011), Original Footnote 15: FCIC staff computations based on data from the Center for Responsive Politics. "Financial sector" here includes insurance companies, commercial banks, securities and investment firms, finance and credit companies, accountants, savings and loan institutions, credit unions, and mortgage bankers and brokers.

> advocated.[15] The *New York Times* reported that Citigroup CEO Sandy Weill hung in his office "a hunk of wood—at least 4 feet wide—etched with his portrait and the words 'The Shatterer of Glass-Steagall.'[16] (FCIC Report)[17]

Note the fact that the FCIC, which was the statutory commission inquiring into the 2008 financial crisis, strongly highlighted the fact that PACs and lobbying indeed played a huge role in the shattering of Glass-Steagall-era restrictions[18].

So how did the sorry saga end? This is what the FCIC report has to say:

> Now, as long as bank holding companies satisfied certain safety and soundness conditions, they could underwrite and sell banking, securities, and insurance products and services. Their securities affiliates were no longer bound by the Fed's 25% limit—their primary regulator, the SEC (Securities and Exchange Commission), set their only boundaries.

---

[15] FCIC Report (2011), Original Footnote 16: U.S. Department of the Treasury, *Modernizing the Financial System* (February 1991); Fed Chairman Alan Greenspan, "H.R. 10, the Financial Services Competitiveness Act of 1997," testimony before the House Committee on Banking and Financial Services, 105th Cong., 1st sess., May 22, 1997.

[16] FCIC Report (2011), Original Footnote 17: Katrina Brooker, Citi's Creator, Alone with His Regrets, *New York Times,* January 2, 2010, http://www.nytimes.com/2010/01/03/business/economy/03weill.html?_r=0

[17] Financial Crisis Inquiry Report, The Financial Crisis Inquiry Commission, http://fcic-static.law.stanford.edu/cdn_media/fcic-reports/fcic_final_report_full.pdf

[18] The **Glass–Steagall Act** has four provisions of the U.S. Banking Act of 1933 which restricted affiliations between banks and securities firms. Efforts to "repeal the Glass–Steagall Act" were numerous - they culminated in the 1999 Gramm–Leach–Bliley Act (GLBA), which repealed the two major provisions restricting affiliations between banks and securities firms. Many experts have openly stated that that the GLBA's repeal of the affiliation restrictions of the Glass–Steagall Act was a very important cause of the financial crisis of 2007–08.

> Supporters of the legislation argued that the new holding companies would be more profitable (due to economies of scale and scope), safer (through a broader diversification of risks), more useful to consumers (thanks to the convenience of one-stop shopping for financial services), and more competitive with large foreign banks, which already offered loans, securities, and insurance products.
>
> The legislation's opponents warned that allowing banks to combine with securities firms would promote excessive speculation and could trigger a crisis like the crash of 1929. John Reed, former co-CEO of Citigroup, acknowledged to the FCIC that, in hindsight, "the compartmentalization that was created by Glass-Steagall would be a positive factor," making less likely a "catastrophic failure" of the financial system.[19] (FCIC Report)[20]

Nevertheless, that was not to be as we saw in 2008 when the financial crisis exploded!

> The new regime encouraged growth and consolidation within and across banking, securities, and insurance. The bank-centered financial holding companies such as Citigroup, JP Morgan, and Bank of America could compete directly with the "big five" investment banks—Goldman Sachs, Morgan Stanley, Merrill Lynch, Lehman Brothers, and Bear Stearns—in securitization, stock and bond underwriting, loan syndication, and trading in over-the-counter (OTC) derivatives.
>
> The biggest bank holding companies became major players in investment banking. The strategies of the

[19] FCIC Report (2011), Original Footnote 18: John Reed, interview by FCIC, March 24, 2010.

[20] Financial Crisis Inquiry Report, The Financial Crisis Inquiry Commission, http://fcic-static.law.stanford.edu/cdn_media/fcic-reports/fcic_final_report_full.pdf

> largest commercial banks and their holding companies came to more closely resemble the strategies of investment banks. Each had advantages: commercial banks enjoyed greater access to insured deposits, and the investment banks enjoyed less regulation. Both prospered from the late 1990s until the outbreak of the financial crisis in 2007.
>
> However, Greenspan's "spare tire" that had helped make the system less vulnerable would be gone when the financial crisis emerged—all the wheels of the system would be spinning on the same axle. (FCIC Report)[21]

Sadly, we are still suffering from the impact of the 2008 financial crisis that affected the United States first and thereafter impacted several other countries globally. Moreover, as the FCIC report argues:

> The financial crisis in the United States was (primarily) caused by lax and laissez-faire regulation coupled with banning of regulation (through legislation) resulting from regular and continuous lobbying as well as huge contributions made by the financial sector to PACs including those of potential presidential candidates!

Read the quote from the FCIC report below:

> We conclude widespread failures in financial regulation and supervision proved devastating to the stability of the nation's financial markets. The sentries were not at their posts, in no small part due to the widely accepted faith in the self-correcting nature of the markets and the ability of financial institutions to effectively police themselves.
>
> More than 30 years of deregulation and reliance on self-regulation by financial institutions, championed by former Federal Reserve chairman Alan Greenspan and

---

[21] Financial Crisis Inquiry Report, The Financial Crisis Inquiry Commission, http://fcic-static.law.stanford.edu/cdn_media/fcic-reports/fcic_final_report_full.pdf

> others, supported by successive administrations and Congresses, and actively pushed by the powerful financial industry at every turn, had stripped away key safeguards, which could have helped avoid catastrophe.
>
> This approach had opened up gaps in oversight of critical areas with trillions of dollars at risk, such as the shadow banking system and over-the-counter derivatives markets. In addition, the government permitted financial firms to pick their preferred regulators in what became a race to the weakest supervisor. ...
>
> Changes in the regulatory system occurred in many instances as financial markets evolved. However, as the report will show, the financial industry itself played a key role in weakening regulatory constraints on institutions, markets, and products. It did not surprise the Commission that an industry of such wealth and power would exert pressure on policy makers and regulators.
>
> From 1999 to 2008, the financial sector expended $2.7 billion in reported federal lobbying expenses. Individuals and political action committees in the sector made more than $1 billion in campaign contributions. What troubled us was the extent to which the nation was deprived of the necessary strength and independence of the oversight necessary to safeguard financial stability. (FCIC Report)[22]

This is what happens when there is a campaign financing system ridden with conflicts of interest. As stated before, there is no free lunch.

If large business interests and/or people with vested interests contribute to the PACs and/or the campaign, they are bound to extract their pound of flesh.

---

[22] Financial Crisis Inquiry Report, The Financial Crisis Inquiry Commission, http://fcic-static.law.stanford.edu/cdn_media/fcic-reports/fcic_final_report_full.pdf

The same argument holds good when a couple pays close to a third of a million dollars to share a table with two celebrities and a potential presidential candidate, as part of the candidate's fund raising process.

Without any doubt, conflicts of interest are indeed being created by a campaign financing strategy that is fundamentally flawed and we all saw from the FCIC report[23] what happens when these conflicts of interest are at play.

Keeping all of this in mind, one has to perforce question the soundness of Hillary Clinton's fund raising strategy (in using George and Amal Clooney as mentioned earlier in this chapter). Candidates who desire to be perceived as "transparent candidates" by the American public should avoid using such fund raising strategies as these could eventually give rise to unnecessary conflicts of interest.

If there is one former president whose famous speech effectively sums up the present discourse in the 2016 U.S. presidential elections with regard to campaign financing, it is that of Abraham Lincoln, who notably said on November 19, 1863, at Gettysburg:

> Four score and seven years ago our fathers brought forth on this continent, a new nation, conceived in Liberty, and dedicated to the proposition that all men are created equal. ...
>
> Now we are engaged in a great civil war, testing whether that nation, or any nation so conceived and so dedicated, can long endure. ...

[23] As an illustration, I gave an example from the financial sector. Media, fossil fuel companies and other large corporations are no exceptions to the conflict of interest phenomenon.

> In a larger sense, we cannot dedicate—we cannot consecrate—we cannot hallow—this ground. The brave men, living and dead, who struggled here, have consecrated it, far above our poor power to add or detract. The world will little note, nor long remember what we say here, but it can never forget what they did here. ...that we here highly resolve that these dead shall not have died in vain—that this nation, under God, shall have a new birth of freedom—and that government of the people, by the people, for the people, shall not perish from the earth.
> *—Abraham Lincoln, November 19, 1863*[24]

Indeed, it is on the one fundamental principle in the above speech that the ethos of modern government and democracy lie—"a government of the people, by the people, for the people"—and one that works for the entire population, without any conflict of interest.

It is in the above context that election 2016 is a watershed in American electoral history and I quote Bernie Sanders, who noted (in this regard):

> In the year 2016, with a political campaign finance system that is corrupt and increasingly controlled by billionaires and special interests, I fear very much that, in fact, government of the people, by the people, and for the people is beginning to perish in the United States of America.[25]

[24] Abraham Lincoln Online, The Gettysburg Address, The Bliss Copy, http://www.abrahamlincolnonline.org/lincoln/speeches/gettysburg.htm
[25] Bernie 2016, Getting Big Money Out of Politics and Restoring Democracy, https://berniesanders.com/issues/money-in-politics/

Indeed, this statement, coupled with various happenings (such as the use of the George and Amal Clooney fund raising strategy by Hillary Clinton), prompted me to look closely at the Federal Election Commission (FEC)[26] and other data[27] to understand whether indeed the political financial system in America is corrupt as has been claimed by many people.

In short, I wanted to explore whether the "big wealthy money in politics" and the "corrupt finance system" arguments are true of the American political milieu today. I decided that the best way to do this would be to analyze the FEC and other data and investigate the backgrounds of those who were contributing to the candidates in three presidential campaign cycles–2016, 2012 and 2008.

And to facilitate this, I created a campaign finance paradigm, based on which the contributions received by a presidential candidate can be analyzed as to whether or not they are *'dirty money.'*

As conceived in this book, this campaign finance paradigm (**see Figure 1.1**) to analyze contributions received focuses on the following aspects:

- Donations by an individual to presidential candidates across three cycles–2016, 2012 and 2008
- Contributions by an individual to PACs supporting presidential candidates across three cycles–2016, 2012 and 2008
- Donations by an individual to foundations (not-for-profits) related to presidential candidates across three cycles–2016, 2012 and 2008

---

[26] Federal Election Commission, www.fec.gov

[27] This would include data from the Securities and Exchange Commission (SEC), Internal Revenue Service (IRS), Federal Bureau of Investigation (FBI), Department of Justice (DoJ) and other federal/state agencies such as the Financial Industry Regulatory Authority (FINRA).

- Contributions received by a presidential candidate and/or his spouse or close relative from an individual/companies through speaking and advisory assignments
- Direct and indirect contributions by an individual's family to presidential candidates across three cycles–2016, 2012 and 2008
- Direct and indirect contributions by an individual's company staff to presidential candidates across three cycles–2016, 2012 and 2008

Figure 1.1: Campaign Finance Paradigm

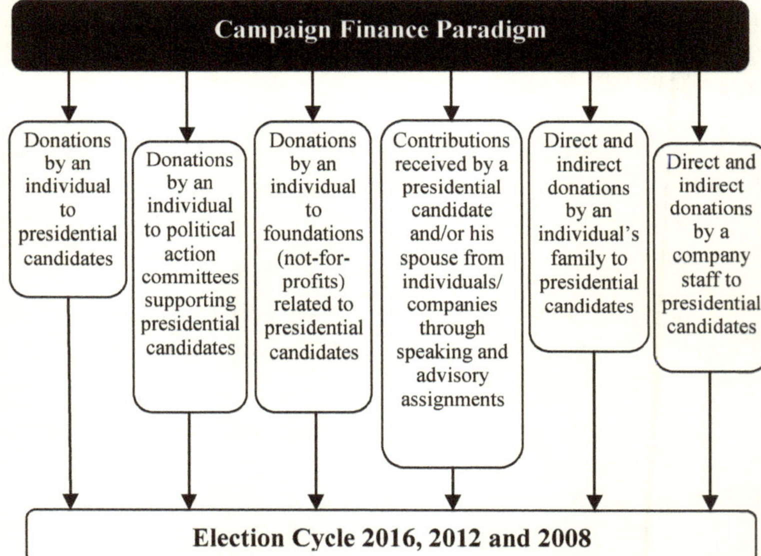

What follows are case studies of several wealthy, and large money billionaire contributors, to candidates in the presidential campaigns of 2016, 2012 and 2008, from Wall Street, the larger financial sector, energy related industries, media and entertainment and so on.

These case studies illustrate how these high profile donors have contributed *'dirty money'* to various presidential and down ballot candidates across the three election cycles– 2016, 2012 and 2008–in the United States of America (USA).

Chapter 2

Campaign Finance and Tax Evasion

Tax evasion has been a huge issue in the American presidential elections. And, indeed, it has become fashionable for candidates to tell their constituents that they would go after those who fail to pay their fair share of taxes in America, provided they are elected as president of the United States. Yet, as this chapter shows, there are many presidential candidates who have taken very large sums of money from people named in various tax-related scandals. **Is this not hypocritical?** Read for yourself to see the truth that the mainstream media has failed to highlight and sustain in the public eye.

What follows here after are four case studies of top donors to various presidential elections in three cycles (2016, 2012 and 2008), who together[28] contributed close to **$100 million** to various presidential candidates across these three election cycles. These case studies provide a microscopic view of these donors in terms of whom they contributed to and how much and what they actually did with regard to tax evasion.

Accepting such *'dirty money'* has become part of America's polity and that is why the campaign finance system is in need of urgent reform. And as long as such *'dirty money'* is part of the

[28] This amount represents the contributions made individually by these top donors. If you include their contributions to the foundations of the presidential candidates, speaking and other assignments and also contributions of their family and staff members (from their various entities), the total contribution will be much larger.

election process, there is no way that President Lincoln's long cherished dream of a '*government by the people, for the people and of the people*' can be realized.

The Case of Renaissance Technologies (RenTec), James Harris Simons and Robert Mercer

The first case that we explore is that of Renaissance Technologies (RenTec), which is named as *thirteenth* in the list of the top hedge funds[29].

RenTec was founded by James Harris Simons, a well-known American mathematician, hedge fund manager, and philanthropist. He served as CEO of this New York-based hedge fund until 2009. Since then, Simons continues to serve RenTec in his capacity as Chairman. James H Simons is also President of Euclidean Capital, supposedly a "family office." Such organizations that handle the financial wealth and affairs of a single family are not required[30] to disclose any details to the U.S. Securities and Exchange Commission (SEC).[31]

While the net worth of James H. Simons stands at about $15.5 billion, according to the Bloomberg Billionaires Index[32], the *Forbes* reported that Simons was *second* in their list of the highest earning hedge fund managers in 2015.[33] RenTec as a company uses the controversial 'Algorithmic Trading'—High Frequency Trading (HFT) approach in its business operation. For

[29] Top Hedge Funds, *Octa Finance*, http://www.octafinance.com/hedge-funds/top-hedge-funds/

[30] Margaret Collins, 'Private Investment Firms Win the Right to Keep Money in the Family', *Bloomberg*, February 10, 2015, http://www.bloomberg.com/news/articles/2015-02-10/meryl-streep-money-stays-with-simon-family-as-sec-grants-in-laws

[31] *Tiger 21*, https://tiger21.com/presenter-bio/1735

[32] Bloomberg Billionaires, *Bloomberg*, http://www.bloomberg.com/billionaires/2016-05-03/cya

[33] Highest Earning Hedge Fund Managers 2016, *Forbes*, http://www.forbes.com/pictures/ghmf45lkdh/2-james-simons#40fafcb32140

those who may have forgotten 'Algorithmic Trading', or 'HFT', the flash crash[34] of May 6, 2010 is one instance that should serve to refresh the memory.

This apart, another interesting fact needs to be highlighted with regard to RenTec. Employees and executives of RenTec supposedly made nearly $13.8 million in campaign contributions over the last three cycles, more than any other high frequency trading company.[35] As per this report, RenTec reportedly contributed $692,300 during the 2008 cycle and nearly $11.8 million during the 2012 cycle, a 1,600 percent increase.

Without a doubt, given the above information, James Harris Simons, his colleagues, affiliates and companies are worthy of closer examination, with regard to whom they have supported in terms of providing campaign finance over the last three presidential cycles in the United States (2008, 2012 and 2016). **Appendix 2.1** provides a summary of the same with regard to James H Simons, his colleagues, affiliates, companies—who together contributed over **$50 million** as contributions to PACs supporting presidential candidates[36] including Hillary Clinton, President Obama (when he was running for the office of the President of the United States on both occasions) Ted Cruz, Donald Trump[37] and others.

---

[34] Wikipedia, '2010 Flash Crash', https://en.wikipedia.org/wiki/2010_Flash_Crash

[35] http://crew.3cdn.net/c1fd518f249f3eef58_8wm6bhouy.pdf

[36] See appendix 1 for a description of candidates across cycles.

[37] See: Nicholas Confessore, 'How One Family's Deep Pockets Helped Reshape Donald Trump's Campaign', *The New York Times,* August 18, 2016, http://www.nytimes.com/2016/08/19/us/politics/robert-mercer-donald-trump-donor.html?hpw&rref=politics&action=click&pgtype=Homepage&module=well-region®ion=bottom-well&WT.nav=bottom-well&_r=0 and, Theodore Schleifer, 'Yet Another Donald Trump super PAC launches, this one with a link to Ted Cruz', *CNN Politics,* June 23, 2016, http://edition.cnn.com/2016/06/23/politics/donald-trump-super-pac-fundraising/

An immediate fact that is discernible from the data is that his Co-CEO, Robert Mercer, has been a big time donor for the Republican campaigns—he has contributed significantly to PACs supporting Mitt Romney, Ted Cruz, Donald Trump and others as noted above. In fact, if you take the total contributions of all RenTec staff to Democrats and Republican presidential candidates over the last three cycles, it is more than a whopping **$50 million**[38]. And if you search the Senate lobbying database it shows that Renaissance Technologies (RenTec) lobbied the Federal Government in the United States at least 80 times during the same time.

Overall, it seems like a fantastic strategy for a Wall Street giant like RenTec! While James Simons gave liberally to PACs supporting Hillary Clinton ($7 million) and President Obama ($5 million), Robert Mercer, his Co-CEO, at the same time, donated very significant amounts to the campaigns of Ted Cruz ($13.5 million) Mitt Romney ($3 million) and Donald Trump.[39]

Thus, both the major parties—in the beltway—were fully covered.

Given this background, where it has been proved that a Wall Street giant like RenTec has made deep inroads through its contributions to the Democratic and Republican Parties, and has also lobbied the federal government eighty times, I was

---

[38] We could not get much data with the 2008 election cycle.

[39] Ted Cruz's – *"Keep The Promise I"* PAC - converted to a *"Make America Number I"* PAC and started working for Donald Trump. The Robert Mercer family is said to be heavily involved in this PAC also as was the case with the Ted Cruz PAC. See: Schleifer, 'Yet Another Donald Trump super PAC launches', *CNN Politics*, June 23, 2016, http://edition.cnn.com/2016/06/23/politics/donald-trump-super-pac-fundraising/
and, Confessore, 'How One Family's Deep Pockets Helped Reshape Donald Trump's Campaign', *The New York Times,* August 18, 2016, http://www.nytimes.com/2016/08/19/us/politics/robert-mercer-donald-trump-donor.html?hpw&rref=politics&action=click&pgtype=Homepage&module=well-region®ion=bottom-well&WT.nav=bottom-well&_r=0

fascinated to read a U.S. Senate report that referred extensively to RenTec.

This very interesting and high profile report on RenTec[40]—a company founded by James Simons and of which he is still the chair and in which Robert Mercer is the Co-CEO—included significant comments on the practices within the company with regard to long and short-term capital gains and avoidance of taxes.

The report that I am referring to is called, "Abuse of Structured Financial Products: Misusing Basket Options to Avoid Taxes and Leverage Limits,"[41] by United States Senate PERMANENT SUBCOMMITTEE ON INVESTIGATIONS (JULY 22, 2014). What follows is an excerpt from the above report[42] of the U.S. Senate Permanent Subcommittee on Investigations on Renaissance Technologies LLC (RenTec):

> For the last decade, the U.S. Senate Permanent Subcommittee on Investigations has presented case histories showing how financial institutions, law firms, accountants, and others have designed and implemented complex financial structures to take advantage of and, at times, abuse or violate U.S. tax statutes, securities regulations, and accounting rules.[43]

---

[40] Pam Martins, 'Senate: Renaissance Hedge Fund Avoided $6 Billion in Taxes in Bogus Scheme With Banks', *Wall Street On Parade,* July 22, 2014, http://wallstreetonparade.com/2014/07/senate-renaissance-hedge-fund-avoided-6-billion-in-taxes-in-bogus-scheme-with-banks/

[41] Report: Abuse Of Structured Financial Products: Misusing Basket Options to Avoid Taxes and Leverage Limits, *Homeland Security and Governmental Affairs, Permanent Subcommittee on Investigations,* July 22, 2014, http://www.hsgac.senate.gov/subcommittees/investigations/hearings/abuse-of-structured-financial-products_misusing-basket-options-to-avoid-taxes-and-leverage-limits

[42] Ibid.

[43] Abuse of Structured Financial Products Report (Basket Options) (2014), Original Footnote 1: See, e.g., U.S. Senate Permanent Subcommittee on Investigations reports and hearings, "Fishtail,

The final phrase is the key, stating the attempt by various stakeholders (including companies) to "*abuse or violate U.S. tax statutes, securities regulations, and accounting rules*" and needs to be carefully noted.

All of us would agree that abusing and/or violating U.S. tax statutes is <u>not</u> a desirable matter and should <u>not</u> be encouraged and/or supported by anyone, least of all candidates aspiring for political office. That people competing for (possibly) the highest office on the planet—i.e., the President of the United States—are willing to compromise and accept campaign funds from those who abuse/violate U.S. tax laws/statues certainly does <u>not</u> represent an acceptable state of affairs. And it goes without saying that it is about time that campaign finance reform is undertaken in full earnest to remove such *'dirty money'* out of American Politics.

That said, let us get back to the Senate report, which further notes:

> This investigation offers yet another detailed case study of how two financial institutions—Deutsche Bank AG and Barclays Bank PLC—developed structured financial products called MAPS and COLT, two types of basket options, and sold them to one or more hedge funds, including <u>Renaissance Technologies LLC</u> (RenTec) and George Weiss Associates, that <u>used</u> them to avoid federal taxes and leverage limits on buying securities with borrowed funds.

Bacchus, Sundance, and Slapshot: Four Enron Transactions Funded and Facilitated by U.S. Financial Institutions," S. Prt. 107-82 (1/2/2003); "U.S. Tax Shelter Industry: The Role of Accountants, Lawyers, and Financial Professionals," S. Hrg. 108-473 (11/18 and 20/2003); "Tax Haven Abuses: The Enablers, The Tools and Secrecy," S. Hrg 109-797 (8/1/2006); "Repatriating Offshore Funds: 2004 Tax Windfall for Select Multinationals," S. Prt. 112-27 (10/11/2011); "Offshore Profit Shifting and the U.S. Tax Code – Part 1 (Microsoft and Hewlett-Packard)," S. Hrg. 112-781 (9/20/2012); and "Offshore Profit Shifting and the U.S. Tax Code - Part 2 (Apple Inc.)," S. Hrg. 113-90 (5/13/2013).

> While that type of option product was identified as abusive in a public memorandum by the Internal Revenue Service (IRS) in 2010, taxes have yet to be collected on many of the basket option transactions and its use to circumvent federal leverage limits has yet to be analyzed or halted.[44]

The point to be clearly emphasized here is that the Senate report talks of RenTec using the 'basket option strategy' to evade not only taxes but also overcome leverage limits on buying securities with borrowed funds. In both cases, it is clear that RenTec used the 'basket option strategy' to defeat the prevailing laws/statutes.

And let us not forget that for most of this period, the CEO of RenTec was its founder, James Harris Simons and top management of RenTec also included Robert Mercer, who is now the Co-CEO. And both of these gentlemen are leading donors to several presidential candidates—across three election cycles (2016, 2012 and 2008).

As the U.S. Senate report further observes:

> The basket option contracts examined by the Subcommittee investigation were used by at least 13 hedge funds to conduct over $100 billion in securities trades, most of which were short-term transactions and some of which lasted only seconds.[45]

The most interesting observation from the Senate report is the fact that most of the transactions were short-term transactions and some lasted a mere few seconds. By default, it means that any profits resulting from these are short-term and should

---

[44] Report: Abuse Of Structured Financial Products: Misusing Basket Options to Avoid Taxes and Leverage Limits, *Homeland Security and Government Affairs,* July 22, 2014, http://www.hsgac.senate.gov/subcommittees/investigations/hearings/abuse-of-structured-financial-products_misusing-basket-options-to-avoid-taxes-and-leverage-limits

[45] Ibid.

therefore not be treated as long term capital gain. That is crystal clear to anyone, including the lay person.

But that is not how things panned out as the Senate report further notes:

> Yet the resulting short-term profits were frequently cast as long-term capital gains subject to a 20% tax rate (previously 15%) rather than the ordinary income tax rate (currently as high as 39%) that would otherwise apply to investors in hedge funds engaged in daily trading. ... specific data supplied by the banks with respect to RenTec, the largest basket option user, suggests that the basket options may have been used to treat short-term capital gains as long-term capital gains, resulting in estimated tax avoidance of more than $6 billion. ...
>
> Over a fourteen-year period from 1999 to 2013, one hedge fund, Renaissance Technologies LLC, held 60 basket option contracts... [and] ...used them to carry out an investment strategy utilizing hundreds of millions of trades, virtually all of which lasted less than 12 months, and characterized the vast majority of the resulting $34 billion in trading profits as long-term capital gains.[46]

The math is very simple. RenTec used the basket option strategy to overcome federal leverage limits and conduct a series of trades. **$34 billion** was the profit from most of these transactions that were short term in nature (<12 months). Some transactions lasted just a few seconds. Technically speaking, **$34 billion** profit was short term and ought to have been taxed at the then prevailing ordinary tax rate (39%)—which makes the taxes payable as $13.26 billion. RenTec, however, claimed these as long term capital gains where were taxed at a reduced tax rate of 20%—taxes paid were a mere $6.8 billion. The difference between the actual taxes payable ($13.26 billion) and taxes paid ($6.8 billion) is a whopping $6.46 billion, which is tax avoided by RenTec.

---

[46] Ibid.

This certainly needs serious consideration as this action perhaps caused a huge loss to the United States (tax) exchequer by RenTec. And as is clear from the above, Renaissance Technologies LLC (RenTec) is one of the major hedge funds named in the U.S. Senate report, for having avoided taxes to the tune of $6.46 billion.

Two questions arise here:

a) Was it right on the part of RenTec to treat profits arising from trades that lasted <12 months (some trades lasted just few seconds) as long term capital gains?
b) Were there any characteristics in these trades that facilitated them to be distinguished from RenTec's regular trading activity?

The answer to both of the above is an emphatic no and in fact, the aforementioned Senate report unequivocally argues and settles the debate as follows:

> While the banks styled the trading arrangement as an "option" under which profits from short-term trades would be treated as long-term capital gains, in essence, the banks loaned the hedge funds money to finance their trading and allowed them to trade for themselves in highly leveraged positions in the banks' proprietary accounts and reap the resulting profits. The banks offering the "options" benefited from the financing, trading, and other fees charged to the hedge funds initiating the trades.
>
> In the end, the trading conducted by the hedge funds using the basket option accounts was virtually indistinguishable from the trading conducted by hedge funds using their own brokerage accounts, and provided no justification for treating the resulting short-term trading profits as long-term capital gains. [47]

[47] Ibid.

Therefore, it is absolutely clear that RenTec was wrong in characterizing its profits of $34 billion as long term capital gain for two reasons: a) they arose from activity very similar to RenTec's regular trading; and b) they lasted <12 months.

The report also notes a second issue related to these events and it pertains to "circumventing Federal Leverage Limits." As the report argues,

> In addition to using basket options to reduce taxes on their short-term capital gains, the hedge funds used them to obtain financing for securities trades far in excess of what federal leverage limits allow. Federal leverage limits were established in response to the stock market crash of 1929, when securities purchased on borrowed funds magnified stock market losses and caused failures of not only the stock speculators, but also the banks and broker-dealers that lent them money.
>
> Federal "margin rules" were enacted to impose a leverage limit of 2:1 on brokerage accounts opened by U.S. broker dealers for their customers. In contrast, because the participating banks seemingly lent money to their own accounts, the basket option accounts examined by the Subcommittee provided the hedge fund option holders with leverage ratios as high as 20:1. RenTec indicated in one document that it had been unable to attain such high leverage levels in any other setting.[48]

This is yet another violation because under normal circumstances companies like RenTec would have been forced to adhere to normal federal leverage limits of 2:1.

A stupendously high leverage of 20:1, a tenfold increase in leverage was possible again became RenTec used the 'basket option strategy' to camouflage the actual leverage. Such enhanced leverage can be detrimental and the seriousness of the

---

[48] Ibid.

issue has been underlined by the financial crisis of 2008 and I quote from the FCIC report,[49] in which it is argued that:

> We conclude a combination of excessive borrowing, risky investments, and lack of transparency put the financial system on a collision course with crisis. …
>
> In the years leading up to the crisis, too many financial institutions, as well as too many households, borrowed to the hilt, leaving them vulnerable to financial distress or ruin if the value of their investments declined even modestly. For example, as of 2007, the five major investment banks—Bear Stearns[50], Goldman Sachs, Lehman Brothers, Merrill Lynch, and Morgan Stanley—were operating with extraordinarily thin capital. By one measure, their leverage ratios were as high as 40 to 1, meaning for every $40 in assets, there was only $1 in capital to cover losses. Less than a 3% drop in asset values could wipe out a firm.
>
> To make matters worse, much of their borrowing was short-term, in the overnight market—meaning the borrowing had to be renewed each and every day. For example, at the end of 2007, Bear Stearns had $11.8 billion in equity and $383.6 billion in liabilities and was borrowing as much as $70 billion in the overnight market. It was the equivalent of a small business with $50,000 in equity borrowing $1.6 million, with $296,750 of that due each and every day.
>
> One can't really ask, "What were they thinking?" when it seems that too many of them were thinking alike. And the leverage was often hidden—in derivatives positions, in

[49] Financial Crisis Inquiry Report, Final Report Of The National Commission On The Causes Of The Financial And Economic Crisis In The United States, The Financial Crisis Inquiry Commission, http://fcic-static.law.stanford.edu/cdn_media/fcic-reports/fcic_final_report_full.pdf

[50] It must be noted that Bear Stearns and RenTec worked closely for several years.

> off-balance-sheet entities, and through "window dressing" of financial reports available to the investing public. (FCIC Report)[51]

Looks like history may repeat itself in terms of another financial crisis, if the above practice of "high leverage" through basket options is allowed to continue.

That said, in summary, the report of the U.S. Senate Permanent Subcommittee on Investigations notes the following:

- Although Deutsche Bank and Barclays established proprietary accounts for the basket options, purportedly to hold assets that would serve as a hedge to cover the option payoffs, those accounts actually functioned as if they were RenTec's own prime brokerage trading accounts, with RenTec acting in the role of trader rather than option holder. The facts show RenTec had active and total control over the trading strategy and executions. …

- The resulting rapid asset turnover in the various option accounts meant that the options purchased by RenTec had no fixed assets and did not function as true options. The accounts existed simply to carry out RenTec's algorithmic trading strategy.

---

[51] Financial Crisis Inquiry Report, The Financial Crisis Inquiry Commission, http://fcic-static.law.stanford.edu/cdn_media/fcic-reports/fcic_final_report_full.pdf

- In the end, for all practical purposes, the accounts functioned as over-leveraged prime brokerage accounts controlled by the hedge fund...to produce trading profits rather than as accounts controlled by the banks to provide a hedge against an option contract. …

- RenTec's control over the trading strategy and related activities, high-volume trading and account turnover, integration of the accounts into a larger investment strategy, and use of the accounts to produce regular cash payments supporting its business operations, contradict a depiction of RenTec as a passive option holder awaiting derivative gains.

- The option structure functioned instead as a vehicle for RenTec to conduct direct trades with leverage at much higher levels than available in normal margin accounts, to aggregate and defer its gains, and to avoid billions of dollars in short-term capital gains taxes.[52]

Thus, it very clear that RenTec misused the 'basket option strategy' to avoid huge taxes (literally, several billion dollars) as well as gain access to unusually high leverage limits—both of which represent an abuse of U.S. statutes/laws (Figure 2.1).

There can be no doubt about that.

---

[52] Report: Abuse Of Structured Financial Products: Misusing Basket Options to Avoid Taxes and Leverage Limits, *Homeland Security and Government Affairs*, July 22, 2014, http://www.hsgac.senate.gov/subcommittees/investigations/hearings/abuse-of-structured-financial-products_misusing-basket-options-to-avoid-taxes-and-leverage-limits

Figure 2.1: Renaissance Technologies (RenTec) and The $6 Billion Tax Avoidance

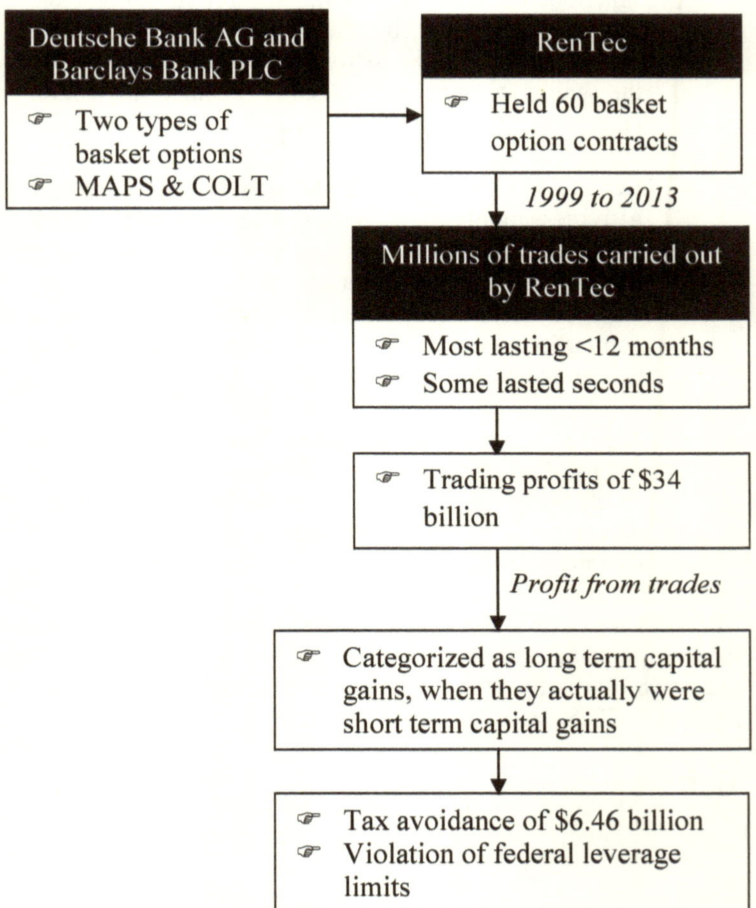

Consequent to the 2014 report by the Senate Permanent Subcommittee on Investigations, reportedly[53] hedge funds like RenTec that used the basket option strategy to avoid billions of dollars in tax faced new scrutiny from the government, in accordance with guidelines issued by the Internal Revenue Service (IRS).

According to the new IRS guideline, basket options—that allowed companies like RenTec to bypass taxes on short-term trades—were to be labeled listed transactions. What this meant was that anyone using the options strategy had to declare them on their tax returns. Failure to do so meant they ran the risk of penalty.

What is even more interesting is the fact that the new IRS guidance was made retroactive, applying to all transactions from January 1, 2011. This fact brought within its ambit transactions by companies like RenTec, which according to a 2014 report by the Senate Permanent Subcommittee on Investigations,[54] was able to avoid more than $6 billion in taxes over a decade through the use of the basket option strategy.

In fact, commenting on the activities, two Democrats reportedly supported the IRS action. Carl Levin, a Michigan Democrat, and chairman of the 2014 Senate Permanent Subcommittee on Investigations supposedly said that the investigations showed that banks and hedge funds used "dubious structured financial products, costing the Treasury billions and bypassing safeguards that protect the economy from excessive bank lending for stock speculation." He further added that the amount of money that hedge funds like Renaissance Technology were able to keep

---

[53] Alexandra Stevenson, I.R.S. Cracks Down on Hedge Fund Tax Strategy, *The New York Times,* July 8, 2015, http://www.nytimes.com/2015/07/09/business/dealbook/irs-cracks-down-on-hedge-fund-tax-strategy.html?_r=0

[54] Alexandra Stevenson, 'Senate Inquiry Faults Hedge Funds' Tax Strategy', *The New York Times,* July 21, 2014, http://dealbook.nytimes.com/2014/07/21/senate-inquiry-faults-hedge-funds-tax-strategy/

back by strategizing and not paying the required taxes, was a very significant amount, even by Washington standards. Likewise, Senator Ron Wyden of Oregon, the ranking Democrat on the Finance Committee, said he was all for the IRS action to crack down on these types of basket option products.[55]

To summarize, without a doubt, as per the report of the U.S. Senate Permanent Subcommittee on Investigations (2014), RenTec used the basket option structure **(for several years starting from 1999)** with hundreds of millions of trades (virtually all of which lasted less than 12 months and some of which lasted just seconds) and characterized the vast majority of the resulting $34 billion in trading profits as long-term capital gains and thereby avoided (paying) billions of dollars in taxes—which the Senate Permanent Subcommittee has estimated as amounting to over $6 billion, a huge number by any standards.

In light of all this, it is baffling how the 2016 Democratic nominee for the U.S. presidential elections, Hillary Clinton, who promises to rein in Wall Street and who has also vowed to penalize (corporate) tax evaders, has no qualms in accepting campaign money from RenTec's founder and current board chair, James Simons.[56]

That President Obama accepted contributions from James H Simons for the 2012 cycle is also astonishing, given that RenTec had been carrying on these practices since 1999 and also given

---

[55] Summarized from: Alexandra Stevenson, 'I.R.S. Cracks Down on Hedge Fund Tax Strategy', *The New York Times,* July 8, 2015, http://www.nytimes.com/2015/07/09/business/dealbook/irs-cracks-down-on-hedge-fund-tax-strategy.html?_r=0

[56] It must be emphasized that James Simons is the founder of RenTec and serves as the current chairman of RenTec. Therefore, whether he donates from RenTec or another company that he runs—Euclidean Capital, which is a family office—is immaterial. In addition, it must be clearly noted that James Simons was CEO of RenTec for much of the period when RenTec used the basket option strategy with Deutsch Bank and Barclays Bank.

that IRS had identified this "type of option product … as abusive in a public memorandum …in 2010."[57]

The problem gets more complicated when one considers the fact that Republicans were equally guilty of accepting *'dirty money'* from RenTec—recall that Robert Mercer[58], Co-CEO of RenTec, has given a whopping $13.5 million to Ted Cruz (2016 cycle), $3 million to Mitt Romney (2012 cycle) and is now supporting Donald Trump.[59]

Besides, RenTec employees, Henry Laufer ($1 million) and Stephen Robert ($1 million) have contributed handsomely to Senate Majority PAC and Priorities USA Action, PAC supporting President Barack Obama.

The Clinton Foundation has also been a beneficiary, getting between $10,001 to $25,000 from Nat Simons[60] and $250,001 to $500,000 from Henry and Marsha Laufer.

---

[57] Tyler Durden, 'How RenTec Made More Than $34 Billion In Profits Since 1998: "Fictional Derivatives"', *Zero Hedge,* July 21, 2014, http://www.zerohedge.com/news/2014-07-21/how-rentec-made-more-34-billion-profits-1998-fictional-derivatives

[58] See appendix 2.2.

[59] Ted Cruz's – *"Keep The Promise I"* PAC - converted to a *"Make America Number I"* PAC and started working for Donald Trump. The Robert Mercer family is said to be heavily involved in this PAC also as was the case with the Ted Cruz PAC. See: Theodore Schleifer, 'Yet another Donald Trump super PAC launches, this one with a link to Ted Cruz', *CNN Politics*, June 23, 2016, http://edition.cnn.com/2016/06/23/politics/donald-trump-super-pac-fundraising/ and, Nicholas Confessore, 'How One Family's Deep Pockets Helped Reshape Donald Trump's Campaign', *The New York Times,* August 18 2016, http://www.nytimes.com/2016/08/19/us/politics/robert-mercer-donald-trump-donor.html?hpw&rref=politics&action=click&pgtype=Homepage&module=well-region®ion=bottom-well&WT.nav=bottom-well&_r=0

[60] Son of James Harris Simons.

Therefore, it is clear that whether Democrat or Republican, RenTec's *'dirty money'* has been welcomed and accepted as part of the various election campaigns across the years.

What would the American people think of their presidential candidates[61] accepting money from a Wall Street giant that has evaded tax to the tune of $6.46 billion? If this is not *'dirty money,'* what is?

The Case of George Soros

The Hungarian-American businessman George Soros is an investor, philanthropist and author of Jewish-Hungarian ancestry. Soros is said to hold dual citizenship (of Hungary and the United States). He is the Chairman of Soros Fund Management and figures in the list of the world's top thirty rich men. A supporter of American progressive and American liberal political causes, Soros is reported to have donated more than $11 billion to various philanthropic causes between 1979 and 2015.[62]

Over three cycles (2016, 2012 and 2008), George Soros has contributed over $15.65 million to the election campaigns of various presidential candidates. Of this, about $8.74 million has gone to Hillary Clinton's 2016 election campaign, the bulk being to pro-Clinton PACs. George Soros has also made a donation in the range of $500,001 to $1,000,000 to the Clinton Foundation through the Soros Foundation.

Other candidates to whom George Soros has contributed are: $1.0 million (2012) to Barack Obama's PAC and $4,600 (2008) to Barack Obama individually; and $2,300 (2008) to Hillary Clinton individually. This apart, Soros has contributed handsomely to PACs support candidates for the U.S. Senate and U.S. House of Representatives. The complete details of George Soros's election donations across three cycles to all presidential

[61] See appendix 1 for details of candidates across three cycles – 2016, 2012 and 2008.

[62] Wikipedia, George Soros, https://en.wikipedia.org/wiki/George_Soros

and other down ballot candidates[63]—along with contributions made by his family members and staff of key entities—is summarized in **appendix 2.3.**

While there seems to be a running competition between mathematician James H Simons, (Euclidean Capital and RenTech CEO) and George Soros for the honor[64] of being the highest contributor to the Hillary Clinton 2016 campaign, it appears that they have yet another pertinent fact in common. There have been allegations of tax avoidance against both Soros and Simons.

As noted earlier, in fact, the company founded by Simons, of which he is still chairman, was named in a Congressional report on tax abuse for having evaded tax to the tune of a cool six billion dollars. Likewise, *Fox News* reported that George Soros could face a $7 billion tax bill, after delaying payment for years.[65] The article also strongly points out that, despite Soros having argued for higher taxes for the super-rich, he himself, a very wealthy billionaire, has used a loophole in the U.S. law and thereby delayed paying his own taxes on client fees. The article further notes that, because this loophole was closed by the Congress in 2008, Soros may have to deal with a tax bill close to $7 billion.

Additionally, George Soros was convicted[66] of insider trading on the French stock market. "His insider-trading conviction was

---

[63] See appendix 1 for a list of candidates across three election cycles.

[64] As of May 28, 2016, both Soros and James Simons have been surpassed by Haim Saban, the media mogul, whose family and institutions have provided more than $10 million to the Hillary Clinton campaign directly and through pro-Clinton PACs.

[65] 'George Soros reportedly could face up to $7B tax bill, after delaying payment for years', *Fox News Politics*, May 1, 2015, http://www.foxnews.com/politics/2015/05/01/george-soros-reportedly-could-face-up-to-7b-tax-bill-after-delaying-payment-for.html — I was, however, unable to get any further information on this matter.

[66] A Paris-based prosecutor reopened the case against Soros and two other French businessmen, disregarding the COB's findings. This

upheld by the highest court in France on June 14, 2006.[67] In December 2006, he appealed to the European Court of Human Rights on various grounds including that the 14-year delay in bringing the case to trial precluded a fair hearing.[68] On the basis of Article 7 of the European Convention on Human Rights, stating that no person may be punished for an act that was not a criminal offense at the time that it was committed, the court agreed to hear the appeal.[69] In October 2011, the court rejected his appeal in a 4–3 decision, saying that Soros had been aware of the risk of breaking insider trading laws."[70, 71]

Likewise, it has also been reported that on September 16, 1992, called "Black Wednesday," the short selling of more than $10 billion pounds was done by the Soros Fund,[72] which essentially profited from the British government's inability and/or reluctance to either raise its interest rates[73] or to float its

---

resulted in Soros's 2005 conviction for insider trading by the Court of Appeals (he was the only one of the three to receive a conviction). The French Supreme Court confirmed the conviction on June 14, 2006, but reduced the penalty to €940,000.

[67] Cited from Soros, Wikipedia, Original Footnote 60: "Insider trading conviction of Soros is upheld." *International Herald Tribune*. June 14, 2006.

[68] Cited from Soros, Wikipedia, Original Footnote 62: *Lichfield, John (December 22, 2002). "Financier Soros fined £1.4m for insider trading." The Independent (London). Retrieved October 12, 2011.*

[69] Cited from Soros, Wikipedia, Original Footnote 63: *Saltmarsh, Matthew (September 15, 2010). "Soros to Get a Day in Court Over Insider Trading Case". The New York Times. Retrieved September 18, 2011.*

[70] Cited from Soros, Wikipedia, Original Footnote 64: *Smith, Heather (October 6, 2011). "Soros Loses Case Against French Insider-Trading Conviction." Bloomberg L.P. Retrieved October 9, 2011.*

[71] https://en.wikipedia.org/wiki/George_Soros

[72] Cited from Soros, Wikipedia — https://en.wikipedia.org/wiki/George_Soros, "George Soros." George Soros. Retrieved, November 25, 2011.

[73] When I talk of raising interest rates, I am making a specific reference to levels comparable to those of other European Exchange Rate Mechanism countries.

currency. Reportedly, the UK finally withdrew from the European Exchange Rate Mechanism, devaluing the pound. It was estimated that Soros's profit on the bet was a whopping $1 billion—really huge money at that time.[74] This led to his being called "the man who broke the Bank of England."[75] It has been reported that the (estimated) cost of Black Wednesday to the UK Treasury was approximately £3.4 billion.[76]

The icing on the cake is what Nobel Prize winning economist, Paul Krugman, said about the "Soros's effect" on financial markets:

> [N]obody who has read a business magazine in the last few years can be unaware that these days there really are investors who not only move money in anticipation of a currency crisis, but actually do their best to trigger that crisis for fun and profit. These new actors on the scene do not yet have a standard name; my proposed term is "Soroi."[77]

---

[74] Wikipedia — https://en.wikipedia.org/wiki/George_Soros, Mallaby, Sebastian, *More Money Than God*, Penguin, 2010, p. 167. ISBN 978-1-59420-255-1

[75] David Litterick, 'Billionaire who Broke the Bank of England', *The Telegraph,* September 13, 2002, http://www.telegraph.co.uk/finance/2773265/Billionaire-who-broke-the-Bank-of-England.html

[76] Phillip Johnston, 'Black Wednesday: The day that Britain went over the edge', *The Telegraph,* September 10, 2012, http://www.telegraph.co.uk/finance/currency/9533474/Black-Wednesday-The-day-that-Britain-went-over-the-edge.html

[77] Cited from Soros, Wikipedia — https://en.wikipedia.org/wiki/George_Soros, Krugman, Paul (1999). The accidental theorist: and other dispatches from the dismal science. New York: *W.W. Norton & Company.* p. 160.

Dirty Money

In an effort to understand the seriousness of the allegations against Soros and his subsequent conviction, it is interesting to recall the case of Rajat Gupta, convicted of insider trading in the U.S. stock markets. Gupta was a powerful man, with far-reaching influence. He served as McKinsey and Company's managing director (worldwide) until his retirement in 2007 and has been on the board of many of today's influential corporations and banks, including most prominently, Goldman Sachs.

Gupta was charged with leaking information from his position on the board of Goldman Sachs, to hedge fund investor Raj Rajaratnam (currently serving an eleven year prison sentence) about internal transactions at Goldman, including Warren Buffet's $5 billion bailout at the height of the crisis. This prompted Rajaratnam to hedge himself against the coming fluctuations in the stock price. Gupta wasn't believed to have had any realistic financial gain and his attorneys say the two friends were discussing the deal in their position as investors themselves. Nevertheless, the timing of it and the fact that the information was revealed before the public announcement, told a more sinister story.

The case was deemed "the big scalp" for the US Federal Reserve in its crusade against insider trading. It was touted as the tale of how public service could not be used as an excuse for white-collar crimes, of boardroom influences not reaching far enough (to ultimately save oneself).

Some might call the case an example of persecution, others might call it profiling by race, but it is above all an example of the sentiment worldwide about Wall Street—the protests, the disillusions, the many accusations of corruption and desire for quick fast money driven by simple greed. It is the tale of a prosperous environment gone terribly wrong and a stark wake-up call to correct it if indeed we are to make an attempt to revive the faltering world economy at all.

Given this context, it is apparent that insider trading is a huge breach of trust, irrespective of conviction or sentencing. Moreover, the same set of standards must be used to judge persons held guilty of the crime, whether in the United States of America or outside of it. If Rajat Gupta, convicted of insider trading and sentenced to two years imprisonment and a fine of five million dollars for being compliant to insider trading, should rightly be regarded as an untouchable in terms of political association, the same standards have to be applied to George Soros.

The argument against association with Soros is further strengthened by latest reports that have emerged indicating that three offshore investment vehicles controlled by him "are catalogued in the Panama Papers."[78]

One is Soros Finance, Inc. incorporated in Panama; another is Soros Holdings Limited that was set up in the British Virgin Islands and the third is a limited partnership called Soros Capital that was created in Bermuda[79].

---

[78] Peter Byrne, 'Panama Papers reveal George Soros' deep money ties to secretive weapons, intel investment firm', *FOX NEWS World*, May 16, 2016, http://www.foxnews.com/world/2016/05/16/panama-papers-reveal-george-soros-deep-money-ties-to-secretive-weapons-intel-firm.html

[79] "Soros Capital is a major investor and corporate officer of AIF (Indonesia) Limited. AIF combines private investments with public funding contributed by Asian governments to develop massive infrastructure projects. The database links Soros Capital to Dongya Ports Limited, owned by a tangle of offshore entities."—Byrne, 'Panama Papers reveal George Soros' deep money ties to secretive weapons, intel investment firm', *FOX NEWS World*, May 16, 2016, http://www.foxnews.com/world/2016/05/16/panama-papers-reveal-george-soros-deep-money-ties-to-secretive-weapons-intel-firm.html. As the *Fox News* article notes, an additional point to note here is that the laws of Panama, Bermuda, the British Virgin Islands and a score of "tax havens" allow foreign firms to shroud (their) ownership of cash, real estate and/or other assets from securities regulators and tax collectors in the countries in which they are physically headquartered.

The details of two of these entities are given in the **table 2.1** below:

Table 2.1: Entities of Soros Named in The Panama Papers		
Name	Soros Finance Inc.	Soros Holdings Limited
Category	Entity	Entity
Incorporation Date	December 27, 1979	December 10, 1996
Address	George de Geofroy 5, Avenue Miremont 1206 Geneva, Switzerland	Management Trustees Group S.A. Rue du Consail General 14 1205 Geneve Switzerland
Country of Incorporation	Panama	British Virgin Islands
Linked Countries	Switzerland	Switzerland
Agent	Mossack Fonseca	Mossack Fonseca
Source: The Panama Papers Data Base, https://offshoreleaks.icij.org/		

To sum up, the achievements of Soros, a global newsmaker, are as follows:

- In 1992, Soros nearly bankrupted the Bank of England through price manipulation of the pound.
- In 1997 or thereabouts, Soros betted against Thai and Malaysian currencies and thereby accelerated a regional economic crisis.
- In 2010, Soros invested in the Indian micro-finance institution SKS Microfinance Ltd (SKSML). It has been reported that SKSML had been involved in a spate of controversies including suicides of poor borrowers in Andhra Pradesh, coercive tactics to recover loans from such poor people and several corporate governance/other violations.

- Indeed, Soros has built a vast empire of off-shore funds with its humongous profits. He is the sole proprietor of Manhattan-based Soros Fund Management LLC, which controls this offshore empire.
- In July 2011, Soros moved to becoming a family office by closing the multibillion-dollar fund to all but immediate family members—this has enabled him to escape disclosure requirements stipulated by the Dodd-Frank Act mandate for hedge funds.
- In 2011, Soros also lost the final appeal of his 2002 (insider trading) conviction by a French court.
- In 2013, it was reported that Soros may end paying $7 billion in taxes that he may have deferred using a loophole in the U.S. law, which the Congress (reportedly) plugged in 2008.[80]
- In 2016, George Soros was named in the Panama Papers expose.[81]

Despite all of the above, he has continued to remain a strong political force. While Soros' companies may not be entirely paying their share of U.S. taxes,[82] he still donates huge amounts to Democrat lawmakers including those who contested against George Bush in 2004.

[80] 'George Soros reportedly could face up to $7B tax bill, after delaying payment for years', *FOX NEWS Politics,* May 1, 2015, http://www.foxnews.com/politics/2015/05/01/george-soros-reportedly-could-face-up-to-7b-tax-bill-after-delaying-payment-for.html

[81] Byrne, 'Panama Papers reveal George Soros' deep money ties to secretive weapons, intel investment firm', *FOX NEWS World*, May 16, 2016, http://www.foxnews.com/world/2016/05/16/panama-papers-reveal-george-soros-deep-money-ties-to-secretive-weapons-intel-firm.html

[82] 'George Soros reportedly could face up to $7B tax bill, after delaying payment for years', *FOX NEWS Politics,* May 1, 2015, http://www.foxnews.com/politics/2015/05/01/george-soros-reportedly-could-face-up-to-7b-tax-bill-after-delaying-payment-for.html

As noted earlier, FEC data[83] shows he contributed significantly to President Obama's campaign. It must be noted that, as of the date of publication of this book, as per FEC data on individual and pro-Clinton PAC contributions, he is among the largest donors to Hillary Clinton's 2016 Presidency run, having donated close to $8.74 million. If you search the Clinton Foundation website, it shows that he contributed up to $1 million to the Clinton Foundation.

Fox News reports that, "Secretary of State Clinton's emails reveal that Soros has lobbied her on behalf of his interests, which encircle the globe, mostly in the dark."[84]Given that the 2016 U.S. presidential campaign is being fought on the issues of "big money in politics" and a "corrupt campaign finance system," continued association with and acceptance of money from a Wall Streeter convicted for insider trading in France and also facing mounting allegations of financial deceit—irrespective of who the person is and how wealthy he may be—is tantamount to compromising the very values the current political battle is being fought on. This is something presidential candidates like Hillary Clinton need to ponder.

A final word is in order here. Given all that Soros has achieved in terms of his notoriety, that Soros has contributed and continues to contribute to many liberals is indeed a cause for worry. This is because many of these liberals ideologically espouse the position of higher taxation of the rich. Given that ideological stance on taxation, how ethical is it for all of them (presidential, senate and house candidates included) to finance their campaigns with the kind of *'dirty money'* that Soros offers? That is a question that begs a serious answer.

---

[83] Federal Election Commission, www.fec.gov

[84] Byrne, 'Panama Papers reveal George Soros' deep money ties to secretive weapons, intel investment firm', *FOX NEWS World*, May 16, 2016, http://www.foxnews.com/world/2016/05/16/panama-papers-reveal-george-soros-deep-money-ties-to-secretive-weapons-intel-firm.html

Especially, Hillary Clinton and President Barack Obama have to answer as to how they could accept money from George Soros, who has been convicted of insider trading in France, been mentioned as a potential tax evader[85] and has also been named in the Panama Papers—all aspects that represent serious examples of corporate crime including tax abuse and tax evasion. If this *'dirty money'* does not represent a nexus between a corrupt campaign finance system and corporate crime, then the billion dollar question is, what does?

The Case of Haim Saban

Haim Saban, an Israeli and American media mogul, investor, philanthropist, musician, record, film and television producer, is a high profile contributor to election campaigns in America. Saban is said to be a very accomplished businessman with wide-ranging business interests—from financial services to entertainment, media, and so on.

His estimated net worth is $3 billion and specifically, he and his wife, Cheryl, have been major donors in the United States. The complete details of Haim Saban's election donations across three cycles to all presidential and other down ballot candidates—along with contributions made by his family members and staff of key entities—are summarized in **appendix 2.4.**

A look at that reveals that, over the last three cycles (2016, 2012 and 2008), Haim Saban has contributed over $12.77 million to the election campaigns of various presidential candidates. Of this, about $11.44 million has gone to Hillary Clinton's 2016 election campaign. Other candidates to whom Haim Saban has contributed are: $10,000 (2012) to Barack Obama and $4,600 (2008) to Hillary Clinton.

---

[85] 'George Soros reportedly could face up to $7B tax bill, after delaying payment for years', *FOX NEWS Politics,* May 1, 2016, http://www.foxnews.com/politics/2015/05/01/george-soros-reportedly-could-face-up-to-7b-tax-bill-after-delaying-payment-for.html

Starting with the 2016 presidential election cycle, it is easy to understand why Cheryl and Haim Saban are such high profile donors. Apart from making individual contributions to Hillary Clinton's 2016 campaign, they have generously donated to the pro-Clinton PACs. Strangely, Haim Saban of the Saban Capital Group is also listed as a contributor to George W Bush—he is said to have contributed on 08/26/2003, a sum of $2,000 as individual contribution to the George Bush election campaign of 2004. Interesting indeed!

Furthermore, the Sabans and their Family Foundation have made donations ranging from $10,000,001 to $25,000,000 to the Clinton Foundation. That is a huge donation by any standards.

Saban however, has not been without his share of controversies, especially with regard to tax evasion. The United States Senate, Permanent Subcommittee On Investigations, Committee on Homeland Security and Governmental Affairs with Norm Coleman, Chairman and Carl Levin, Ranking Minority Member released a report titled: "*Tax Haven Abuses: The Enablers, The Tools And Secrecy*", Minority & Majority Staff Report by the Permanent Subcommittee on Investigations. This report was released in conjunction with the Permanent Subcommittee on Investigations August 1, 2006 hearing.

The report dated 2007 observes the following:

> POINT: Offshore Securities Portfolio. This case history examines a complex securities transaction used to shelter over $2 billion in capital gains from U.S. taxes, relying in part on offshore secrecy to shield its workings from U.S. law enforcement. In contrast to the case histories examining offshore structures used over a period of years, this inquiry focuses on the use of offshore secrecy jurisdictions to facilitate one-time tax shelter transactions.[86]

---

[86] Tax Haven Abuses: The Enablers, the Tools And Secrecy, Minority & Majority Staff Report, Permanent Subcommittee On Investigations, *Homeland Security and Government Affairs,* August 1, 2006,

Please note the emphasis of the report on the one-time use of tax shelters, which clearly suggests the motivation was tax evasion and abuse rather than anything else.

As the report further notes,

> The tax shelter was designed, promoted, and implemented by a Seattle-based securities firm, Quellos Group, LLC, (Quellos), with the assistance of lawyers, bankers, and other professionals. Quellos sold the shelter, called POINT (Personally Optimized INvestment Transaction), to six wealthy clients in six separate transactions. Together, the tax shelters were used in an effort to erase over $2 billion in capital gains that would otherwise have been taxed, costing the U.S. Treasury lost revenue of about $300 million.[87]

The interesting point to note here is that the U.S. Treasury lost close to $300 million in 2006, which in terms of money value is a huge sum of money back then. These are grave observations on tax haven abuses and coming from the United States Senate, they are even more serious. In a related suit[88], Matthew Krane made a strong claim that, "Saban defrauded the government out of tax money when he sold his company to the Walt Disney Company in October 2001 for $5.3 billion." As per the suit, Saban (reportedly) demanded that Krane put together a tax plan that ensured that Saban would pay nil (zero) taxes on his $1.5 billion profit from the forthcoming sale. Back to the POINT transactions, let us look at the detailed mechanism of how they were structured, especially to help U.S. tax payers avoid taxes.

---

http://www.hsgac.senate.gov/subcommittees/investigations/hearings/tax-haven-abuses-the-enablers-the-tools-and-secrecy

[87] Ibid.

[88] Brent Lang, 'Haim Saban Loses Court Round; Former Tax Lawyer Can Sue Him', *The Wrap,* April 12, 2011, http://www.thewrap.com/haim-saban-loses-court-round-former-tax-lawyer-can-sue-him-26386/

Figure 2.2 illustrates the same diagrammatically.

Figure 2.2: Point Transactions Haim Saban and others Permanent Subcommittee on Investigations U.S. Senate

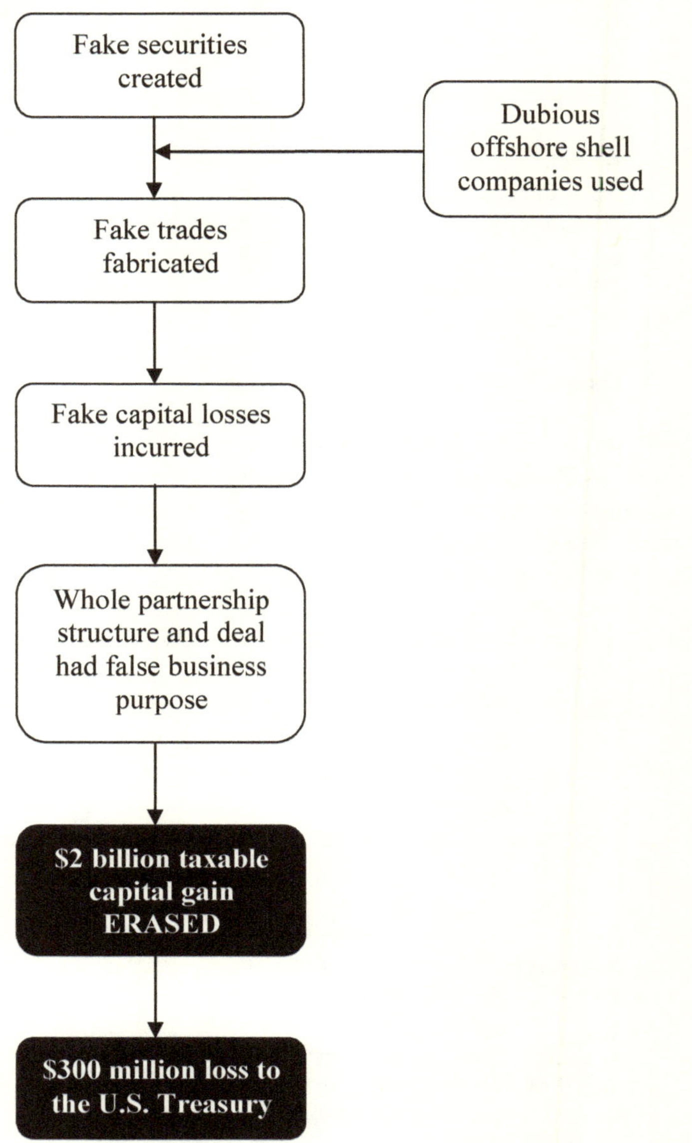

To be precise, the Subcommittee's investigation[89] clearly found that:

- Quellos, a Seattle based tax shelter promoter, invented a tax shelter that used the fabrication of billions of dollars worth of fake securities transactions, which in turn, were used to generate billions of dollars in fake capital losses so as to offset real tangible taxable capital gains of U.S. taxpayers so they could avoid paying taxes to the U.S. Treasury.

- The entire POINT transaction was carried out under offshore secrecy laws through the help of compliant trust and corporate management companies located in the Isle of Man and the Cayman Islands. These shrouded entities facilitated the true nature of the securities transactions and the persons/institutions that conducted them to remain hidden and away from the public eye.

- The POINT strategy was promoted by Quellos to individuals as a tax avoidance product, but the possibility of realizing some income to cover a part of the fees always remained.

- Quellos, charged, for designing and implementing the scheme, fees that depended on the amount of tax loss generated in each transaction; The fees that Quellos collected was commensurate with the money that the transaction lost - the more money the transaction "lost," the greater fees that Quellos collected.

- Two other aspects are significant in the Senate Subcommittee's findings: a) Well established and known law firms worked with Quellos to develop the legal rationale to provide support to the legitimacy of the "tax losses generated by the POINT transactions"; and b) Formal U.S. and foreign financial institutions provided "the financing, planning, and technical assistance" for executing the transactions—despite knowing full well that

[89] The Subcommittee Report (2006).

they were designed to avoid taxes payable in the United States.

To summarize, the POINT strategy used **fake securities transactions** worth billions of dollars to generate **fake capital losses** amounting to billions of dollars with the sole objective of offsetting real taxable capital gains of U.S. taxpayers. The objective was tax evasion which according to the IRS is a crime. That is not all.

OK, who were the U.S. taxpayers? Six U.S. taxpayers, including Haim Saban and Robert Wood Johnson IV, purchased the tax shelter, paying fees totaling approximately $65 million. Note the fact that Haim Saban is a key member of the group of six individuals who were involved in purchasing the tax shelter created in a nefarious manner. For such powerful and educated individuals to argue that they did know what was going on, is a matter that cannot be taken at face value.

Three more aspects are disturbing[90] from the POINT case:

- Cravath, Swaine & Moore and Bryan Cave, prominent law firms, gave "written tax opinion letters affirming that it was 'more likely than not' that the Quellos plan would produce the favorable tax consequences promised, and collaborated with Quellos on its design or implementation."

- It can be clearly discerned from the report that "The factual statements used to support the legal analysis in the opinion letters inaccurately described the nature of the securities transactions generating the capital losses. The law firms accepted the representations of Quellos on these matters without inquiring behind them."

- What is very interesting is the fact that well known "U.S.

[90] The Subcommittee Report (2006).

and foreign financial institutions, including HSBC Bank, provided financing for the POINT transactions, without conducting adequate due diligence into the underlying transactions." Not at all surprised that HSBC's name figures in one more scandal!

In addition, there were several critical impacts from the POINT transactions, which are highlighted in Table 2.2 below:

Table 2.2: Critical Impacts of the POINT Transactions	
Impact	**Description**
Fake Transactions and Fake Capital Losses	☞ Fake transactions worth billions of dollars were crafted to create billions of dollars of fake capital losses to avoid legitimate taxes to be paid in the United States.
Shrouding of Real Capital Gains	☞ Real capital gains of United States taxpayers were therefore shrouded illegally.
Tax Avoidance	☞ United States taxpayers avoided paying taxes to the U.S. Treasury.
Use of Secrecy Laws	☞ Corporate and financial secrecy laws and practices in offshore tax havens made it easy to conceal and obscure the economic and other realities underlying these fake financial transactions.
Offshore Tax Haven Abuses	☞ U.S. persons, with the assistance of lawyers, brokers, bankers, offshore service providers, and others, used offshore entities in offshore tax havens to circumvent U.S. tax, securities, and anti-money laundering requirements.
Anti-Money Laundering Abuses	☞ U.S. financial institutions have failed to identify the beneficial owners of offshore trusts and corporations

Table 2.2: Critical Impacts of the POINT Transactions	
Impact	**Description**
	that opened U.S. securities accounts, and have accepted W-8 forms in which offshore entities represented that they beneficially owned the account assets, even when the financial institutions knew the offshore entities were being directed by or were closely associated with U.S. taxpayers.
Securities Abuses	☞ Corporate insiders at U.S. publicly traded corporations have used offshore entities to trade in the company's stock, and these offshore entities have taken actions to circumvent U.S. securities safeguards and disclosure and trading requirements.
Stock Option Abuses	☞ Because stock option compensation is taxed when exercised, and not when granted, stock options have been used in potentially abusive transactions to defer and in some cases avoid U.S. taxes.
Hedge Fund Transfers	☞ U.S. persons who transferred assets to allegedly independent offshore entities in a tax haven have then directed those offshore entities to invest the assets in a hedge fund controlled by the same U.S. persons, thereby regaining investment control of the assets.
Source: Compiled from The Subcommittee Report (2006)	

And Haim Saban, one of the largest donors in the 2016 presidential elections, evaded the legitimate taxes that had to be paid using the POINT transaction route[91]. Let us be clear on that aspect.

Another interesting fact emerges with regard to the POINT transactions. Quellos, the firm identified in the above Senate Subcommittee Report, is also reported to have, "In the mid to late 1990s … helped accounting firm KPMG LLP design, develop, market, and implement tax shelter products for sale to U.S. clients."[92]

In fact, other reports[93] by the Permanent Sub Committee identified that two investment advisory firms, Presidio Advisory Services and the Quellos Group (formerly doing business as Quadra Capital Management LLP and QA Investments LLC), "assisted in the design, development, marketing, and implementation of tax shelters promoted by KPMG."

Specifically, as per the above report, these firms are supposed to have helped develop, design, market, and execute potentially abusive or illegal tax shelters such as FLIP, OPIS, and BLIPS.

Likewise, the report identifies that Deutsche Bank, HVB Bank, and UBS Bank "provided billions of dollars in lending critical to transactions which the banks knew were tax motivated, involved

---

[91] See The Subcommittee Report (2006) and: David Cay Johnston, 'Tax Cheats Called Out of Control', *The New York Times,* August 1, 2006, http://www.nytimes.com/2006/08/01/business/01tax.html

[92] Tax Haven Abuses: The Enablers, the Tools And Secrecy, Minority & Majority Staff Report, *Homeland Security and Government Affairs*, August 1, 2006, http://www.hsgac.senate.gov/subcommittees/investigations/hearings/tax-haven-abuses-the-enablers-the-tools-and-secrecy

[93] The Role of Professional Firms in the U.S. Tax Shelter Industry Report, Prepared by the Permanent Subcommittee on Investigations Of the Committee on Homeland Security and Governmental Affairs United States Senate, April 13, 2005.

little or no credit risk, and facilitated potentially abusive or illegal tax shelters known as FLIP, OPIS, and BLIPS."

A crucial aspect deserves mention here. While some of people who were involved in the POINT transactions got away lightly, for almost the same issue, "KPMG LLP (KPMG)… admitted to criminal wrongdoing and agreed to pay $456 million in fines, restitution and penalties as part of an agreement to defer prosecution of the firm, the Justice Department and the Internal Revenue Service announced, August 29, 2005."[94]

As the IRS release noted,

> In the largest criminal tax case ever filed, KPMG has admitted that it engaged in a fraud that generated at least $11 billion dollars in phony tax losses which, according to court papers, cost the United States at least $2.5 billion dollars in evaded taxes. In addition to KPMG's former deputy chairman, the individuals indicted today include two former heads of KPMG's tax practice and a former tax partner in the New York, NY office of a prominent national law firm. The criminal information and indictment together allege that from 1996 through 2003, KPMG, the nine indicted defendants and others conspired to defraud the IRS by designing, marketing and implementing illegal tax shelters. The charging documents focus on four shelters that the conspirators called FLIP, OPIS, BLIPS and SOS. …
>
> KPMG also admitted that the clients' motivations were to get a tax loss.[95]

The key issue here is that while the Quellos facilitated FLIP transactions got KPMG into serious trouble with the federal

---

[94] 'KPMG to Pay $456 Million for Criminal Violations', IR-2005-83, *IRS,* August 29, 2005, https://www.irs.gov/uac/kpmg-to-pay-456-million-for-criminal-violations

[95] 'KPMG to Pay $456 Million for Criminal Violations', IR-2005-83, *IRS,* August 29, 2005, https://www.irs.gov/uac/kpmg-to-pay-456-million-for-criminal-violations

authorities and led to a criminal tax case, how was it that those who used the POINT transactions—to evade tax as per a U.S. Senate report—were able to get away lightly?

As Senator Levin is reported to have said, the law "should assume that any transaction in a tax haven is a sham." In fact, Senator Levin puts things in proper perspective when he says that some people use tax havens to not pay their taxes while "the average guy has to pay his taxes because they are taken out of his pay before he gets it."[96]

Indeed, it is perplexing to think that Hillary Clinton[97] and other candidates like President Obama and President George W Bush did not take cognizance of all of this while taking contributions from Haim Saban who had used known and well established tax offenders like Quellos, which has been sequentially named as an abettor and facilitator in creating 'tax shelters for tax abuse' by U.S. Senate Permanent Subcommittee on Investigations.

Wonder how these candidates accept Saban's contributions given his involvement in POINT transactions and the use of tax shelters by him? If this not the nexus between *'dirty money'* and politics, what is?

The Case of Donald Sussman

An interesting presidential campaign donor who has not only been linked to off-shore entities but also named in the Panama Papers is Donald Sussman.

---

[96] David Cay Johnston, 'Tax Cheats Called Out of Control', *The New York Times,* August 1, 2006, http://www.nytimes.com/2006/08/01/business/01tax.html

[97] It needs to be remembered that Hillary Clinton and Barack Obama were members of the United States Senate while George W Bush was President at the time when the United States Senate Permanent Subcommittee on Investigations came out with reports concerning the POINT transactions and the KPMG tax shelter case.

Sussman has indeed contributed handsomely to various liberal initiatives. Recently, in the 2016 election, Sussman has contributed $2,700 to Hillary Clinton directly as an individual. He has also given huge donations **(about $8.786 million)** to pro-Clinton PACs that are supporting her campaign as per details given in **appendix 2.5**. Additionally, he has contributed to $2,000,000 to Women Vote PAC, $2,000,000 to House Majority PAC, $1,100,000 to Working for Us PAC apart from $20,000 to 21st Century Leaders PAC.

Apart from this, Sussman also contributed $5,000 individually to Barack Obama's 2012 campaign. He also gave $2,300 to Barack Obama's 2008 presidential run, apart from providing an individual contribution of $4,600 to Hillary Clinton's 2008 presidential campaign as well as $2,300 to Bill Richardson's election run.

Besides, the Sussman Family Foundation has also donated between $50,000 and $100,000 to the Clinton Foundation. Totally, Donald Sussman has contributed over $13.9 million in the 2016 cycle alone which represents a jump of 1008 per cent as compared to his donations in the 2012 cycle, which stood at a measly $1.255 million.

Overall, Donald Sussman has contributed in excess of $17.5 million, which is a huge sum indeed and that includes donations to the presidential candidates as well as those standing for the U.S. House of Representatives and the U.S. Senate.

Appendix 2.5 provides a comprehensive listing of his financing of various election campaigns and this includes contributions of his family members as well as staff of key entities.

As noted above, Sussman was named in the Panama Papers[98] and he has been linked to Simply Radiant Ltd., which is

[98] Offshore Leaks Database, Tax haven secrecy revealed, *ICIJ*, https://offshoreleaks.icij.org/search?utf8=%E2%9C%93&q =Sussman+&e= &commit=Search and, 'Major Hillary Clinton Donor Caught Up in Fresh Panama Papers Scandal', *News World*,

incorporated in the British Virgin Islands, as a director. Paloma Partners LP is listed as a shareholder of Simply Radiant Ltd. and Paloma Partners International Investors Corp is listed as an intermediary of Simply Radiant Ltd. This Paloma Partners International Investors Corp. (incorporated in the United States) is linked to another Paloma Partners International Investors Corp. whose jurisdiction is unknown. Selwyn Donald Sussman,[99] has also been linked to New China Technology Licensing Inc., which is also incorporated in the British Virgin Islands. Selwyn Donald Sussman is listed as a director.

Several questions remain unanswered here:

a) Who incorporated Simply Radiant Ltd., and why?
b) Likewise, who established New China Technology Licensing Inc., and why?
c) What is Donald Sussman's real relationship with these entities?
d) Why were both companies incorporated in the British Virgin Islands?
e) What activities did they carry on?
f) Were they used in abusive tax shelter operations—an aspect so often mentioned by the United States Permanent Subcommittee on Investigations[100]—that have been used to avoid paying legitimate taxes in the United States?

These and other questions need clear and straight answers not only from Donald Sussman but also those candidates, listed in **appendix 2.5**, who could have received '*dirty money*' from him for their election campaigns.

---

http://www.telesurtv.net/english/news/Major-Clinton-Donor-Caught-Up-in-Fresh-Panama-Papers-Scandal-20160510-0033.html

[99] Offshore Leaks Database, Tax haven secrecy revealed, *ICIJ*, https://offshoreleaks.icij.org/search?utf8=%E2%9C%93&q =Sussman+&e= &commit=Search

[100] The Role of Professional Firms in the U.S. Tax Shelter Industry Report, Prepared by the Permanent Subcommittee on Investigations Of the Committee on Homeland Security and Governmental Affairs United States Senate, April 13, 2005

If his name appearing in the Panama papers expose was not embarrassing enough for Donald Sussman, there is another interesting and related issue with regard to Donald Sussman as revealed by a *New York Times* article[101] titled "Tax Break Bringing Businesses, and Fraud, to the Virgin Islands" (by Stephanie Strom and Lynnley Browning).

According to the article, the principal threat to the United States mainland tax coffers could come from the emigration of extremely well compensated hedge fund managers—such as Donald Sussman, the founder of Paloma Partners of Greenwich which manages capital of about $3 billion—who had started claiming tax benefits under the Virgin Island program.

Further, it must also be noted that Sussman, in September 1997 as per a Securities and Exchange Commission order under the Investment Advisers Act of 1940 (Release No. 1653/September 2, 1997), accounting and auditing enforcement (Release No. 948 / September 2, 1997) and administrative proceeding (File No. 3-9382) had been charged with several violations.

> C. Sussman violated Section 206(2) in the following manner. As to 99 River Road, Sussman failed to disclose the Initial Loan that enabled him to buy 99 River Road for his wholly-owned corporation and the potential conflicts of interest that resulted. Sussman's interests were in potential conflict with those of his clients in that the documentation concerning the building indicated that Sussman was now Paloma Limited's landlord and stood to profit on any resale of the building, even though Paloma Limited had loaned to Sussman, interest free, the money needed to purchase the building.[102]

---

[101] Stephanie Strom and Lynnley Browning, 'Tax Break Bringing Businesses, and Fraud, to the Virgin Islands', *The New York Times,* September 18, 2004, http://www.nytimes.com/2004/09/18/us/tax-break-bringing-businesses-and-fraud-to-the-virgin-islands.html?_r=0

[102] United States of America, Before the Securities Exchange Commission, In the matter of Donald Sussman, https://www.sec.gov/litigation/admin/ia1653.txt

How is this permissible? Does this not constitute a serious conflict of interest?

As the SEC order further observes,

> This conflict created a risk that Sussman's decisions regarding 99 River Road would not be disinterested and that the arrangement at 99 River Road might as a result be less favorable to Paloma Limited than an arrangement reached at arms' length with a third party would be. Sussman should have disclosed these potential conflicts to the limited partners of Paloma Limited.
>
> Sussman's subsequent statement in the Paloma Limited financial statements that he intended for the limited partners to benefit on resale did not inform them that there were no formal documents legally binding Sussman to provide them with this benefit.
>
> Sussman also failed to inform the limited partners that they were at a risk of loss if there were insufficient funds from a resale to enable Lamda Holdings to repay the mortgage or the Lamda Receivable.
>
> Information concerning these potential conflicts of interest and Sussman's use of Paloma Limited's funds for his own benefit would be material to a limited partner.[103]

---

[103] United States of America, Before the Securities Exchange Commission, In the matter of Donald Sussman, https://www.sec.gov/litigation/admin/ia1653.txt

That is not all. According to the SEC, Section 206 (2) was further violated as outlined below:

> D. With respect to the bonus expense accounting, Sussman violated Section 206(2) by failing to charge $3.35 million in expenses in 1992, which resulted in a 36% understatement of operating expenses. If it had been charged in 1992, it would have reduced the investors' rate of return for the year from 11% to 10.6%. As a result of the foregoing, Sussman willfully violated Section 206(2) of the Advisers Act, which is a serious matter.[104]

Section 206 (2) says that "It shall be unlawful for any investment adviser, by use of the mails or any means or instrumentality of interstate commerce, directly or indirectly— (2) to engage in any transaction, practice, or course of business which operates as a fraud or deceit upon any client or prospective client."[105]

Accordingly, the SEC ORDERED that Sussman:

A. shall cease and desist from committing or causing any violation and any future violation of Section 206(2) of the Advisers Act;

B. shall, within ten days of any sale of 99 River Road, disgorge to Paloma Limited any net profits earned on such sale;

C. shall comply with his undertakings, as specified in his Offer of Settlement:

1. not to impose on Paloma Limited any losses incurred in connection with the resale of 99 River Road;

---

[104] United States of America, Before the Securities Exchange Commission, In the matter of Donald Sussman, https://www.sec.gov/litigation/admin/ia1653.txt
[105] Investment Advisers Act Of 1940 as Amended, https://www.sec.gov/about/laws/iaa40.pdf

2. not to impose on Paloma Limited any future costs of future capital improvements, if any, to 99 River Road; and

3. within ten days of any sale of 99 River Road, to pay any remaining indebtedness due from Lamda Holdings to Paloma Limited; and

D. shall, within ten days of the date of this Order, pay a civil money penalty in the amount of $40,000 to the United States Treasury.[106]

The civil money penalty of $40,000 is indeed substantial, given that it was ordered in 1997, almost two decades ago. It was certainly 'big money' by any standards then.

Given all of this information about Donald Sussman, his violations, conflicts of interest, his being linked to tax havens and also being named in the 2016 Panama Papers Expose, how can candidates for the office of the President of the United States, supposedly the highest office on the face of this planet, touch his *'dirty money'*?

The same goes for down ballot candidates including those contesting for the United States House of Representatives and United States Senate.

Given that over $17.5 million has been contributed to various candidates as part of this corrupt campaign finance system, what and who can rescue American democracy from its fatal embrace of money power?

---

[106] United States of America, Before the Securities Exchange Commission, In the matter of Donald Sussman, https://www.sec.gov/litigation/admin/ia1653.txt

The Case of Donald Trump

Before concluding this chapter, I thought it is important to focus on Donald Trump because of several issues related to his campaign finance and its structure.

First is the fact that his campaign has, by and large, been self-funded although people like Robert Mercer, Co-CEO of Renaissance Technologies (RenTec) are beginning to support him now.[107] As noted earlier, RenTec was named in a United States Senate Permanent Subcommittee on Investigations Report for evading taxes to the tune of $6 billion.[108]

Clearly Donald Trump has no moral right what-so-ever to criticize Hillary Clinton because they represent two sides of the same coin. While Hillary Clinton has been heavily funded by Rentec's former CEO and present chair, James Harris Simons, Donald Trump is being supported by Robert Mercer, the present Co-CEO of RenTec.

That is not all, as chapter 7 will reveal. Both Hillary Clinton and Donald Trump are extremely close to the fracking fund billionaire, Marc Lasry, who is not only a major fund raiser for Hillary Clinton but also a key business partner of Donald Trump.

---

[107] Nicholas Confessore, 'How One Family's Deep Pockets Helped Reshape Donald Trump's Campaign, *The New York Times,* August 18 2016, http://www.nytimes.com/2016/08/19/us/politics/robert-mercer-donald-trsump-donor.html?hpw&rref=politics&action=click&pgtype=Homepage&module=well-region®ion=bottom-well&WT.nav=bottom-well&_r=0 and, Theodore Schleifer, 'Yet another Donald Trump super PAC launches, this one with a link to Ted Cruz', CNN Politics, June 23, 2016, http://edition.cnn.com/2016/06/23/politics/donald-trump-super-pac-fundraising/

[108] Report: Abuse Of Structured Financial Products: Misusing Basket Options to Avoid Taxes and Leverage Limits, *Homeland Security and Governmental Affairs,* July 22, 2014, http://www.hsgac.senate.gov/subcommittees/investigations/hearings/abuse-of-structured-financial-products_misusing-basket-options-to-avoid-taxes-and-leverage-limits

Incidentally, as the New York Times[109] noted, James Harris Simons and Robert Mercer are fighting huge tax cases with the IRS. And by taking money from both Robert Mercer and James Simons, both Donald Trump and Hillary Clinton have indeed accepted *'dirty money'* without a doubt.

In fact, if you look at the cost benefit of what RenTec has done with regard to tax evasion and contributions to the presidential candidates and other campaigns, it is clear that the benefits to RenTec far outweigh the costs.

The math is clear and simple. While together, Rentec Co-CEO (Robert Mercer) and Chair (James Simons) have contributed over $50 million across the last three election cycles to various campaigns, they have been able to reportedly get away by evading taxes close to $6.46 billion. *In other words, for every $1 contributed to campaigns (the cost), they have (notionally) gained $129 (the benefit).* **That is phenomenal returns, by any standards!**

Second, Donald Trump has not released his taxes and this is not acceptable for a candidate running for office of the President of the United States. Donald Trump is making excuses, and, to the best of my knowledge, there appears to be no legal basis for his claiming that *'because his taxes are being audited, they cannot be released'*.

Two issues deserve mention here. One, again, to the best of my knowledge, the law is crystal clear and it does not prohibit anyone from releasing taxes, even if they are being audited. Two, even assuming Trump's statement to be true, the next question is why is he not releasing taxes for the years that are not under audit. Donald Trump seems to have no explanation for that.

[109] Noam Scheiber and Patricia Cohen, 'For the Wealthiest, a Private Tax System That Saves Them Billions', *The New York Times,* December 29, 2015, http://www.nytimes.com/2015/12/30/business/economy/for-the-wealthiest-private-tax-system-saves-them-billions.html

From the above, it appears that Donald Trump has something to hide with regard to his taxes and a couple of articles in the press in the run up to the 2016 election suggest that all may not be clean with Donald Trump and his taxes.

A *New York Times* article[110] suggests that Donald Trump received almost $885 million in tax breaks (using inside connections) to support his real estate ventures. Another article cites Donald Trump and his children as having been named in a $250 million tax scam[111]. Yet another article claims that there is "new evidence that Donald Trump didn't pay taxes."[112] In fact, another recent *New York Times* article[113] claims that Donald Trump reportedly declared "a $916 million loss on his 1995 income tax returns". The article goes on to argue that this huge tax deduction may have helped him to legally avoid paying any (federal) income taxes for up to 18 years. These are all serious claims and coming from reputed organizations like the *New York Times* and other well known news agencies, they should not be taken lightly. And when coupled with Donald Trump's refusal to release his tax returns, it naturally leads us to ask as to what is Donald Trump really hiding?

---

[110] Charles V Bagli, 'A Trump Empire Built on Inside Connections and $885 Million in Tax Breaks', *The New York Times,* September 17, 2016, http://mobile.nytimes.com/2016/09/18/nyregion/donald-trump-tax-breaks-real-estate.html?emc=edit_th_20160918&nl=todaysheadlines&nlid=73858581&referer=

[111] David Cay Johnston, 'Donald Trump and Kids Named in $250M Tax Scam', *The Daily Beast,* July 15, 2016, http://www.thedailybeast.com/articles/2016/07/14/donald-trump-junior-and-ivanka-material-witnesses-in-huge-tax-scam-case.html

[112] David Cay Johnston, 'New Evidence Donald Trump Didn't Pay Taxes', *The Daily Beast,* June 15, 2016, http://www.thedailybeast.com/articles/2016/06/15/new-evidence-donald-trump-didn-t-pay-taxes.html

[113] David Barstow et al, 'Trump Tax Records Obtained by The Times Reveal He Could Have Avoided Paying Taxes for Nearly Two Decades' *The New York Times*, October 1, 2016, http://www.nytimes.com/2016/10/02/us/politics/donald-trump-taxes.html?_r=0

Further, if the above claims are true, it again goes to show that the billionaires like Donald Trump, Robert Mercer and James Simons are able to use various means to avoid paying taxes whereas the ordinary average American has his taxes deducted first and has to claim any excess deductions back subsequently.

This indeed has been a central issue in this 2016 U.S. presidential election and I am not sure that Donald Trump or, for that matter, Hillary Clinton perform well in terms of not using *'dirty money'*—in this case, money tainted by tax evasion, tax abuse and tax breaks.

Indeed, as this chapter has clearly shown, Donald Trump, Hillary Clinton and many other candidates like Ted Cruz, Mitt Romney and Barack Obama, have accepted and used *'dirty money'* in their election campaigns. In this context, by *'dirty money'*, I am referring to money that is tainted because of tax abuse, tax evasion and tax breaks. That being the case, will the much needed campaign finance reform—to eliminate *'dirty money'* from electoral politics in America—that the people have been long aspiring for, ever become a reality? Only time can provide the answer.

Chapter 3

Campaign Finance and Corporate Crime

Corporate crime[114] typically takes any of the following forms: a) misrepresentation in financial statements of corporations; b) manipulation in the stock market; c) securities fraud; d) conflicts of interests; e) commercial bribery; f) bribery of public officials directly or indirectly; g) misrepresentation in advertisement and salesmanship; h) embezzlement and misappropriation of funds; i) misapplication of funds in receiverships and bankruptcies; j) violations of the Federal Election Act and so on. While taxation issues are a part of corporate crime, they are omitted from the analysis in this chapter because they have been discussed in the earlier chapter.

The entities primarily dealing with the above crimes are the Securities and Exchange Commission (SEC), Internal Revenue Service (IRS), Federal Bureau of Investigation (FBI) and Department of Justice (DoJ).

The laws[115] that govern these crimes include:

- Securities Act of 1933;
- Securities Exchange Act of 1934;
- Trust Indenture Act of 1939;

[114] This adapts Edwin Sutherland's definition of white collar crime to corporate crime.
[115] As noted above, tax laws and tax issues are omitted from the discussion on corporate crime in this chapter as they are the focus of an earlier chapter.

- Investment Company Act of 1940;
- Investment Advisers Act of 1940;
- Sarbanes-Oxley Act of 2002;
- Dodd-Frank Wall Street Reform and Consumer Protection Act of 2010;
- Jumpstart Our Business Startups Act of 2012;
- Federal Election Campaign Act of 1971;
- Foreign Corrupt Practices Act (FCPA) of 1977; and
- Various Rules and Regulations pertaining to the different Acts.

Having set the context about corporate crime, let us now look at specific cases in so far as they relate to huge contributions to presidential candidates in 2016 and other election cycles, and the antecedents and consequences of these cases therein.

The Case of Pat and Jon Stryker

Pat Stryker and her brother, Jon Stryker, the grandchildren of the famous Homer Stryker, surgeon and founder of Stryker Corporation (a medical technology company), are major contributors to the election campaign of 2016. According to *Forbes*, Patricia Stryker, has an estimated net worth of around $1.6 billion (March 2013) and much of it comes from the Stryker Corporation mentioned above.

Born in Michigan, Pat Stryker now lives in Fort Collins, Colorado. She is also the owner of Bohemian Companies which is a diversified group engaged in venture capital, real estate, and other industries. She has floated the Bohemian Foundation, which works with youth and has community development programs.[116] Her brother, Jon L Stryker,[117] a self-employed

---

[116] Paraphrased from: The World's Billionaires, *Forbes,* http://www.forbes.com/profile/pat-stryker/, and Pat Stryker Net Worth, *The Richest*, http://www.therichest.com/celebnetworth/celebrity-business/women/pat-stryker-net-worth/

[117] Jon L Stryker & Slobodan Randjelovic have also donated between $250,001 and $500,000 to the Clinton Foundation.

architect, is said to be worth $2.1 billion and his wealth is also said to partially come from the Stryker Corporation.

Over three cycles (2016, 2012 and 2008 including 2014 down ballot races), Pat Stryker has contributed over $3.5 million to the election campaigns of various presidential candidates (**appendix 1**). Of this, around $2.67 million has gone to Hillary Clinton's 2016 election campaign alone—i.e., pro-Clinton PACs. Other candidates to whom Pat Stryker has contributed individually are: $5,000 (2012) to Barack Obama; $4,600 (2008) to Barack Obama and $4,600 (2008) to Hillary Clinton. Pat Stryker has not offered any speaking assignments to any of the presidential candidates.

Likewise, across three cycles (2016, 2012 and 2008 including 2014 down ballot races), Jon Stryker has contributed a whopping $8.87 million to the election campaigns of various presidential and down ballot candidates. Of this, about $2.68 million has gone to Hillary Clinton's 2016 election campaign alone—mainly to PACs supporting Hillary Clinton. Jon Stryker has also made a donation to the Clinton Foundation through the Arcus Foundation (in the range of $25,001 to $50,000) as well as individually in the names of Jon L Stryker & Slobodan Randjelovic (in the range of $250,001 to $500,000). Other candidates[118] to whom Jon Stryker has contributed are: a huge $2 million (2012) to PACs supporting Barack Obama and $5000 (2012) to Barack Obama individually and $2,300 (2008) to Barack Obama. Jon Stryker has not offered any speaking assignments to any of the presidential candidates.

The complete details of Pat and Jon Stryker's election donations across three cycles to all presidential and other down ballot candidates—along with contributions made by their family members and staff of key entities—is summarized in **appendices 3.1 and 3.2.** A point that needs emphasis again is that much of these election donations are possible because of the substantial wealth that Pat and Jon Stryker have derived from Stryker

[118] See appendix 1 for a list of candidates across election cycles.

Corporation, which they partly and jointly own. Stryker Corporation, which has its principal executive offices in Kalamazoo, Michigan, is reported[119] to manufacture and distribute medical devices and products in more than 100 countries around the world. It has its common stock registered with the Securities and Exchange Commission pursuant to Section 12(b) of the Exchange Act.

Stryker sold its medical products—including implants, surgical equipment, and neuro technology devices—around the world through wholly-owned regional subsidiaries as well as through third-party dealers and distributors. The financial results of all of the Stryker subsidiaries are consolidated into Stryker's financial statements. In 2008, approximately 36 percent of Stryker's over $6.7 billion in total sales (about $2.41 billion) occurred outside of the United States. This is huge by any standards.

A word on how Stryker's foreign subsidiaries were organized. Typically, a Stryker subsidiary took the form of a decentralized, country-based structure, wherein a manager of a particular country's operations had primary responsibility for all business within a given country. Thus, each of Stryker's foreign subsidiaries operated pursuant to the individual policies and directives as implemented by country and/or regional management. All of the above clearly show that Stryker Corporation is a large multi-national medical technology products manufacturer partly owned by Pat and Jon Stryker,[120] from which they derive their immense wealth.

---

[119]United States of America before the Securities and Exchange Commission, in the Matter of Stryker Corporation, https://www.sec.gov/litigation/admin/2013/34-70751.pdf

[120] Dr. Homer Stryker's three grandchildren—Jon, Pat, and Rhonda Stryker—are said to partly own the Stryker Corporation. Excluding other stock holdings, it has also been reported that the siblings have control over a trust that owns about 25 percent of the $6 billion company. 'Medical supplier Stryker probed', *The Washington Times,* March 11, 2008, http://www.washingtontimes.com/news/2008/mar/11/medical-supplier-stryker-probed/?page=all

While all of this makes good reading, what does not is the fact that in 2013, as shown in **figure 3.1** and described in **table 3.2.3** in **appendix 3.2**, the SEC charged Stryker Corporation under the Foreign Corrupt Practices Act (FCPA) for violations including bribery, which is a very serious matter.

Figure 3.1: Stryker Violations of FCPA with Bribery

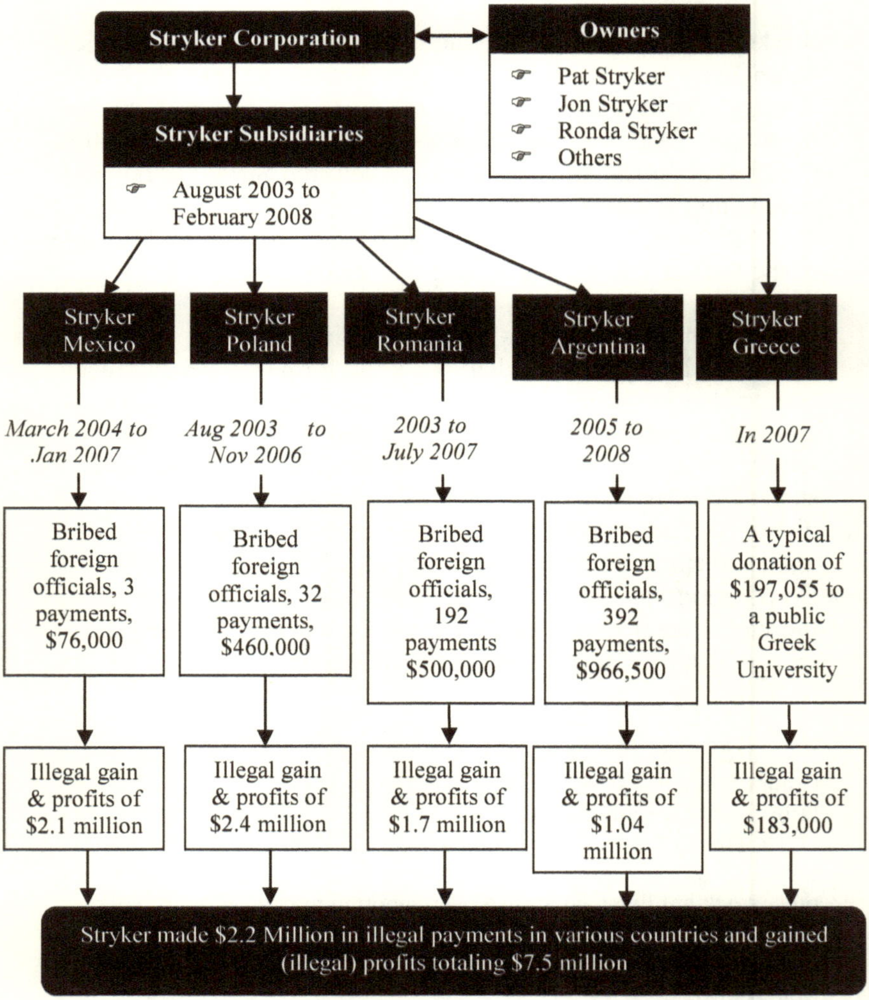

Stryker Corporation

Owners
- Pat Stryker
- Jon Stryker
- Ronda Stryker
- Others

Stryker Subsidiaries
- August 2003 to February 2008

Stryker Mexico	Stryker Poland	Stryker Romania	Stryker Argentina	Stryker Greece
March 2004 to Jan 2007	*Aug 2003 to Nov 2006*	*2003 to July 2007*	*2005 to 2008*	*In 2007*
Bribed foreign officials, 3 payments, $76,000	Bribed foreign officials, 32 payments, $460.000	Bribed foreign officials, 192 payments $500,000	Bribed foreign officials, 392 payments, $966,500	A typical donation of $197,055 to a public Greek University
Illegal gain & profits of $2.1 million	Illegal gain & profits of $2.4 million	Illegal gain & profits of $1.7 million	Illegal gain & profits of $1.04 million	Illegal gain & profits of $183,000

Stryker made $2.2 Million in illegal payments in various countries and gained (illegal) profits totaling $7.5 million

A look at the SEC order[121] reveals the following:

> Stryker failed to devise and maintain an adequate system of internal accounting controls sufficient to provide reasonable assurance that the company maintained accountability for its assets and that transactions were executed in accordance with management's authorization.
>
> Stryker's foreign subsidiaries made over $2.2 million in unlawful payments to foreign officials that were incorrectly described in the company's books and records. Stryker improperly recorded these payments as legitimate consulting and service contract payments, business travel expenses, charitable donations, or commissions.
>
> As a result of the conduct described above, Stryker violated Section 13(b)(2)(A) of the Exchange Act, which requires every issuer with a class of securities registered pursuant to Section 12 of the Exchange Act to make and keep books, records, and accounts, which, in reasonable detail, accurately and fairly reflect the transactions and dispositions of the assets of the issuer. Public companies are responsible for ensuring that their foreign subsidiaries comply with Exchange Act Section 13(b)(2)(A).

The specific details from the SEC order are summarized in **table 3.2.3** in **appendix 3.2**. In the order, SEC noted that:

> Pursuant to Section 21C of the Exchange Act, Respondent Stryker shall cease and desist from committing or causing any violations and any future violations of Sections 13(b)(2)(A) and 13(b)(2)(B) of the Exchange Act;

[121] Paraphrased and quoted from the SEC Order: United States of America, before the Securities and Exchange Commission, In the Matter of Stryker Corporation, https://www.sec.gov/litigation/admin/2013/34-70751.pdf

> Respondent shall, within ten days of the entry of this Order, pay $13,283,523 to the United States Treasury, including $7,502,635 in disgorgement, $2,280,888 in prejudgment interest thereon, and a civil monetary penalty of $3,500,000. If timely payment is not made, interest shall accrue pursuant to SEC Rule of Practice 600.

Subsequently, in a press release, the SEC summarized[122] that:

> Stryker has agreed to pay more than $13.2 million to settle the SEC's charges. "Stryker's misconduct involved hundreds of improper payments over a number of years during which the company's internal controls were fatally flawed," said Andrew M. Calamari, director of the SEC's New York Regional Office. "Companies that allow corruption to occur by failing to implement robust compliance programs will not be allowed to profit from their misconduct."

The above are not the only instances where Stryker Corporation was in legal trouble. It has been reported[123] that there are several other situations where Stryker Corporation was having legal issues—indeed, a look at Stryker's history of legal problems certainly does not make for good reading:

a) In 2008, the company faced a criminal probe with regard to two of its salesmen who reportedly pleaded guilty to "distributing misbranded devices and bone drugs and actually giving doctors instructions on how to use them."

---

[122] 'SEC Charges Stryker Corporation with FCPA Violations', *U.S. Securities and Exchange Commission,* October 24, 2013, https://www.sec.gov/News/PressRelease/Detail/PressRelease/1370540044262

[123] Jim Edwards, 'As Stryker's Legal Troubles Grew Its Management Got Richer', *CBS Money Watch,* February 20, 2009, http://www.cbsnews.com/news/as-strykers-legal-troubles-grew-its-management-got-richer/

b) In 2008, three warning letters were issued by the Food and Drug Administration (FDA) to Stryker regarding quality at three of its manufacturing plants.
c) In 2008, Stryker received subpoena with regard to compliance of the company with a previous agreement "not to pay kickbacks to bone doctors."
d) In 2008, Stryker received a Department of Justice (DOJ) subpoena on whether it violated the Foreign Corrupt Practices Act (FCPA) that prohibits companies "from paying bribes to do business in foreign countries."
e) In 2007, Stryker settled the DOJ probe into "kickbacks paid to knee doctors."
f) In 2007, there was also an SEC inquiry into whether Stryker violated the Foreign Corrupt Practices act, that prohibits companies from paying bribes to do business overseas.

To top it all off, there is the payment of $80 million to resolve criminal and civil investigations by OtisMed Corp, which had been acquired by Stryker Corporation and was its subsidiary thereafter. OtisMed reportedly[124] "pleaded guilty before U.S. District Judge Claire C. Cecchi," for "distributing—with the intent to defraud and mislead—adulterated medical devices into interstate commerce in violation of the Food, Drug, and Cosmetic Act (FDCA)." Judge Cecchi also sentenced the company, fining OtisMed $34.4 million and ordering $5.16 million in criminal forfeiture. In a separate civil settlement, OtisMed agreed to pay $40 million plus interest to resolve its civil liability.[125]

---

[124] OtisMed Corporation and former CEO Plead Guilty to Distributing FDA-Rejected Cutting Guides for Knee Replacement Surgeries, *U.S. Food and Drug Administration,* December 8, 2014, http://www.fda.gov/ICECI/CriminalInvestigations/ucm426475.htm

[125] OtisMed Corporation and former CEO Plead Guilty to Distributing FDA-Rejected Cutting Guides for Knee Replacement Surgeries, *U.S. Food and Drug Administration,* December 8, 2014, http://www.fda.gov/ICECI/CriminalInvestigations/ucm426475.htm

Dirty Money

Given the above background, how is it that the various presidential candidates and also down ballot candidates-who talk so much about eliminating corporate crime-accept money from Pat and Jon Stryker who have derived their major wealth from Stryker Corporation that has admitted to having given huge bribes to gain business overseas.

Without a doubt, corporate bribery is bad for the business environment, especially in a free market system that America and many countries so strongly believe in, where fair competition should determine who wins at the market place. Indeed, products should compete on the basis of price, quality, service, and other factors.

Corporate bribery destroys this basic tenet and Stryker's indulgence of bribery of foreign officials to assist its subsidiaries in gaining business overseas is bad practice. Period!

Therefore, accepting money for election campaigns from those who own Stryker Corporation is tantamount to using *'dirty money'* in election campaigns. That is to set the record straight.

The Case of David Elliot Shaw (D. E. Shaw)

David Elliot Shaw (born 1951) is an American computer scientist and computational biochemist who founded D. E. Shaw & Co., a hedge fund company, in 1988. The *Fortune* magazine called it "the most intriguing and mysterious force on Wall Street."[126] Employing algorithmic trading, it is reported that D. E. Shaw made $700 million in 2015, in comparison to James H. Simons of Renaissance Technologies who is said to have made $1.65 billion.[127] Indeed, D. E. Shaw is said to be among the top 5 earners in the hedge fund industry in 2015.[128]

Given his huge earning capacity, D. E. Shaw has been a significant contributor to election campaigns in the United States—specifically, he has given $5.37 million to various presidential and down ballot candidates[129] over three cycles (2016, 2012 and 2008). Of this, around $3.16 million has gone to pro-Clinton PACs in the 2016 election campaign. D. E. Shaw has also made a donation to the Clinton Foundation individually—Beth and David Shaw are listed as having contributed in the range of $500,001 to $1,000,000. Other candidates to whom D.E. Shaw has contributed are: $1.37 million (2012) to Barack Obama's PACs and $2,300 (2008) individually to Joseph R Jr Biden. D. E. Shaw has not offered any speaking assignments to any of the presidential candidates. The complete details of D. E. Shaw's election donations across three cycles to all presidential and other down ballot candidates—along with contributions made by his family members and staff of key entities—is summarized in **appendix 3.3.**

---

[126] Stacy-Marie Ishmael, 'The 25 Most Intriguing Hedge Funds', *FT Alphaville,* January 31, 2007, http://ftalphaville.ft.com/2007/01/31/2195/the-25-most-intriguing-hedge-funds/

[127] Highest Earning Hedge Fund Managers 2016, *Forbes,* http://www.forbes.com/pictures/mdg45ejfhd/2-james-simons/#7b6fb4b373f3

[128] Ibid.

[129] See appendix 1 for a list of candidates.

While D. E. Shaw's performance as a hedge fund manager is great, as also is his generosity in contributing to election campaigns, what is not so positive is the Securities and Exchange Commission order, under the Securities Exchange Act of 1934 (Release No. 70396 / September 16, 2013) and Administrative Proceeding (File No. 3-15476)[130] which instituted "cease-and-desist proceedings... pursuant to Section 21C of the Securities Exchange Act of 1934 ("Exchange Act"), against **D. E. Shaw & Co., L.P.** ("D. E. Shaw" or "Respondent"). The SEC order[131] notes:

> 1. These proceedings arise out of violations of Rule 105 of Regulation M of the Exchange Act by D. E. Shaw, a New York-based registered investment adviser. Rule 105 prohibits buying an equity security made available through a public offering, conducted on a firm commitment basis, from an underwriter or broker or dealer participating in the offering after having sold short[132] the same security during the restricted period as defined therein.
>
> 2. On five occasions, from May 2010 through March 2012, D. E. Shaw bought offered shares from an underwriter or broker or dealer participating in a follow-on public offering after having sold short the same security during the restricted period. The violations resulted in profits of $447,794.

Figure 3.2 captures these five occasions where D. E. Shaw violated Rule 105 of Regulation M of the Exchange Act

---

[130]United States of America before the Securities and Exchange Commission, in the Matter of D.E. Shaw & Co., L.P., https://www.sec.gov/litigation/admin/2013/34-70396.pdf

[131] Ibid.

[132] "*Short selling* is the sale of a security that is not owned by the seller, or that the seller has borrowed. *Short selling* is motivated by the belief that a security's price will decline, enabling it to be bought back at a lower price to make a profit." What is Short Selling?, *Investopedia,* http://www.investopedia.com/terms/s/shortselling.asp

Figure 3.2: Short Selling Instances of D. E. Shaw & Co., L.P. (Called as D. E. Shaw Hereafter)

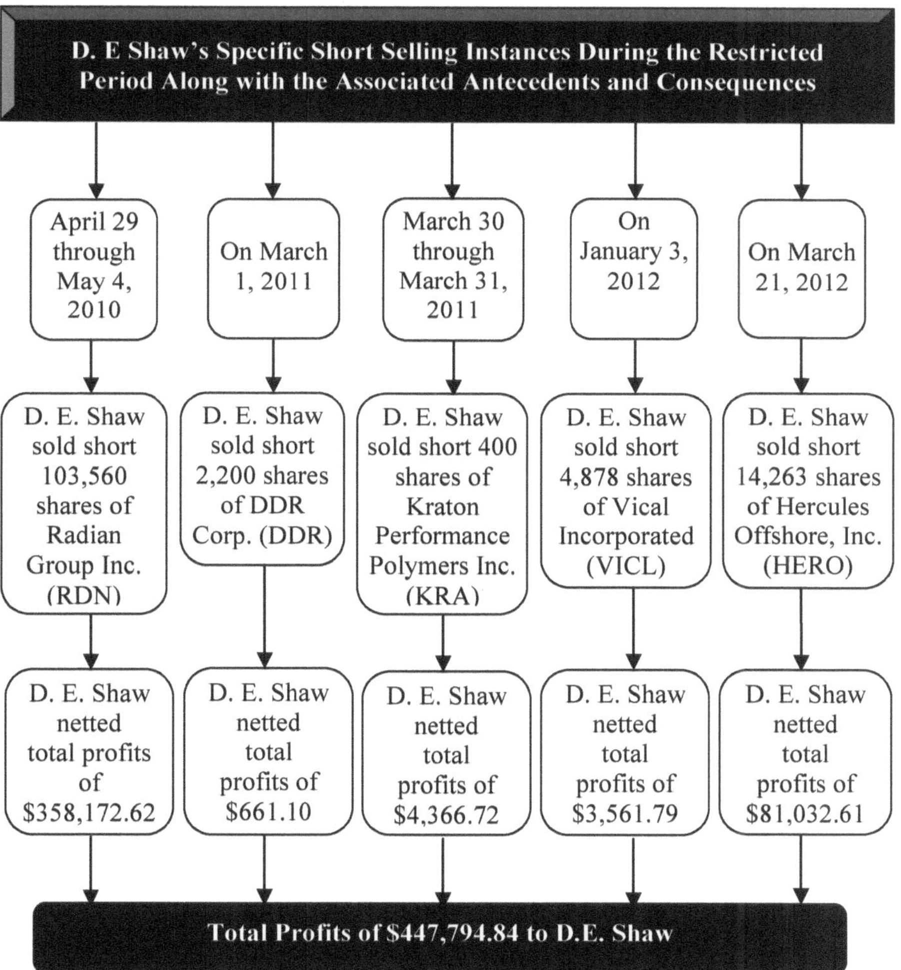

The SEC[133] further notes,

> Accordingly, it is hereby ORDERED that:
>
> A. Pursuant to Section 21C of the Exchange Act, Respondent D. E. Shaw cease and desist from committing or causing any violations and any future violations of Rule 105 of Regulation M of the Exchange Act;
>
> B. D. E. Shaw shall within fourteen (14) days of the entry of this Order, pay disgorgement of $447,794 prejudgment interest of $18,192.37, and a civil money penalty in the amount of $201,506.00 (for a total of $667,492.37) to the United States Treasury. If timely payment is not made, additional interest shall accrue pursuant to SEC Rule of Practice 600.

Without a doubt, short selling is certainly not the most ethical strategy and the **table 3.3.6** in **appendix 3.3** illustrates this as it lays out the specific instances along with the associated antecedents and consequences.

All in all, **D. E. Shaw & Co., L.P.** violations of Rule 105 resulted in profits to certain funds advised by **D. E. Shaw & Co., L.P.** of $447,794.

Ok, let us understand this properly.

Why is Rule 105 of Regulation M such a big deal?

---

[133] United States of America before the Securities and Exchange Commission, in the Matter of D.E. Shaw & Co., L.P., https://www.sec.gov/litigation/admin/2013/34-70396.pdf

As the SEC notes[134], the primary goal of Rule 105 of Regulation M is:

> Protecting the independent pricing mechanisms of the securities markets so that offering prices result from the natural forces of supply and demand unencumbered by artificial forces. The Rule is particularly concerned with short selling that could artificially depress market prices. Generally, the offering prices of follow-on and secondary offerings are set at a discount to a stock's closing price just prior to pricing. A person who expects to receive offering shares may attempt to profit by aggressively short-selling the security just prior to the pricing of the offering, thereby depressing the offering price, and then purchasing lower-priced securities in the offering.
>
> In 2007, the Commission amended Rule 105 in order to address the proliferation of trading strategies designed to conceal violations of the prior rule and in light of evolving trading strategies. **As amended, Rule 105 makes it unlawful for a person to purchase securities in a firm commitment equity offering from an underwriter or broker-dealer participating in the offering *if* that person sold short the security that is the subject of the offering during the Rule 105 restricted period,** absent an available exception.[135]

---

[134] Rule 105 of Regulation M: Short selling in connection with a public offering, *National Exam Program Risk Alert,* https://www.sec.gov/about/offices/ocie/risk-alert-091713-rule105-regm.pdf

[135] Rule 105 Of Regulation M (2013), Original Footnote 4: The Rule 105 restricted period is typically the period beginning five days before the pricing of the offered securities and ending with such pricing. Specifically, Rule 105(a) provides as follows: In connection with an offering of equity securities for cash pursuant to a registration statement or notification on Form 1-A or Form 1-E filed under the Securities Act of 1933 ("offered securities"), it shall be unlawful for any person to sell short (as defined in Rule 200(a) of Regulation SHO) the security that is the subject of the offering and purchase the offered securities from an underwriter or broker or dealer participating in the offering if such short sale was effected during the period ("Rule 105

Thus, as observed above, the above activity by **D. E. Shaw & Co., L.P. violated the federal securities laws** as defined by **Rule 105 of Regulation M.**[136]

This is not the only short selling case with **D. E. Shaw & Co., L.P.** In fact, short selling seems to have become a regular feature of the company's strategy as espoused by the following:

> DE Shaw subsidiary has been fined $13,000 by the Securities & Futures Commission of Korea for short-selling violations.[137]

What clearly emerges from the above is the purposeful intent and strategy of a company like D. E. Shaw to engage in short selling which has been deemed as detrimental in many places across the world.

You may ask why SEC is so interested in this type of violation—i.e., short selling?

First understand that "Rule 105 is sort of a cousin to Rule 10b-5, the Securities and Exchange Commission's better known **general anti-fraud rule.** Rule 105 forbids firms from 'improperly participating in public stock offerings.'"[138] That makes it a very serious matter.

---

restricted period") that is the shorter of the period: (1) Beginning five business days before the pricing of the offered securities and ending with such pricing; or (2) Beginning with the initial filing of such registration statement or notification on Form 1-A or Form 1-E and ending with the pricing. 17 CFR 242.105(a)

[136] Rule 105 of Regulation M: Short selling in connection with a public offering, *National Exam Program Risk Alert,* https://www.sec.gov/about/offices/ocie/risk-alert-091713-rule105-regm.pdf

[137] Jasmin Leitner, 'DE Shaw fined for short-selling violations in South Korea', *HFMWeek,* November 30, 2015, https://hfm.global/hfmweek/news/de-shaw-fined-for-short-selling-violations-in-south-korea/

[138] Kirsten Grind, 'SEC Short Selling Crackdown: What is Rule 105?', *The Wall Street Journal,* September 18, 2013,

Because of the above, the SEC's continued focus on Rule 105 has significant implications for hedge funds because of the rule's "strict liability nature". Merely citing the lack of manipulative intent is no defence. Likewise, the magnitude of the violation seems irrelevant. What is remarkable is that the SEC has pursued Rule 105 enforcement actions even in cases that involved a small number of shares sold short and rather meagre resultant profits. **Why is that the case?**

This is because Rule 105 is an anti-fraud provision contained in Regulation M under Section 10(b) of the Securities Exchange Act.[139] Regulation M is a set of rules designed to protect the integrity of the U.S. equity market by restricting trading behavior that might artificially affect a security's price around the time of a public offering. Rule 105 specifically is concerned with pre-offering short sales, which, by exerting downward pressure on an issuer's stock price, could cause the issuer to receive lower offering proceeds than independent market dynamics would produce. Rule 105 attempts to prevent that outcome by prohibiting the purchase of offering securities by investors that have shorted securities of the offered class during a defined period preceding the offering.

You can now appreciate the kind of violations that **D. E. Shaw & Co., L.P.** has been committing globally. It does not auger well for the fairness in the functioning of markets and that is a real fundamental issue. That is why the SEC has zero tolerance on such violations.

If short selling is one serious issue with **D. E. Shaw & Co., L.P.**, the management of pension funds is another aspect that has become controversial for the D. E. Shaw group.

---

http://blogs.wsj.com/moneybeat/2013/09/18/sec-short-selling-crackdown-what-is-rule-105/

[139] SEC Release No. 34-38067, "Anti-manipulation Rules Concerning Securities Offerings" (Dec. 20, 1996). Regulation M replaced a former series of trading practices rules in the 10b series.

Along with several other funds, the D. E. Shaw group has participated in the management of the $7 billion Employee Retirement System of the State of Rhode Island, which is embroiled in a huge controversy as noted below.

In an article titled "Rhode Island Public Pension "Reform" Looks More Like Wall Street Feeding Frenzy," Edward Siedle succinctly notes[140] that Rhode Island Treasurer, Gina Raimondo's changes to the investment portfolio of the $7 billion Employee Retirement System of the State of Rhode Island will undoubtedly cause a huge increase not just in fees paid to the (eclectic) Wall Street-based investment managers (read hedge funds and private equity companies), but will also result in a significant enhancement of the risk of the pension fund portfolio. This in effect seems to indicate that while the alternative investment strategy pursued by Gina Raimondo would increase the risk several fold, the returns will also be lower because the fees would be much higher—clearly, if this is true, then, something is amiss here.

Siedle further argues that the key problem in the Rhode Island Public Pension Reform controversy is the payment of "undisclosed and/or illegal placement agent fees" related to alternative investments by the new fund managers.

This, he emphasizes, should be investigated by the SEC. While claiming he is all for public pension reform that calls for proper, safe, and prudent investing coupled with sustainable returns, he says he just cannot sit quiet while Wall Street takes control of a huge state pension fund and recklessly dumps such hard earned money into very high cost, alternative, and risky investments, all of which, he says, will simply erode the workers' benefit. He

---

[140] Edward Siedle, 'Rhode Island Public Pension "Reform" Looks More Like Wall Street Feeding Frenzy', *Forbes,* April 4, 2013, http://www.forbes.com/sites/edwardsiedle/2013/04/04/rhode-island-public-pension-reform-looks-more-like-wall-street-feeding-frenzy/#e5aea312db00

signs off by calling this pension reform, initiated by Gina Raimondo, as nothing but a money grab[141].

In fact, Siedle claims he has asked for an FBI, SEC, and DoJ investigation.[142]

The data on fees[143] released by Raimondo has been cast into a table for easy reading below:

Table 3.1: Management and Performance Fees in Rhode Island Public Pension Fund		
Type of Fees	General Norms for Fees	• Fees in Rhode Island Public Pension Fund after Alternative Investment Using Hedge Funds
Management Fees	1.5 to 2% of money invested.	• 10 funds charge 1.5%, 8 charge 2% and D.E. Shaw charges 2.5% w3hich is the highest.
Performance Fees	Generally, 20% of any gains	• 16 funds charge 20% of any gains and this is deducted once a year. • 2 funds take 17.5%. • D.E. Shaw and Brevan Howard take 25% each, which is among

[141] Edward Siedle, 'Rhode Island Public Pension "Reform" Looks More Like Wall Street Feeding Frenzy', *Forbes,* April 4, 2013, http://www.forbes.com/sites/edwardsiedle/2013/04/04/rhode-island-public-pension-reform-looks-more-like-wall-street-feeding-frenzy/#e5aea312db00 -the same article is available here, http://ricouncil94.org/Portals/0/Uploads/Documents/Public/2013Forbes SiedleMediaCoverage2.pdf

[142] Edward Siedle, 'Will Rhode Island Pension Looters Be Prosecuted?', *Forbes,* December 16, 2015, http://www.forbes.com/sites/edwardsiedle/2015/12/16/will-sec-fbi-and-doj-prosecute-any-hedge-fund-and-private-equity-looting-of-rhode-island-pension/#a0134162b976

[143] Mike Stanton, 'R.I. Treasurer Raimondo releases data about pension hedge funds', *Providence Journal,* May 23, 2013, http://www.providencejournal.com/article/20130523/BUSINESS/305239879

Table 3.1: Management and Performance Fees in Rhode Island Public Pension Fund		
		the highest.
Sample of Combined Fees for a year[144] over $ 1 million	-	• OZ Domestic partners — $ 1.9 million • D. E Shaw — $ 1.8 million • Viking Global — $ 1.5 million • Elliot — $ 1.3 million • Davidson Kempner[145] — $1.1 million • Brevan Howard $ 1 million

Two observations gleaned from the above data must be shared—owners of three of the above funds have contributed to the Hillary Clinton campaign[146] with D. E. Shaw being the major

[144] "Rhode Island paid six of its 20 hedge-fund managers more than $1 million each in fees last year, and a total of $15.9 million on its $1 billion hedge-fund portfolio. Those numbers reflect only about six months of the 2012 fiscal year—which ended June 30, 2012—because the state Investment Commission didn't start moving money into hedge funds until November 2011, building them up to 15 percent of the state's $7.7 billion pension fund. However, the state treasurer's office does not know the dollar amount for how much the state has paid in fees since last summer because of how the information is reported. Because performance fees are not billed directly to the state and are deducted only once a year, those numbers won't be available until after the current fiscal year, which ends June 30."
Mike Stanton, 'R.I. Treasurer Raimondo releases data about pension hedge funds', *Providence Journal,* May 23, 2013, http://www.providencejournal.com/article/20130523/BUSINESS/305239879

[145] Davidson Kempner Capital Management has $25.4 billion in assets under management (as of March 2015). The firm is led by Thomas L Kempner, Jr., who has contributed to the Hillary Clinton campaign. Yet another large hedge fund where the senior management has contributed to the Hillary Clinton campaign. What is interesting is that Hillary Clinton seems to be the preferred choice of Wall Street firms and hedge funds undoubtedly.

[146] The three funds that participate in the management of the $7 billion Employee Retirement System of the State of Rhode Island and have

contributor and the fact that the management and performance fees charged by the D. E Shaw group are among the highest.

In fact, the level of fees paid has reportedly prompted the Rhode Island Retired Teachers Association (RIRTA) to retain Edward Siedle to "bring potential civil and criminal malfeasance"[147] suits in relation to the Employees' Retirement System of Rhode Island (ERSRI)". Siedle claims that he has investigated this so as to provide base information for the benefit of the FBI, SEC, and DOJ so that they can further investigate and prosecute, if required.[148] He also notes that he has "sent a letter to key officials at these agencies on RIRTA's behalf."[149] Siedle further emphasizes that the potential legal violations elaborated on in his letter would also impact other stakeholders in ERSRI, such as taxpayers and general participants.

In fact, it has been reported that the impact of Gina Raimondo's pension wealth transfer scheme that "cut workers' 3 percent COLAs to pay 4 percent to Wall Street hedge fund and private equity managers"[150] supposedly amounted to a reduction of "$1

---

contributed to the Hillary Clinton campaign, are OZ Domestic Partners via its parent company (Och-Ziff), Davidson Kempner and D. E Shaw. There are several issues with regard to the Och-Ziff as well including very serious allegations against it under the Foreign Corrupt Practices Act (FCPA). It must also be noted that Och-Ziff Capital Management Group has also donated $10,001 to $25,000 to the Clinton Foundation

[147] Edward Siedle, 'Will Rhode Island Pension Looters Be Prosecuted?', *Forbes,* December 16, 2015, http://www.forbes.com/sites/edwardsiedle/2015/12/ 16/will-sec-fbi-and-doj-prosecute-any-hedge-fund-and-private-equity-looting-of-rhode-island-pension/#742e96cc596f

[148] Ibid.

[149] Ibid.

[150] Edward Siedle, 'Rhode Island Retired Teachers Association Turns Up the Heat on Pension Looting', *Forbes,* November 20, 2015, http://www.forbes.com/sites/edwardsiedle/2015/11/20/rhode-island-retired-teachers-association-turning-up-the-heat-on-pension-looting/#5192917f7170

million a day or $1.4 billion."[151] Again, a claim worthy of investigation by the SEC, FBI, and DoJ.

Therefore, given the above context of the Rhode Island Public Pension Reform controversy, which is serious if found to be true, and also given the SEC violation committed by **D. E. Shaw & Co., L.P.**, how comfortable are presidential candidates in taking (huge) campaign contributions from D. E. Shaw[152] directly and through PACs. The same goes for down ballot candidates. Would this not contribute to the American public viewing their campaign finance strategies with suspicion? Without a doubt, a potential conflict of interest has been created here.

Take for example the following. Come next year, as President of the United States, Hillary Clinton for that matter, may have to take (strong) action to protect the peoples' (pension) money in the $7 billion Employee Retirement System of the State of Rhode Island. How can she do this when the fund is managed by the D. E. Shaw group (and others) from whom she has received huge campaign contributions? More importantly, how can she do what needs to be done given that her close associate Gov. Raimondo may be one of those Hillary will have to take action against after all? There are indeed serious questions that require a clear and transparent answer.

Overall, given the above background about D. E. Shaw and his companies, I am not sure that it is appropriate to take money from him and/or his companies. Without a doubt, candidates taking donations from such Wall Street veterans who have many skeletons in their cupboard are surely feeding on *'dirty money'*.

---

[151] Ibid.

[152] It has also been reported that with regard to D. E. Shaw and Company as follows—"The $24bn fund recently made headlines when it hired Lawrence Summers, former Treasury Secretary with the Clinton administration": Stacy-Marie Ishmael, 'The 25 Most Intriguing Hedge Funds', *FT Alphaville*, January 31, 2007, http://ftalphaville.ft.com/2007/01/31/2195/the-25-most-intriguing-hedge-funds/

The Case of the Blackstone Group

The Blackstone Group L.P. was founded in 1985 as a mergers and acquisitions specialist. Today, Blackstone has grown into one of the world's largest private equity firms. Headquartered at 345 Park Avenue in Manhattan, New York City, Blackstone has eight other offices in the United States. Globally, it has offices in London, Paris, Düsseldorf, Sydney, Tokyo, Hong Kong, Singapore, Beijing, Shanghai, Madrid, Mumbai, and Dubai.

Among its noteworthy achievements is a $4 billion initial public offering (IPO) completed in 2007, making it one of the first major private equity firms to list shares on a public exchange. Another aspect about Blackstone worthy of mention here is that it has been one of the largest investors in leveraged buyout transactions over the last ten years. [153]

Blackstone staff have been politically active and contributed almost $1,017,773 to the campaigns of various presidential candidates over the three recent election cycles (2016, 2012 and 2008). Of this, about $128,100 has gone to Hillary Clinton's 2016 election campaign while $252,700 went to Jeb Bush's 2016 primary run and $18,452 to Marco Rubio's 2016 election campaign. In addition, Blackstone's President is reported[154] to have held a fundraiser for Clinton and the money is said to have been donated to Hillary Clinton's 2016 campaign.

Other candidates[155] to whom Blackstone has contributed include: $316,406 (2012) to Mitt Romney; $61,436 (2012) to Barack Obama; $4,500 (2012) to Newt Gingrich; $79,050 (2008) to

---

[153] The Blackstone Group, *Wikipedia,* https://en.wikipedia.org/wiki/The_Blackstone_Group

[154] David Sirota and Andrew Perez, 'Hillary Clinton Denounces Corporate Crime While Accepting Cash From Blackstone, Firm Sanctioned By SEC', *International Business Times,* December 16, 2015, http://www.ibtimes.com/political-capital/hillary-clinton-denounces-corporate-crime-while-accepting-cash-blackstone-firm

[155] See appendix 1 for a list of candidates across election cycles.

John S McCain; $58,578 (2008) to Barack Obama; and $43,500 (2008) to Christopher J Dodd.

The Blackstone Group L.P. has also made a donation in the range of $250,001 to $500,000 to the Clinton Foundation. The complete details of Blackstone's senior management staffs' election donations across three cycles to all presidential and other down ballot candidates—along with contributions made by their family members—is summarized in **appendix 3.4**.

While the above achievements look good, two issues have sullied Blackstone's image.

One, its executives have repeatedly stated that state pension funds are too generous and this has got them into controversy time and again. For example, such a comment was made on January 5, 2010, (at a webcast for Blackstone's clients) by Byron R. Wien, vice chairman, Blackstone Advisory Partners LP, Blackstone's global advisory business, who said:

> The retirement benefits for state workers, really not only in New York, California and New Jersey, but throughout the country, are very generous. Too generous. And it is very hard to change that. ... But I think we have to be more realistic. We literally can't afford the benefits we have given our retirees in state and local governments. And we have to change that.[156]

Second, is the Securities and Exchange Commission (SEC) order against Blackstone. Specifically, the SEC—under the Investment Advisers Act Of 1940 (Release No. 4219 / October 7, 2015) and Administrative Proceeding (File No. 3-16887), in the Matter of Blackstone Management Partners L.L.C., Blackstone Management Partners III L.L.C., and Blackstone Management Partners IV L.L.C., Respondents—has given an order instituting

---

[156]Arleen Jacobius, 'Blackstone in repair mode after Wein flap', *Pensions & Investments,* June 28, 2010, http://www.pionline.com/article/20100628/PRINT/306289980/blackstone-in-repair-mode-after-wien-flap

cease-and-desist proceedings pursuant to section 203(k) of the investment advisers act of 1940.[157]
The SEC order notes that:

> These proceedings arise from inadequate disclosures that involved two distinct breaches of fiduciary duty by private equity fund advisers Blackstone Management Partners L.L.C. (BMP), Blackstone Management Partners III L.L.C. (BMP III), and Blackstone Management Partners IV L.L.C. (BMP IV) (collectively, "Blackstone").
>
> First, from at least 2010 through March 2015, upon either the private sale of a portfolio company or an initial public offering ("IPO"), Blackstone terminated certain portfolio company monitoring agreements and accelerated the payment of future monitoring fees as set forth in the agreements. Although Blackstone disclosed that it may receive monitoring fees from portfolio companies held by the funds it advised, and disclosed the amount of monitoring fees that had been accelerated following the acceleration, Blackstone failed to disclose to its funds, and to the funds' limited partners prior to their commitment of capital, that it may accelerate future monitoring fees upon termination of the monitoring agreements.

This is a serious lapse indeed. That is not all, there is more as evident from the SEC order below:

> Second, in late 2007, Blackstone negotiated a single legal services arrangement with its primary outside law firm (the "Law Firm") on behalf of itself and the funds. For the majority of legal services performed by the Law Firm beginning in 2008 and continuing through early 2011, Blackstone received a discount that was substantially greater than the discount received by the funds. The

[157] United States of America, before the Securities and Exchange Commission, in the matter of Blackstone et al., https://www.sec.gov/litigation/admin/2015/ia-4219.pdf

> disparate legal fee discounts were not disclosed to the funds or the funds' limited partners until August 2012. Because of its conflict of interest as the recipient of the accelerated monitoring fees and the beneficiary of the disparate legal fee discounts, Blackstone could not effectively consent to either of these practices on behalf of the funds it advised. As a result, Blackstone breached its fiduciary duty to the funds in violation of Section 206(2) of the Advisers Act and also violated Section 206(4) of the Advisers Act and Rule 206(4)-8 there under.
>
> Blackstone separately violated Section 206(4) of the Advisers Act and Rule 206(4)-7 there under by failing to adopt and implement written policies and procedures reasonably designed to prevent violations of the Advisers Act arising from the undisclosed receipt of fees and conflicts of interest.

It is crucial to note that Section 206(2) of the Advisers Act prohibits investment advisers from directly or indirectly engaging **"in any transaction, practice, or course of business which operates as a fraud or deceit upon any client or prospective client."**[158]

Likewise, as per Section 206(4) of the Advisers Act and Rule 206(4)-8, it is unlawful for any investment adviser to a pooled investment vehicle to "make any untrue statement of a material fact or omit to state a material fact necessary to make the statements made, in the light of the circumstances under which they were made, not misleading, to any investor or prospective investor in the pooled investment vehicle" or "engage in any act, practice, or course of business that is fraudulent, deceptive, or manipulative with

[158] United States of America, before the Securities and Exchange Commission, in the matter of Blackstone et al., https://www.sec.gov/litigation/admin/2015/ia-4219.pdf

respect to any investor or prospective investor in the pooled investment vehicle."[159]

Thus, as the SEC order further notes,

> As a result of the conduct described above, BMP, BMP III, and BMP IV violated Section 206(4) of the Advisers Act and Rule 206(4)-8 thereunder.
>
> Section 206(4) of the Advisers Act and Rule 206(4)-7 thereunder require registered investment advisers to adopt and implement written policies and procedures reasonably designed to prevent violations of the Advisers Act and its rules. As a result of the conduct described above, BMP, BMP III, and BMP IV violated Section 206(4) of the Advisers Act and Rule 206(4)-7 thereunder.

Accordingly, pursuant to Section 203(k) of the Advisers Act, the SEC ORDERED that:

A. Respondents BMP, BMP III, and BMP IV cease and desist from committing or causing any violations and any future violations of Sections 206(2) and 206(4) of the Advisers Act and Rules 206(4)-7 and 206(4)-8 thereunder.

B. Respondents BMP, BMP III, and BMP IV shall pay, jointly and severally, disgorgement and prejudgment interest as follows:

   i. Respondents shall pay a total of $28,911,756 consisting of disgorgement of $26,225,203 and prejudgment interest of $2,686,553 (collectively, the "Disgorgement Fund") to compensate the Funds and limited partners therein that invested in private equity transactions from 2010 to

---

[159] United States of America, before the Securities and Exchange Commission, in the matter of Blackstone et al., https://www.sec.gov/litigation/admin/2015/ia-4219.pdf

March 2015 that resulted in payment of undisclosed accelerated monitoring fees;

ii. Within ten (10) days of the entry of this Order, Respondents shall deposit the full amount of the Disgorgement Fund into an escrow account acceptable to the Commission staff and shall provide the Commission staff with evidence of such deposit in a form acceptable to the Commission staff. If timely deposit of the Disgorgement Fund is not made, additional interest shall accrue pursuant to SEC Rule of Practice 600;

C. Respondents BMP, BMP III, and BMP IV shall pay, jointly and severally, within ten (10) days of the entry of this Order, a civil monetary penalty in the amount of $10,000,000 to the Securities and Exchange Commission for transfer to the general fund of the United States Treasury, subject to Section 21F(g)(3) of the Securities Exchange Act of 1934. If timely payment is not made, additional interest shall accrue pursuant to 31 U.S.C. § 3717."

What is important to note is that the investors[160] in the Blackstone funds who were apparently harmed were the major public pension systems in the states of California, Florida, and New Jersey, all of which hold the retirement savings of educators, police officials, fire fighters, and other government workers. Reportedly[161], municipal and state pension systems that

---

[160] David Sirota and Andrew Perez, 'Hillary Clinton Denounces Corporate Crime While Accepting Cash From Blackstone, Firm Sanctioned By SEC', *International Business Times,* December 16, 2015,
http://www.ibtimes.com/political-capital/hillary-clinton-denounces-corporate-crime-while-accepting-cash-blackstone-firm

[161] David Sirota and Andrew Perez, 'Hillary Clinton Denounces Corporate Crime While Accepting Cash From Blackstone, Firm Sanctioned By SEC', *International Business Times,* December 16, 2015,

had invested close to $9.7 billion were supposedly affected in the three Blackstone funds case. In other words, Blackstone settled with the Securities and Exchange Commission on charges that it had used monitoring fees to enrich itself at the expense of these investors.

Recall that this practice of Wall Street firms enriching themselves at the expense of investors was also reported in the case of the $7 billion Employee Retirement System of the State of Rhode Island where D. E. Shaw, Davidson Kempner, OZ Domestic Partners, and other Wall Street firms are managing[162] the said pension fund. Looks like it's the same old story again and perhaps this is how Wall Street builds its own wealth? Also recall what happened in the case of Calpers,[163] the $200 billion California Pension and Retirement System, where again $500 million was lost due to the carelessness of a Wall Street asset manager, namely BlackRock.[164]

What is interesting in all of the above is that these very same presidential candidates, who have taken money from the Blackstone group and its staff, have received the endorsement of different public unions (that have employees as their constituents) at various points in time. They need to remember that these public employees rely almost exclusively on the various public pension systems for their life after retirement.

What will these presidential candidates tell the unions when they find out that they (the candidates) are backed by major Wall Street firms, many of whom have eroded savings and returns of various employee pension funds? That would be a difficult question to answer under any circumstances.

---

http://www.ibtimes.com/political-capital/hillary-clinton-denounces-corporate-crime-while-accepting-cash-blackstone-firm

[162] Refer case study of D. E. Shaw given earlier in this chapter.

[163] Suzanna Andrews, 'Larry Fink's $12 Trillion Shadow', *Vanity Fair,* April, 2010, http://www.vanityfair.com/news/2010/04/fink-201004

[164] Refer case study of BlackRock given later in this chapter.

The above excerpt clearly indicates that the Blackstone Group has been charged with serious violations by the SEC and the question that begs to be asked all over again is: "How and why did the various candidates take 'dirty money' from such an institution? This is an especially critical question given what many candidates have been saying in terms of reining in Wall Street professionals engaging in financial crime. On the face of it, this is once again proof that high-sounding rhetoric and the actual action on the ground don't match at all.

The Case Study of BlackRock

When on the topic of corporate crime, it is important to discuss the very "special" case study of BlackRock, the world's largest asset management company, headed by Larry Fink and this is the last case study in this chapter.

Over three cycles (2016, 2012 and 2008), BlackRock key staff have contributed over $496,791 million to the election campaigns of various presidential candidates. Of this, over $120,510 has gone to Hillary Clinton's 2016 election campaign. Fink's staff members have indeed been at the forefront raising money for the Clinton campaign in a big way.

For example, BlackRock's senior Managing Director Matthew Mallow is a "Hillblazer"[165] who has helped raise $100,000 or more in donations. Clinton even held a fundraiser[166] at Mallow's New York City home. Joshua A. Fink, the son of Larry Fink has made a donation in the range of $10,001 to $25,000 to the Clinton Foundation.

Other candidates to whom staff (of BlackRock) have contributed include: $9,100 (2016) to Jeb Bush; $3,034 (2016) to Bernard Sanders; $104,444 (2012) to Mitt Romney; $54,221 (2012) to

---

[165] Hillblazers, https://www.hillaryclinton.com/page/hillblazers/

[166] Zaid Jilani, 'Hillary Clinton Doing Finance Industry Fundraiser Just Before Iowa', *The Intercept,* January 27, 2016, https://theintercept.com/2016/01/26/hillary-clinton-doing-back-to-back-finance-industry-fundraisers-just-before-iowa/

Barack Obama; $5,500 (2012) to Jon Huntsman; $45,191 (2008) to Barack Obama; $20,300 (2008) to John S McCain; $16,475 (2008) to Hillary Clinton. The complete details of election donations by BlackRock and its entities across three cycles to all presidential candidates including contributions made by staff of BlackRock and their family members is summarized in **appendix 3.5.**

There are several aspects about BlackRock that deserve mention:

First, BlackRock has a huge global presence—while it reportedly manages $3.3 trillion worth of assets directly, it is said to indirectly advise in the management of $9 trillion worth assets.[167] Thus, BlackRock is also a firm that has become too big to fail—an issue central to the 2016 presidential elections with regard to Wall Street firms.[168] Indeed, BlackRock itself is therefore an institution that poses significant systemic risk, not just for the United States economy but the global economy as well.

Second, given the trillions that flow through BlackRock, the question that needs asking is whether it is indeed appropriate to have the "global market influenced by one firm and the

---

[167] Suzanna Andrews, 'Larry Fink's $12 Trillion Shadow', *Vanity Fair,* April, 2010, http://www.vanityfair.com/news/2010/04/fink-201004 Other estimates put the total of managed + advised assets at 15 trillion — see: Jessica Toonkel, 'BlackRock executive Charles Hallac, dies at 50', *Reuters,* September 9, 2015, http://www.reuters.com/article/us-blackrock-copresident-idUSKCN0R92J320150909#4TSASgekEB6rCw3G.97

[168] The too-big-to-fail issue concerns the size of the already large financial institutions. In this context, it should be noted that many of today's financial institutions of 2016 are much larger than their counterparts of 2008, for which the financial crisis occurred. In addition, several of them hold much riskier assets than in 2008. Therefore, the argument is that the large financial institutions of today represent a huge systemic risk to the economy and therefore have to be broken into institutions that are less risky. This is the essence of the too-big-to-fail argument which is dominating the discussion in the United States Presidential elections of 2016.

perspective of one man—Larry Fink."[169] This is especially relevant when one consider(s) the fact that Fink and BlackRock committed several blunders in the past:

a) Fink and BlackRock were strong backers of the 'Lehman Brothers' management, even as the bank was crashing. We need to remember that BlackRock purchased a huge amount of Lehman stock (at $28/share), three months before Lehman went bust;
b) BlackRock, is also said to have had close to $8 billion of collateralized-debt-obligation deals that defaulted in 2007 and 2008, thereby contributing to the 2008 financial crisis in the United States; and
c) BlackRock's purchase of the well-known Manhattan housing complex, Stuyvesant Town and Peter Cooper Village—a $5.4 billion deal that went into default and resulted in investors who bought equity losing large amounts of money—a case in point is that of the $200 billion California Pension and Retirement System (Calpers), the largest pension fund in the United States, which lost close to $500 million.[170]

Third, Clinton's long-term aide Cheryl Mills, who is also embroiled in the private email/server controversy that is being investigated by the Federal Bureau of Investigation (FBI), is a member of the board of BlackRock as well as the Clinton Foundation. Again, it raises serious conflict of interest issues, given what happened in the 2008 financial crisis, and BlackRock's own past as well as the issues that are dominating the Clinton Foundation discourse in the present 2016 election.

Fourth, BlackRock is a very strange entity that manages a huge amount of global assets spanning many countries and several industries. Yet, despite its humongous size and widespread influence, BlackRock remains virtually unregulated. That is why BlackRock is best referred to as a "hidden giant" that very few of

---

[169] Suzanne Andrews, 'Larry Fink's $12 Trillion Shadow', *Vanity Fair,* April, 2010, http://www.vanityfair.com/news/2010/04/fink-201004
[170] Ibid.

us have knowledge about[171]—a Goliath that is so powerful it could even wreck the United States and the global economy in a jiffy, if and when things actually go wrong.

Fifth, there is much of this revolving door phenomenon going on at BlackRock itself with key personnel[172] moving to and from government/public policy positions and so on—a further case of huge conflicts of interest summarized in **table 3.2**:

Table 3.2: From Government to BlackRock, People and Positions		
Name	**Former Position**	**Position at BlackRock**
Christopher Meade	☞ Former general counsel at the Treasury Department. He spent 2010–2015 at Treasury, with three years as general counsel	☞ Serves in a similar capacity at BlackRock
Katheryn Rosen	☞ Senior policy adviser to Barney Frank (adviser to the Clinton campaign) on the House Financial Services Committee, helping to write Dodd-Frank. She became deputy assistant secretary at Treasury in February 2011 working to build the Financial Stability Oversight Council, the Treasury-led super-regulator monitoring	☞ Is managing director at BlackRock. Prior to government work, Rosen spent 14 years as a managing director with JPMorgan Chase

[171] Andrew Gavin Marshall, 'Exposing BlackRock: Who's Afraid of Lawrence Fink?', *counterpunch,* December 11, 2015, http://www.counterpunch.org/2015/12/11/exposing-blackrock-whos-afraid-of-lawrence-fink/

[172] Blackrock, http://www.blackrock.com/corporate/en-in/investor-relations/company-overview-and-governance/board-of-directors

Table 3.2: From Government to BlackRock, People and Positions		
Name	**Former Position**	**Position at BlackRock**
	systemic risk	
Kendrick Wilson	☞ Advised Treasury while it managed the financial crisis and its fallout in 2008 and 2009. Advised the merger of Bank of America and failed subprime lender Countrywide while at Treasury	☞ Is a vice chairman at BlackRock since 2010
Michael Pyle	☞ Was a senior adviser to Lael Brainard when she served as undersecretary to the Treasury for international affairs. Worked at the White House for the National Economic Council and the Office of Management and Budget. Said to be an economic policy adviser to the Clinton campaign	☞ He worked as a director at BlackRock until at least October 2015
Cheryl Mills	☞ Clinton's chief of staff at the State Department. ☞ Previously, Mills was, was deputy White House counsel in the Bill Clinton administration	☞ Cheryl Mills is presently on the board of directors of the Clinton Foundation[173] as well as BlackRock. She is Clinton's

[173] Board of Directors, Clinton Foundation, https://www.clintonfoundation.org/about/board-directors

Table 3.2: From Government to BlackRock, People and Positions		
Name	**Former Position**	**Position at BlackRock**
		closest and most trusted (former) aide
Source: Compiled from Larry Fink and His BlackRock Team Poised to Take Over Hillary Clinton's Treasury Department — https://theintercept.com/2016/03/02/larry-fink-and-his-blackrock-team-poised-to-take-over-hillary-clintons-treasury-department/		

Sixth, an added reason is BlackRock's nature of business and its role in shaping regulation, post 2008 crisis. The kind of work that BlackRock does, as an asset manager, poses a systemic risk to the financial system. Yet, BlackRock and Larry Fink do not accept the view that asset managers are systemically important financial institutions as this could lead to capital requirements being made larger.

Further, BlackRock reportedly is against the reinstatement of the Glass-Steagall Act whereas, even the man who was widely reported to be responsible for the shattering of The Glass-Steagall Act, Sanford Weill[174] himself wants it brought back . . . today!

---

[174] Kevin Wack, 'Weill Puts Glass-Steagall Back on Washington's Agenda', *American Banker,* July 25, 2012, http://www.americanbanker.com/issues/177_143/sandy-weill-puts-glass-steagall-back-on-washingtons-agenda-1051271-1.html and Heather Long, 'Former Citigroup CEO: Big banks don't work', *CNN Money,* November 12, 2015, http://money.cnn.com/2015/11/12/investing/citigroup-john-reed-glass-steagall/

Finally, see what the SEC says in its order[175] about BlackRock and its ability to manage conflict of interest—an issue of great concern in the 2016 presidential election.

> This matter concerns investment adviser BlackRock's[176] failure to disclose a conflict of interest involving the outside business activity of one of its portfolio managers. Daniel J. Rice, III was a well-known, long-standing, top-performing energy-sector portfolio manager.
>
> Rice joined BlackRock in 2005 and managed BlackRock energy-focused registered funds, private funds, and separate accounts. In 2007, Rice founded Rice Energy, L.P.—a Rice family-owned-and-operated oil and natural gas production company. Rice was the general partner of Rice Energy and personally invested approximately $50 million in the company. Rice's three sons were the CEO, CFO, and VP of Geology of Rice Energy.
>
> In February 2010, Rice Energy formed a joint venture with Alpha Natural Resources, Inc. ("ANR"), a publicly-traded coal company held in the BlackRock funds and accounts managed by Rice. By June 30, 2011, ANR stock was the largest holding (9.4%) in the Rice-managed $1.7 billion BlackRock Energy & Resources Portfolio, primarily as a result of ANR acquiring two other public companies held in that portfolio. BlackRock knew of Rice's involvement with and investment in Rice Energy as well as the joint venture with ANR, but failed to disclose Rice's conflict of interest to the BlackRock

---

[175] United States of America before the Securities and Exchange Commission, in the Matter of Blackrock Advisors et al., https://www.sec.gov/litigation/admin/2015/ia-4065.pdf

[176] BlackRock Advisors, LLC, a Delaware limited liability company headquartered in Wilmington, Delaware, is an investment adviser registered with the Commission. According to its Form ADV filed in June 2014, BlackRock has assets under management of approximately $452 billion. BlackRock is a subsidiary of BlackRock, Inc., an investment management firm with assets under management of approximately $4.3 trillion as of December 31, 2013.

> funds' boards of directors or to BlackRock advisory clients.
>
> BlackRock also failed to adopt and implement written compliance policies and procedures reasonably designed to prevent violations of the Advisers Act and the rules thereunder, as required by Section 206(4) of the Advisers Act and Rule 206(4)-7 thereunder, concerning the outside activities of its employees, including how they should be assessed and monitored for conflict purposes, and when an employee's outside activity should be disclosed to the BlackRock funds' board of directors or to BlackRock advisory clients. BlackRock's chief compliance officer ("CCO"), Bartholomew A. Battista, caused BlackRock's compliance-related violations.
>
> BlackRock and Battista also caused the registered funds' failure to have the funds' chief compliance officer report to the funds' boards of directors — in violation of Rule 38a-1(a)(4)(iii)(B) under the Investment Company Act of 1940 — Rice's violations of BlackRock's private investment policy. BlackRock and Battista knew about Rice's violations, and knew or should have known that they were not reported to the funds' boards.

Thus, as the SEC order unequivocally notes in its order, BlackRock willfully[177] violated Section 206(2) of the Advisers Act, "which prohibits an investment adviser from engaging in any transaction, practice, or course of business that operates as a fraud or deceit upon a client or prospective client."[178]

---

[177] SEC order Original Footnote 1: A willful violation of the securities laws means merely "that the person charged with the duty knows what he is doing." *Wonsover v. SEC*, 205 F.3d 408, 414 (D.C. Cir. 2000) (quoting *Hughes v. SEC*, 174 F.2d 969, 977 (D.C. Cir. 1949)). There is no requirement that the actor 'also be aware that he is violating one of the Rules or Acts.' Id. (quoting *Gearhart & Otis, Inc. v. SEC*, 348 F.2d 798, 803 (D.C. Cir. 1965)).

[178] SEC order Original Footnote 2: A violation of Section 206(2) of the Advisors Act does not require scienter, but, rather, may rest on a

The SEC order further notes,

> BlackRock breached its fiduciary duty by failing to disclose a conflict of interest—namely Rice's involvement with and investment in Rice Energy—to the BlackRock funds' boards of directors or to advisory clients.
>
> As a result of the conduct described above, BlackRock willfully violated Section 206(4) of the Advisers Act and Rule 206(4)-7 thereunder by failing to adopt and implement written policies and procedures reasonably designed to prevent violations of the Advisers Act and its rules.
>
> BlackRock failed to adopt and implement written policies and procedures to assess and monitor the outside activities of its employees and to disclose conflicts of interest to the funds' boards and to advisory clients. Battista caused BlackRock's compliance-related violations.
>
> As a result of the conduct described above, BlackRock and Battista caused certain BlackRock funds' violations of Rule 38a-1(a) under the Investment Company Act. Rule 38a-1(a)(4)(iii)(B) requires registered investment companies, through their chief compliance officer, to provide a written report at least annually to the fund's board of directors that addresses each material compliance matter that occurred since the date of the last report. Rule 38a-1, in pertinent part, defines a "material compliance matter" as any compliance matter about which the fund's board of directors would reasonably need to know to oversee fund compliance, and that involves, without limitation, a violation of the policies and procedures of its investment adviser. BlackRock and Battista caused the failures by certain BlackRock funds to

---

finding of simple negligence. *SEC v. Steadman*, 967 F.2d 636, 643 n.5 (D.C. Cir. 1992) (citing *SEC v. Capital Gains Research Bureau*, Inc., 375 U.S. 180, 195 (1963)).

> report all material compliance matters—namely Rice's violations of BlackRock's private investment policy—to their boards of directors.

Accordingly, pursuant to Sections 203(e) and 203(k) of the Advisers Act and Sections 9(b) and 9(f) of the Investment Company Act with respect to BlackRock, and pursuant to Section 203(k) of the Advisers Act and Section 9(f) of the Investment Company Act with respect to Battista, the SEC ORDERED that:

> D. Respondent BlackRock shall, within thirty (30) calendar days of the entry of this Order, pay a civil money penalty in the amount of $12 million to the Securities and Exchange Commission. ... If timely payment is not made, additional interest shall accrue pursuant to 31 U.S.C. 3717.

Given the above background on BlackRock, its humongous size, its various past blunders and recent settlement with SEC on conflicts of interest, how appropriate is it for presidential candidates to accept money from BlackRock and/or its senior management/staff for an election campaign.

The above apart, there is one another point that deserves mention. Many presidential candidates (including Hillary Clinton and Donald Trump) have called for tougher action on financial crime. What is really ironical though is the fact that, while many of these candidates, like Hillary Clinton and Donald Trump, talk tough and promise action against "corporate wrongdoers and shadow banks" as well as cracking down on "investment firms that offer banking services outside the purview of traditional financial regulations and other Wall Street entities," their own campaigns still continue to be funded largely by Wall Street firms—many of whom have either been fined by the SEC for supposedly "ripping off" their clients and/or named in Senate reports for tax abuse and tax evasion.

One final issue is in order here. Hillary Clinton echoes ideas very similar[179] to those of Larry Fink as far as prescriptions go for Wall Street and the larger United States economy. She is said to rely on Fink's ideas, at least with regard to Wall Street and its regulation. There is also a strong rumor[180] that Larry Fink could become treasury secretary in a new Clinton Administration. If true, there are serious issues including conflicts of interest in this. And given the Wells Fargo case[181] that just occurred during the 2016 election run up, without a doubt, the consequences of such a reverse revolving door appointment would be disastrous not only for the United States of America but the world economy as a whole. One of major reasons for the 2008 financial crisis is the fact that Wall Street lobbied[182] so hard to have the industry

---

[179] Stephen Gandel, 'BlackRock's Larry Fink May Be Stepping Up his Play for Treasury Secretary', *Fortune,* February 4, 2016, http://fortune.com/2016/02/04/blackrock-larry-fink-treasury-secretary/ (In a recent letter to CEOs, the BlackRock CEO took a page out of Hillary Clinton's playbook.) and, Heather Long, 'Wall Street CEO sounds a lot like Hillary Clinton', *CNN Money,* February 3, 2016, http://money.cnn.com/2016/02/03/investing/hillary-clinton-larry-fink-blackrock/

[180] David Dayen, 'Larry Fink and His BlackRock Team Poised to Take Over Hillary Clinton's Treasury Department', *The Intercept,* March 3, 2016, https://theintercept.com/2016/03/02/larry-fink-and-his-blackrock-team-poised-to-take-over-hillary-clintons-treasury-department/

[181] Gina Chon, 'In Wells Fargo Case, Watchdogs Didn't Play Team Ball', *The New York Times,* September 20, 2016, http://www.nytimes.com/2016/09/21/business/dealbook/in-wells-fargo-case-watchdogs-didnt-play-team-ball.html?_r=0

[182] "Changes in the regulatory system occurred in many instances as financial markets evolved. However, as the report will show, the financial industry itself played a key role in weakening regulatory constraints on institutions, markets, and products. It did not surprise the Commission that an industry of such wealth and power would exert pressure on policy makers and regulators. From 1999 to 2008, the financial sector expended $2.7 billion in reported federal lobbying expenses; individuals and political action committees in the sector made more than $1 billion in campaign contributions. What troubled us was the extent to which the nation was deprived of the necessary strength and independence of the oversight necessary to safeguard financial stability." — (Final Report Of The National Commission On

de-regulated (including the shattering of the Glass-Steagall Act). In light of this, the idea of having Wall Street industry insiders[183] make policy does not appear sound.

The potential Treasury Secretary appointment aside, there are several other issues related to Larry Fink and BlackRock that make it extremely inappropriate for Hillary Clinton and other candidates to even accept contributions from BlackRock/Larry Fink or use BlackRock staff as bundlers for collecting campaign contributions.

In an election where the key issues are "big money in politics," "corrupt campaign finance system" and "conflicts of interest and campaign funding," any association with an entity like BlackRock is a definite no-no, let alone getting them to mobilize campaign funds. That being the case, how is it that the various presidential candidates have accepted money for a company like BlackRock, about which serious concerns have been raised above.

The Causes Of The Financial And Economic Crisis In The United States, Submitted by The Financial Crisis Inquiry Commission, Pursuant to Public Law 111-21, January 2011, Page number 18)

[183] We know what happened when Paulson of Goldman Sachs fame was in charge of the treasury during 2006–2009—the crisis burgeoned and exploded as there were huge conflicts of interest.

Chapter 4

Campaign Finance and Wall Street

While on the topic of corporate crime, there is growing concern over the lack of regulation and supervision of Wall Street, the vulnerability of small investors is of particular concern. This is one of the key issues of the 2016 presidential election. One must perforce mention here that the position of various presidential candidates on the subject has been ambiguous to say the least, especially because of a mismatch between words and action. Only Senator Bernie Sanders during the primaries addressed this issue head on and said that existing systems for Wall Street regulation are very weak. How right he is proving to be is borne out by the Wells Fargo[184] case that unfolded recently.

One of the biggest reasons for the existing weak regulatory system is the near seamless shift of key people from Wall Street to regulatory and supervisory bodies through the "reverse revolving door" phenomenon. Top executives of Wall Street firms (and representatives of special interest groups including lobbyists) have been known to take up positions in the Government or the regulatory set up. Paulson, for example, the Treasury Secretary of the United States during the years 2006–2009 is a classic case. He came to the Treasury after nearly 32

---

[184] Gina Chon, 'In Wells Fargo Case, Watchdogs Didn't Play Team Ball', *The New York Times,* September 20, 2016, http://www.nytimes.com/2016/09/21/business/dealbook/in-wells-fargo-case-watchdogs-didnt-play-team-ball.html?_r=0

years at Goldman Sachs. (See **Table 4.1** below for other examples.) Others have likewise built up extremely close working relationships with the regulators and supervisors, in particular those who oversee or regulate Wall Street.

Table 4.1: Henry Paulson			
Name	**Designation**	**Period**	**Previous Position**
Henry Paulson	United States Secretary of the Treasury	July 10, 2006–January 20, 2009	• Chairman and Chief Executive Officer, Goldman Sachs in 1974. His compensation package, according to reports, was $37 million in 2005, and $16.4 million projected for 2006. His net worth has been estimated at over $700 million.
Source: Compiled from Wikipedia — https://en.wikipedia.org/wiki/Henry_Paulson			

Robert Rubin (**table 4.2**) is yet another of those who made the switch from Wall Street to government. It must be recalled here that much of the foundations for the de-regulation that took place during former President Bill Clinton's second term, were laid during Rubin's tenure. It is of course common knowledge what this de-regulation ultimately did in terms of repealing the Glass-Steagall Act, thereby resulting in the 2008 financial crisis.[185]

[185] This is an opinion expressed in the Financial Crisis Inquiry Report, Final Report Of The National Commission On The Causes Of The Financial And Economic Crisis In The United States, The Financial Crisis Inquiry Commission, 2011, http://fcic-static.law.stanford.edu/cdn_media/fcic-reports/fcic_final_report_full.pdf

Table 4.2: Robert Rubin			
Name	**Designation**	**Period**	**Previous Position**
Robert Rubin	United States Secretary of the Treasury	January 11, 1995– July 2, 1999	• Before his government service, Rubin spent 26 years at Goldman Sachs, eventually serving as a member of the board and co-chairman from 1990 to 1992. • As Treasury Secretary during 1995–99, Rubin oversaw the loosening of financial industry underwriting guidelines, which had been intact since the 1930s. • From November to December 2007, he served temporarily as chairman of Citigroup and resigned from the company on January 9, 2009. He received more than $126 million in cash and stock during his tenure at Citigroup, up through and including Citigroup's bailout by the U.S. Treasury. • Rubin received over $17 million in compensation from Citigroup and a further $33 million in stock options as of 2008 and total compensation of $126 million from Citigroup between 1999 and 2009.`
Source: Compiled from Wikipedia — https://en.wikipedia.org/wiki/Robert_Rubin			

Often called "the reverse revolving door" phenomenon, these people have established a very strong pro-financial sector/Wall Street bias in policy formulation and regulatory enforcement by regulators and supervisors that oversee their (former) industry, former employers and/or related institutions. This oftentimes results in de-regulation to the detriment of the end user.

Next is the shift of key people from government institutions to Wall Street through the normal revolving door phenomenon. There are the cases where key people from regulatory and supervisory bodies and governments have moved (either through a permanent or temporary relationship) to lucrative private-sector positions at Wall Street firms.

An example is relevant here. People like Lawrence Summers (**table 4.3**), Timothy Geithner (**table 4.3**), or Robert Rubin (**table 4.2**) for that matter, who, after having served as Treasury Secretary, went on to work with Wall Street firms like D. E. Shaw, Warburg Pincus,[186] and Citigroup respectively.

Table 4.3: Lawrence Summers and Timothy Geithner			
Name	**Designation**	**Period**	**Previous Position**
Lawrence Summers	United States Secretary of the Treasury	July 2, 1999– January 20, 2001	• Post Government, Summers has worked as an advisor to hedge fund D. E. Shaw & Co, Citigroup and the NASDAQ OMX Group while resuming his role as a tenured, Harvard professor. • In June 2011, Summers joined the board of directors of Square, a company

[186] A Wall Street private equity firm.

Table 4.3: Lawrence Summers and Timothy Geithner			
Name	**Designation**	**Period**	**Previous Position**
			developing an electronic payment service, and became a special adviser at venture capital firm Andreessen Horowitz. • He joined the board of person-to-person lending company Lending Club in December 2012.
Timothy Geithner	United States Secretary of the Treasury	January 26, 2009–January 25, 2013	• American economic policy maker and central banker. He was previously the president of the Federal Reserve Bank of New York from 2003 to 2009. He now serves as president of Warburg Pincus, a Wall Street private equity firm.
Source: Compiled from Wikipedia — https://en.wikipedia.org/wiki/Lawrence_Summers and https://en.wikipedia.org/wiki/Timothy_Geithner			

Typically, such people use their regulatory and government experience and long-standing connections to benefit their new employer or industry directly as well as indirectly (e.g. through lobbying for a supportive regulatory policy environment,[187] in public procurement and so on). This has not only led to a lax

[187] The case of the Dodd Frank legislation is one example here and the lobbying database is replete with examples of lobbying by various Wall Street firms with former government staff.

regulatory environment and poor supervision by their former colleagues (with regard to Wall Street) but has also resulted in the drafting and framing of policies hugely supportive to Wall Street, and a de-regulated environment, especially at the expense of end user client protection and well being. Again, as noted before, we all know that the 2008 financial crisis resulted from a massive de-regulation due lobbying, campaign contributions, PAC activity, and other similar efforts.[188]

There have also been situations where former decision makers (including policy makers and executive decision makers) have become paid advocates and use their knowledge of, and connections with, governmental agencies, regulators, and supervisors to advance the interests of Wall Street companies. This again would be part of Wall Street lobbying which has been discussed above.

Finally, we have the paid speeches delivered by former Government position holders—all the Wall Street speeches by Hillary and Bill Clinton would come under this category. In fact, to the best of my knowledge, of the candidates still in the fray in the 2016 election cycle, Hillary Clinton is the only presidential candidate who has delivered such a large number of speeches after taking money for her speaking assignments. Indeed, Hillary and Bill Clinton have had a packed schedule of speaking assignments across the globe in the last decade or so, especially during times when either or both of them have not held any political office. But what is interesting is the fact that they have given almost 39 speeches to the Wall Street firms and the big banks. A brief analysis of the 39 speeches given by Bill Clinton and Hillary Clinton[189] over the years to six big banks and

---

[188] This is an opinion expressed in the Financial Crisis Inquiry Report, Final Report Of The National Commission On The Causes Of The Financial And Economic Crisis In The United States, The Financial Crisis Inquiry Commission, 2011, http://fcic-static.law.stanford.edu/cdn_media/fcic-reports/fcic_final_report_full.pdf

[189] The website, http://www.releasethetranscripts.com/ provides a complete listing of all 91 speeches given by Hillary Clinton to 84

numerous large Wall Street firms is given below and the complete details can be found in **appendix 4.**

Of the 39 speeches given to big banks and Wall Street firms, 8 speeches were delivered by Hillary (2013–2014) and 31 by Bill (2001–2015). While Hillary received $1,835,000 for her 8 speeches, Bill was paid $5,910,000 for his 31 speeches. Together, Bill and Hillary made about a total of $7.75 million from the 39 speeches that were delivered to the 6 big banks and to large Wall Street firms. Further, Hillary Clinton made a total of $21.14 million from 91 speeches[190] (given to 84 organizations) that she delivered post her laying down office as Secretary of State in 2013. In terms of individual institutions, Goldman Sachs (12 speeches) and UBS (10 speeches) had the maximum number. Interestingly, 5 out of the 6 institutions listed—Citigroup, Goldman Sachs, Morgan Stanley, Bank of America/Merrill Lynch and Deutsch Bank—were involved and in some ways responsible for the 2008 financial crisis. Most of these institutions were also recipients of the United States taxpayer bailout. The data given in **table 4.4** below is very revealing in that the six major Wall Street firms and big banks paid a settlement of just $45.31 billion while receiving tax payer bailouts to the tune of $110 billion—which is almost 2.43 times the settlement paid.

Table 4.4: Settlement and Bailout of Key Wall Street Firms and Large Banks in USA

Wall Street Entity	Settlement in Billions of $ for Role in Financial Crisis (Fines)	Tax Payer Bailout	Bailout/ Settlement
Goldman	$5.06 billion	$10 billion	1.98

organizations after she left the position of Secretary of State in 2013. A full listing of the 39 speeches that Hillary and Bill Clinton delivered to 6 large banks and Wall Street firms can be found at- http://edition.cnn.com/2016/02/05/politics/hillary-clinton-bill-clinton-paid-speeches/

[190] This figure includes her 8 Wall Street speeches given above for which she received $1.835 million.

Table 4.4: Settlement and Bailout of Key Wall Street Firms and Large Banks in USA			
Sachs			
Bank of America	$16.65 billion	$45 billion	2.70
Citigroup	$7 billion	$45 billion	6.43
Deutsche Bank	$14 billion	N/A	N/A
Morgan Stanley	$2.6 billion	$10 billion	3.85
UBS AG	$19.5 million	N/A	N/A
All	**$45.31 billion**	**$110 billion**	**2.43**

Interestingly, all the above institutions have donated significant amounts to the Clinton Foundation as evident from **table 4.5**. The Foundation has only indicated the range of the donations made on their website[191] and not the exact amounts.

Table 4.5: Contributions of Wall Street and Big Banks to the Clinton Foundation	
Name	**Contributions**
Citigroup Inc.	$500,001 to $1,000,000
Goldman Sachs Group, Inc.	$1,000,001 to $5,000,000
Goldman Sachs Philanthropy Fund	$250,001 to $500,000
Bank of America	$100,001 to $250,000
Bank of America Foundation	$500,001 to $1,000,000
Merrill Lynch & Company Foundation, Inc.	$100,001 to $250,000
UBS AG	$50,000 to $100,000,
UBS Wealth Management USA	$500,001 to $1,000,000
Morgan Stanley	$100,001 to $250,000
Morgan Stanley Global Impact Funding Trust	$250,001 to $500,000
Morgan Stanley Bank AG	$10,001 to $25,000

[191] Please see Clinton Foundation, https://www.clintonfoundation.org/contributors

Table 4.5: Contributions of Wall Street and Big Banks to the Clinton Foundation	
Deutsche Bank AG	$250,001 to $500,000
Deutsche Bank Americas	$250,001 to $500,000.
Wells Fargo Foundation	$100,001 to $250,000
Wells Fargo Bank	$10,001 to $25,000

Appendix 4 also lists contributions of senior management/staff of some of these firms to various presidential and down ballot candidates.

Another interesting fact is that all of these institutions were lobbying with various government departments in the United States and several of them had issues and cases pending with the Securities and Exchange Commission (SEC), Internal Revenue Service (IRS) and other departments at various points in time.

It must also be mentioned that all the speeches made by Bill and Hillary Clinton to UBS, an organization that ran into severe problems with the IRS, for example, happened at a time when either the IRS problem persisted or after it had been resolved.

As per the official lobbying database, these six institutions had directly lobbied the government 2,411 times during a 16-year period[192] (1999–2015), spending over $400 million.[193] This does not include what their trade associations lobbied nor does it include the money each of their employees had contributed to political action committees (PACs) and campaign financing, nor the money that they had paid for celebrity speeches and the like. This is also the number that is officially reported to the lobbying

[192] Data is not uniformly available across the years and therefore, taking the number of years as 16 is indeed an overestimate. In reality, the number of years for which data is available would be closer to 10 years. This data comes from just one database—The United States Senate, http://soprweb.senate.gov/index.cfm?event=selectfields

[193] It must be noted that many of the entries in the lobbying database had blank entries for expenses.

database[194] and it is expected that the actual figures could have been even higher. Please note that[195] from 1999 to 2008, the financial sector is said to have expended $2.7 billion in reported federal lobbying expenses and individuals/political action committees in the financial sector made more than $1 billion in campaign contributions.

Similarly, the 84 organizations[196] to which Hillary Clinton delivered 91 speeches (since she moved on from her position as Secretary of State in 2013), had directly lobbied the government on 11,628 occasions, spending about $1.95 billion,[197] which is an incredible amount by any standards. Taken together, the above data clearly indicate that the influence of corporate America in lobbying the government should not be underestimated in any way. Their power to influence is huge indeed.

There have been several demands, by Bernie Sanders and others, asking Hillary Clinton to immediately release the transcripts of these Wall Street speeches, most notably the ones made to Goldman Sachs. While there have been arguments for and against this practice (of releasing speech transcripts), it is about time that we looked objectively at this issue from a larger standpoint. To do so, we need to understand the context of the 2008 financial crisis better and this chapter is devoted to that

---

[194] The United States Senate, http://soprweb.senate.gov/index.cfm?event=selectfields

[195] Financial Crisis Inquiry Report, Final Report Of The National Commission On The Causes Of The Financial And Economic Crisis In The United States, The Financial Crisis Inquiry Commission, 2011, http://fcic-static.law.stanford.edu/cdn_media/fcic-reports/fcic_final_report_full.pdf

[196] This includes the 8 speeches by Hillary Clinton to the six big banks and large Wall Street firms.

[197] The time period is 1999–2015. However, data is not uniformly available across the years and therefore, taking the number of years as 16 is indeed an overestimate. In reality, the number of years for which data is available would be closer to 10 years. This data comes from just one database—The United States Senate, http://soprweb.senate.gov/index.cfm?event=selectfields

even as it tries to answer the question of whether or not Hillary Clinton is duty-bound to release the transcripts of her speeches.

If there is one thing that stands out about the 2008 financial crisis, it is the fact that weak, lax and laissez-faire regulation—caused by lobbying, PACs, campaign financing, and the power of Wall Street to influence policy makers, regulators and others—served as an important factor that triggered the meltdown. There are no two opinions on this and this is what the Financial Crisis Inquiry Commission (FCIC) Final Report[198] dated January 2011 has said over and over again.

What exactly did the FCIC say in its final report and what is the connection with the requests by Bernie Sanders and others urging Hillary Clinton to immediately release the transcripts of her Goldman Sachs speech?

Transparency and accountability in public life and electoral politics are at the root of a healthy democracy and they call for sharing of information (with the electorate) in a clear manner by all potential law makers[199] now and in the future. That is precisely why Hillary Clinton needs to release her Wall Street speeches immediately. Without a doubt, she owes this disclosure to the American people.[200] What she told Wall Street during her

---

[198] Financial Crisis Inquiry Report, Final Report Of The National Commission On The Causes Of The Financial And Economic Crisis In The United States, The Financial Crisis Inquiry Commission, 2011, http://fcic-static.law.stanford.edu/cdn_media/fcic-reports/fcic_final_report_full.pdf

[199] A candidate who could get elected as The President of the United States is a potential law maker.

[200] From the perspective of the democratic presidential nomination race, Hillary Clinton and Bernie Sanders are the only candidates. And Hillary's immediate Democratic Party opponent Bernie Sanders has been very forthright and the least that one can expect of Hillary Clinton is the same. Hillary's argument that let the others (i.e., Republicans etc.) do so first and I will follow suit and then release my speeches does not hold any water. Her refusal to release the speeches would only make the American people more curious and perhaps, even a tad suspicious.

speeches has huge ramifications for the future of financial regulation in America (including that of Wall Street firms), which, in turn, will have a significant bearing on what happens in the global economy—in reality, I don't think that any of us want another financial crisis[201] caused by Wall Street . . . period!

In addition, it goes without saying that much water has passed under the Wall Street bridge since then and the regulation and orderly growth of Wall Street firms (including investment banks, commercial banks, financial conglomerates etc.) has a very important stake in the American Presidency with gigantic implications for the global economy. And financial regulation—especially regulation of Wall Street—has become as important a topic as campaign financing, foreign policy, trade and jobs, homeland security and terrorism (and the like) in the American Presidential election. Therefore, if any of the candidates have delivered speeches at Wall Street, be it Hillary Clinton, Bernie Sanders, or Donald Trump, they should provide full and complete disclosure on these paid/unpaid speeches that they have made to Wall Street firms as well as other corporations.[202] This is imperative from the point of view of "good" electoral and political governance that calls for minimum standards in transparency and accountability.

Please see what the Financial Crisis Inquiry Commission (FCIC) Final Report[203] says about the 2008 Financial Crisis and its causes (including the role of Wall Street firms). Then decide on whether or not Hillary Clinton, who is fighting for the

---

[201] This is because of the lax and laissez-faire regulation and supervision (due to conflicts of interests), which resulted in the financial crisis in 2008, which had global ramifications as well.

[202] Firms from other industries and large corporations have been mentioned in the context of the campaign funding process, which is discussed later.

[203] Financial Crisis Inquiry Report, Final Report Of The National Commission On The Causes Of The Financial And Economic Crisis In The United States, The Financial Crisis Inquiry Commission, 2011, http://fcic-static.law.stanford.edu/cdn_media/fcic-reports/fcic_final_report_full.pdf

Democratic presidential nomination, is correct in refusing to release the text of speeches made by her at Wall Street firms (like Goldman Sachs etc.). You can see multiple references to Goldman Sachs and other Wall Street firms in the FCIC report as it dwells on the causes that led to the Financial Crisis of 2008.

If one looks closely at many of the past financial crisis situations (like the 2008 global financial crisis fueled by the U.S. sub-prime and other crisis situations before that), it is clear that they can be linked to lax and laissez-faire regulatory and supervisory frameworks. Frameworks that were either developed by industry insiders with commercial interests or created with significant input from such insiders—both with a view to benefit the overall financial industry concerned.

In other words, these regulatory and supervisory frameworks had serious "conflict of interest situations" that led to such lax and laissez-faire regulatory and supervisory frameworks being developed in the first place. In effect, they were regulating their own industry. There can be no doubt that this was corruption at its worst.

Despite all that has happened, even today, there is a puzzling lack of attention given to the role played by conflicts of interest in the corruption saga and especially with regard to the larger financial sector. Look at the United Nations Convention Against Corruption (UNCAC). Even the UNCAC only makes a fleeting mention of the role played by conflicts of interests, despite it being the very important keystone to unearthing corruption and supporting the structure to fight against corruption worldwide.

It is not just my opinion; many scholars, academics, economists, politicians, and business people worldwide also agree that the close regulation and monitoring of conflicts of interest are of great importance to regulatory ethics. Moreover, this is something that all of us need to note with urgency because, if not eliminated, these conflict of interest situations could spell disaster for the larger financial sector as they will inevitably lead to corruption and, ultimately, to financial crisis caused by laissez-faire regulation and supervision.

That said, let us now look at what is meant[204] by "conflict of interest." A "conflict of interest" is a conflict between the duty, roles, responsibilities, and private interests of any official that could improperly and unfairly influence the performance of his/her official roles and responsibilities.

By private interests, I mean the following: Private interests include financial, pecuniary and other interests[205] which generate a direct personal benefit to the public official as also personal affiliations, associations, and family ties, that could (practically be considered as likely to) improperly and unfairly influence the official's performance of his/her roles, duties and responsibilities.

Defined in this way, conflict of interest has the potential to undermine the proper functioning of institutions (public, private, not-for-profit), governments and the like by:

- Weakening adherence by officials to the ideals of impartiality, objectivity, fairness, and legitimacy, in decision making, and
- Distorting the rule of law, the development and application of policy, the functioning of organizations and markets, as well as the allocation of resources.

Indeed, what is the difference between conflict of interest and corruption?

---

[204] These definitions have been compiled from several sources including OECD and other material found on the web, which are far too numerous to quote. These are gratefully and sincerely acknowledged.

[205] The negotiation of future employment by an official (for himself/family/friends) prior to his leaving his present office is one example here and there are many more examples that I could provide. This is like negotiating a job with a vendor. For example, an official may say, "I will make rules governing X and Y situations very lenient provided you make my nephew the CEO in another project of yours."

Conflict of interest situations exist where officials, because of their position, have the *opportunity* to abuse the power and authority of their position for personal and private gain. On the other hand, corruption exists where officials *have abused* their position for personal and private gain. Put differently, conflicts of interest situations do not always lead to corruption. However, where there is corruption, you can be sure that conflicts of interest indeed exist.

Why do we need to attach so much importance to conflicts of interest with regard to regulation and supervision in the financial sector? Because if conflicts of interest are not entirely eliminated and/or at least properly monitored by independent bodies, or reduced, the situation can easily lead to corruption in regulation and supervision and thereby threaten the entire financial system.

This is not new. This is what past crisis situations have taught us. In fact, if there is a single most recurring theme in financial crises and scandals globally, it is the failure to manage conflicts of interest. The following are some well-known examples.

Let us look this with regard to the larger financial sector in the United States, which provides a very useful lesson with regard to conflicts of interest and their relationship to crisis situations. They hold very important lessons for how the United States politicians, including Hillary Clinton, deal with Wall Street.

As described[206] by former SEC Chairman Arthur Levitt:

> Bank involvement in the securities markets came under close scrutiny after the 1929 market crash. The Pecora hearings of 1933 …uncovered a wide range of abusive practices on the part of banks and bank affiliates. These included a variety of conflicts of interest; the underwriting of unsound securities in order to pay off bad

[206] Testimony of Arthur Levitt, Chairman U.S. Securities and Exchange Commission,
http://www.sec.gov/news/testimony/testarchive/1995/spch029.txt

bank loans; and "pool operations" to support the price of bank stocks.

In fact, as Levitt has further argued,[207] and please note this carefully, it is the significant revelations of "uncontrolled conflicts of interest" that provided the basis and rationale for the passing of many subsequent regulations—the Securities Act (1933), the Securities Exchange Act (1934), and the Glass-Steagall Banking Act (1933). In fact, it appears that conflicts of interest were also the major reason for the enactment of the Investment Company Act (1940) and the Investment Advisor Act (1940).

Closer to the 1990s, I see numerous examples of conflicts of interest that led directly to financial crisis:

- The insider trading scandals (such as, the Ivan Boesky and Dennis Levine scandals in the 1980s), the closure of Drexel Burnham Lambert (the investment bank) and the associated (criminal) conviction of its famous employee (Michael Milken) are still fresh in my memory.

- Later, there were more financial scandals in the early 2000s—for example, the internet bubble in 2000/2001 exposed problems with dubious high-flying research analysts (with significant conflicts of interest), whose reports were in fact, influenced by their own institutions' investment banking interests. This, in fact, led to specific provisions in the Sarbanes-Oxley Act that dealt with conflicts of interest among research analysts.

- Then, just over a decade ago, in 2003, the SEC found that the use of brokerage commissions to facilitate the sales of fund shares [was] widespread among funds that relied on

[207] Ibid.

broker-dealers to sell fund shares. This led to the adoption of new rules to prohibit funds from this practice.[208]

- Then, even closer to home, we had the mother of all financial crises in recent times—the global financial crisis of 2008—which was again based on significant conflicts of interest in many areas and I quote from the FCIC report hereafter which identifies several key aspects that caused the 2008 financial crisis, including conflicts of interest.

First Cause

The first key point from the FCIC report is given below:

> The captains of finance and the public stewards of our financial system ignored warnings and failed to question, understand, and manage evolving risks within a system essential to the well-being of the American public. Theirs was a big miss, not a stumble. …
>
> The prime example is the Federal Reserve's pivotal failure to stem the flow of toxic mortgages, which it could have done by setting prudent mortgage-lending standards. The Federal Reserve was the one entity empowered to do so and it did not. The record of our examination is replete with evidence of other failures: financial institutions made, bought, and sold mortgage securities they never examined, did not care to examine, or knew to be defective; firms depended on tens of billions of dollars of borrowing that had to be renewed each and every night, secured by subprime mortgage securities; and major firms and investors blindly relied on credit rating agencies as their arbiters of risk. What else could one expect on a

[208] Please see: Prohibition on the Use of Brokerage Commissions to Finance Distribution, Investment Company Act Release 26591 (Sept. 2, 2004), 69 Fed. Register 54728, 54728 (Sept. 9, 2004), http://www.sec.gov/rules/final/ic-26591.pdf

> highway where there were neither speed limits nor neatly painted lines? (FCIC Report)[209]

The reader will note the emphasis on the "pivotal failure" of the regulator—the Federal Reserve. The reader will also note that the FCIC report mentions the fact that:

> Financial institutions made, bought, and sold mortgage securities they never examined, did not care to examine, or knew to be defective; firms depended on tens of billions of dollars of borrowing that had to be renewed each and every night, secured by subprime mortgage securities; and major firms and investors blindly relied on credit rating agencies as their arbiters of risk. (FCIC Report)[210]

And surely, as the FCIC report argues in the next point (given below), law/policy makers and regulators, for reasons best known to them, did have a huge say in creating such a "highway where there were neither speed limits nor neatly painted lines"[211] and where reckless driving was the norm (rather than the exception).

Given the above, you will now understand why it is important that current as well as future law and policy-makers and politicians who participate in the American electoral process, especially for the office of the President of the United States, must come clean on their relationships with Wall Street firms. There should be no question about this.

---

209 Financial Crisis Inquiry Report, Final Report Of The National Commission On The Causes Of The Financial And Economic Crisis In The United States, The Financial Crisis Inquiry Commission, 2011, http://fcic-static.law.stanford.edu/cdn_media/fcic-reports/fcic_final_report_full.pdf

210 Financial Crisis Inquiry Report, Final Report Of The National Commission On The Causes Of The Financial And Economic Crisis In The United States, The Financial Crisis Inquiry Commission, 2011, http://fcic-static.law.stanford.edu/cdn_media/fcic-reports/fcic_final_report_full.pdf

211 Ibid.

Second Cause

Let us move to the next key point identified by FCIC:

> We conclude widespread failures in financial regulation and supervision proved devastating to the stability of the nation's financial markets. The sentries were not at their posts, in no small part due to the widely accepted faith in the self-correcting nature of the markets and the ability of financial institutions to effectively police themselves. More than 30 years of deregulation and reliance on self-regulation by financial institutions, championed by former Federal Reserve chairman Alan Greenspan and others, supported by successive administrations and Congresses, and actively pushed by the powerful financial industry at every turn, had stripped away key safeguards, which could have helped avoid catastrophe. This approach had opened up gaps in oversight of critical areas with trillions of dollars at risk, such as the shadow banking system and over-the-counter derivatives markets. In addition, the government permitted financial firms to pick their preferred regulators in what became a race to the weakest supervisor. ...
>
> Changes in the regulatory system occurred in many instances as financial markets evolved. Nevertheless, as the report will show, the financial industry itself played a key role in weakening regulatory constraints on institutions, markets, and products. It did not surprise the Commission that an industry of such wealth and power would exert pressure on policy makers and regulators. From 1999 to 2008, the financial sector expended $2.7 billion in reported federal lobbying expenses; individuals and political action committees in the sector made more than $1 billion in campaign contributions. What troubled us was the extent to which the nation was deprived of the necessary strength and independence of the oversight

> necessary to safeguard financial stability. (FCIC Report)[212]

Please note the comment on the failure of financial regulation and supervision in causing the crisis as well as the reference to lobbying expenses, campaign contributions and the power and wealth of Wall Street to "exert pressure on policy makers and regulators." For a moment I thought that it was Bernie Sanders who had written this report but I was mistaken. These words appear in the final report of the FCIC, the Statutory Commission that inquired into the Financial Crisis of 2008. Now, tell me whether, as an American, you feel comfortable when a potential law/policy maker talks of reining in Wall Street but refuses to release the paid speeches that she made to a key Wall Street firm like Goldman Sachs, which has been repeatedly cited in the FCIC report.

Third Cause

Alright, let us move on to the next point cited by FCIC and it is about self-regulation — an idea sold by large Wall Street Firms, Financial Conglomerates, Big Banks and Corporations to Law/Policy Makers and Regulators, who readily bought this idea and faced the consequences via the financial crisis of 2008:

> We conclude dramatic failures of corporate governance and risk management at many systemically important financial institutions were a key cause of this crisis. There was a view that instincts for self-preservation inside major financial firms would shield them from fatal risk-taking without the need for a steady regulatory hand, which, the firms argued, would stifle innovation. Too many of these institutions acted recklessly, taking on too much risk, with too little capital, and with too much

[212] Financial Crisis Inquiry Report, Final Report Of The National Commission On The Causes Of The Financial And Economic Crisis In The United States, The Financial Crisis Inquiry Commission, 2011, http://fcic-static.law.stanford.edu/cdn_media/fcic-reports/fcic_final_report_full.pdf

dependence on short-term funding. In many respects, this reflected a fundamental change in these institutions, particularly the large investment banks and bank holding companies, which focused their activities increasingly on risky trading activities that produced hefty profits. They took on enormous exposures in acquiring and supporting subprime lenders and creating, packaging, repackaging, and selling trillions of dollars in mortgage-related securities, including synthetic financial products. Like Icarus,[213] they never feared flying ever closer to the sun.

Many of these institutions grew aggressively through poorly executed acquisition and integration strategies that made effective management more challenging. The CEO of Citigroup told the Commission that a $40 billion position in highly rated mortgage securities would "not in any way have excited my attention," and the co-head of Citigroup's investment bank said he spent "a small fraction of 1%" of his time on those securities. In this instance, too big to fail meant too big to manage.

Financial institutions and credit rating agencies embraced mathematical models as reliable predictors of risks, replacing judgment in too many instances. Too often, risk management became risk justification.

Compensation systems—designed in an environment of cheap money, intense competition, and light regulation—too often rewarded the quick deal, the short-term gain—without proper consideration of long-term consequences. Often, those systems encouraged the big bet—where the payoff on the upside could be huge and the downside

---

[213] In Greek mythology, Icarus is the son of the master craftsman Daedalus, the creator of the Labyrinth. Icarus and his father attempted to escape from Crete by means of wings that his father had constructed from feathers and wax. Icarus's father warns him first of complacency and then of hubris, asking that he fly neither too low nor too high, so the sea's dampness would not clog his wings or the sun's heat melt them. Icarus ignored his father's instructions not to fly too close to the sun, whereupon the wax in his wings melted and he fell into the sea.

> limited. This was the case up and down the line—from the corporate boardroom to the mortgage broker on the street.
>
> Our examination revealed stunning instances of governance breakdowns and irresponsibility. You will read, among other things, about AIG senior management's ignorance of the terms and risks of the company's $79 billion derivatives exposure to mortgage-related securities; Fannie Mae's quest for bigger market share, profits, and bonuses, which led it to ramp up its exposure to risky loans and securities as the housing market was peaking; and the costly surprise when Merrill Lynch's top management realized that the company held $55 billion in "super-senior" and supposedly "super-safe" mortgage-related securities that resulted in billions of dollars in losses. (FCIC Report)[214]

Yet the law/policy makers and regulators swore by self-regulation. Why were they so dogmatic and shortsighted? Self-regulation is an oxymoron and has never worked … ever! It pushes people to fly like Icarus who did not fear flying closer to the sun and simply perished.

Now, this again, is a clear failure on the part of policy and law-makers who were convinced by these large Wall Street firms, financial conglomerates, banks and corporations to bring in the paradigm of self-regulation as a key component of the regulatory and supervisory process. Again, as before, the cost of this decision was very high and it resulted in the financial crisis of 2008, the impact of which we are still feeling today.

---

[214] Financial Crisis Inquiry Report, Final Report Of The National Commission On The Causes Of The Financial And Economic Crisis In The United States, The Financial Crisis Inquiry Commission, 2011, http://fcic-static.law.stanford.edu/cdn_media/fcic-reports/fcic_final_report_full.pdf

Fourth, Fifth and Sixth Causes

The FCIC report talks of three more critical aspects that led to the financial crisis of 2008 and each of these is highlighted below:

> We conclude a combination of excessive borrowing, risky investments, and lack of transparency put the financial system on a collision course with crisis.
>
> Clearly, this vulnerability was related to failures of corporate governance and regulation, but it is significant enough by itself to warrant our attention here. In the years leading up to the crisis, too many financial institutions, as well as too many households, borrowed to the hilt, leaving them vulnerable to financial distress or ruin if the value of their investments declined even modestly. For example, as of 2007, the five major investment banks—Bear Stearns, Goldman Sachs, Lehman Brothers, Merrill Lynch, and Morgan Stanley—were operating with extraordinarily thin capital. By one measure, their leverage ratios were as high as 40 to 1, meaning for every $40 in assets, there was only $1 in capital to cover losses. Less than a 3% drop in asset values could wipe out a firm. To make matters worse, much of their borrowing was short-term, in the overnight market—meaning the borrowing had to be renewed each and every day. For example, at the end of 2007, Bear Stearns had $11.8 billion in equity and $383.6 billion in liabilities and was borrowing as much as $70 billion in the overnight market. It was the equivalent of a small business with $50,000 in equity borrowing $1.6 million, with $296,750 of that due each and every day. One can't really ask, "What were they thinking?" when it seems that too many of them were thinking alike. (FCIC Report)[215]

[215] Financial Crisis Inquiry Report, Final Report Of The National Commission On The Causes Of The Financial And Economic Crisis In The United States, The Financial Crisis Inquiry Commission, 2011, http://fcic-static.law.stanford.edu/cdn_media/fcic-reports/fcic_final_report_full.pdf

Anyone with financial sense will argue that such leverage is ridiculous, and yet it was consciously allowed by the powers that be. Where were regulators and law policy-makers? I don't know. No one seems to know!

> We conclude over-the-counter derivatives contributed significantly to this crisis. The enactment of legislation in 2000 to ban the regulation by both the federal and state governments of over-the-counter (OTC) derivatives was a key turning point in the march toward the financial crisis. …
>
> OTC derivatives contributed to the crisis in three significant ways. First, one type of derivative—credit default swaps (CDS)—fueled the mortgage securitization pipeline. CDS were sold to investors to protect against the default or decline in value of mortgage-related securities backed by risky loans. Companies sold protection—to the tune of $79 billion, in AIG's case—to investors in these newfangled mortgage securities, helping to launch and expand the market and, in turn, to further fuel the housing bubble.
>
> Second, CDS were essential to the creation of synthetic CDOs. These synthetic CDOs were merely bets on the performance of real mortgage-related securities. They amplified the losses from the collapse of the housing bubble by allowing multiple bets on the same securities and helped spread them throughout the financial system.
>
> Goldman Sachs alone packaged and sold $73 billion in synthetic CDOs from July 1, 2004, to May 31, 2007. Synthetic CDOs created by Goldman referenced more than 3,400 mortgage securities, and 610 of them were referenced at least twice. This is apart from how many times these securities may have been referenced in synthetic CDOs created by other firms. …
>
> While financial institutions surveyed by the FCIC said they do not track revenues and profits generated by their derivatives operations, some firms did provide estimates.

> For example, Goldman Sachs estimated that between 25% and 35% of its revenues from 2006 through 2009 were generated by derivatives, including 70% to 75% of the firm's commodities business, and half or more of its interest rate and currencies business. From May 2007 through November 2008, $133 billion, or 86%, of the $155 billion of trades made by Goldman's mortgage department were derivative transactions.[216] (FCIC Report)[217]

Here we go once again with another example where regulation was banned *by legislation* and as the FCIC report argues, and I quote, "the enactment of legislation in 2000 to ban the regulation by both the federal and state governments of over-the-counter (OTC) derivatives was a key turning point in the march toward the financial crisis."

Why on earth would the Federal Government ban regulation with legislation and thereby purchase a crisis? The answer eludes me. I simply don't understand why this happened or how it could happen. Was no one watching? Was it lobbying, friendly relationships between policy and law-makers with Wall Street firms, paid speeches, and/or campaign donations that did the trick? I'm not sure, and I simply cannot fathom why this banning of regulation happened in the year 2000. Now you will understand why people like Bernie Sanders and others are asking for Hillary Clinton's paid speeches to be released and why I fully support this demand.

> Removing barriers helped consolidate the banking industry. Between 1990 and 2005, 74 "megamergers" occurred involving banks with assets of more than $10

---

[216] FCIC Report (2011), Original Footnote 57: Data provided to the FCIC by Goldman Sachs.

[217] Financial Crisis Inquiry Report, Final Report Of The National Commission On The Causes Of The Financial And Economic Crisis In The United States, The Financial Crisis Inquiry Commission, 2011, http://fcic-static.law.stanford.edu/cdn_media/fcic-reports/fcic_final_report_full.pdf

billion each. Meanwhile the 10 largest jumped from owning 25% of the industry's assets to 55%. From 1998 to 2007, the combined assets of the five largest U.S. banks—Bank of America, Citigroup, JP Morgan, Wachovia, and Wells Fargo—more than tripled, from $2.2 trillion to $6.8 trillion.[218] And investment banks were growing bigger, too. Smith Barney acquired Shearson in 1993 and Salomon Brothers in 1997, while Paine Webber purchased Kidder, Peabody in 1995. Two years later, Morgan Stanley merged with Dean Witter, and Bankers Trust purchased Alex. Brown & Sons. The assets of the five largest investment banks —Goldman Sachs, Morgan Stanley, Merrill Lynch, Lehman Brothers, and Bear Stearns—quadrupled, from $1 trillion in 1998 to $4 trillion in 2007.[219]

In the spring of 1996, after years of opposing repeal of Glass-Steagall, the Securities Industry Association—the trade organization of Wall Street firms such as Goldman Sachs and Merrill Lynch—changed course. Because restrictions on banks had been slowly removed during the previous decade, banks already had beachheads in securities and insurance. Despite numerous lawsuits against the Fed and the OCC, securities firms and insurance companies could not stop this piecemeal process of deregulation through agency rulings.[220] Edward Yingling, the CEO of the American Bankers Association (a lobbying organization), said, "Because we had knocked so many holes in the walls separating commercial and investment banking and insurance, we were able to aggressively enter their businesses—in some cases more

---

[218] FCIC Report (2011), Original Footnote 2: These were the largest banks as of 2007. See FCIC, "Preliminary Staff Report: Too-Big-to-Fail Financial Institutions," August 31, 2010, p. 14.
[219] FCIC Report (2011), Original Footnote 3: Data from SNL Financial (www.snl.com/).
[220] FCIC Report (2011), Original Footnote 12: Securities Industry Association v. Board of Governors of the Federal Reserve System, 627 F. Supp. 695 (D.D.C. 1986); Kathleen Day, "Reinventing the Bank; With Depression-Era Law about to Be Rewritten, the Future Remains Unclear," *Washington Post,* October 31, 1999.

> aggressively than they could enter ours. So first the securities industry, then the insurance companies, and finally the agents came over and said let's negotiate a deal and work together.[221] [222]

In addition, the FCIC Report stated:

> The new regime encouraged growth and consolidation within and across banking, securities, and insurance. The bank-centered financial holding companies such as Citigroup, JP Morgan, and Bank of America could compete directly with the "big five" investment banks — Goldman Sachs, Morgan Stanley, Merrill Lynch, Lehman Brothers, and Bear Stearns—in securitization, stock and bond underwriting, loan syndication, and trading in over-the-counter (OTC) derivatives. The biggest bank holding companies became major players in investment banking. The strategies of the largest commercial banks and their holding companies came to more closely resemble the strategies of investment banks. Each had advantages: commercial banks enjoyed greater access to insured deposits, and the investment banks enjoyed less regulation. Both prospered from the late 1990s until the outbreak of the financial crisis in 2007. However, Greenspan's "spare tire" that had helped make the system less vulnerable would be gone when the financial crisis emerged—all the wheels of the system would be spinning on the same axle. (FCIC Report)[223]

---

[221] FCIC Report (2011), Original Footnote 13: Edward Yingling, quoted in "The Making of a Law," *ABA Banking Journal*, December 1999.

[222] Financial Crisis Inquiry Report, Final Report Of The National Commission On The Causes Of The Financial And Economic Crisis In The United States, The Financial Crisis Inquiry Commission, 2011, http://fcic-static.law.stanford.edu/cdn_media/fcic-reports/fcic_final_report_full.pdf

[223] Financial Crisis Inquiry Report, Final Report Of The National Commission On The Causes Of The Financial And Economic Crisis In The United States, The Financial Crisis Inquiry Commission, 2011, http://fcic-static.law.stanford.edu/cdn_media/fcic-reports/fcic_final_report_full.pdf

Again, the above represents a classic case where, in the name of innovation and consolidation, regulatory safeguards were removed, resulting in the system being more vulnerable when the financial crisis actually emerged (as all the wheels of the system were indeed spinning on the same axle, which eventually broke under the load). Please note that, as the FCIC report argues very clearly, the financial crisis was essentially caused by a regulatory and policy failure that occurred because regulation and supervision were either lax and/or regulatory safeguards had been removed through lobbying, legislation and the like. We simply cannot afford more of this in the future. That is why, with the backdrop of the 2008 financial crisis (and its aftermath) and the role played by Wall Street (including investment banks, commercial banks, financial conglomerates etc.) in creating and sustaining this crisis, we simply cannot have presidential nominees cozy up to Wall Street and refuse to release transcripts of their paid for speeches. Sorry, but that is unacceptable and is not good electoral governance in any form or manner . . . anywhere!

Seventh Cause

Let's move on further and get to the governance of compensation, which played a very important role in the 2008 financial crisis. Indeed, compensation is one factor among many that contributed to the financial crisis in the United States, and elsewhere. Moreover, the FCIC report has also mentioned the same and this is quoted below:

> Both before and after going public, investment banks typically paid out half their revenues in compensation. For example, Goldman Sachs spent between 44% and 49% a year between 2005 and 2008, when Morgan Stanley allotted between 46% and 59%. Merrill paid out

similar percentages in 2005 and 2006, but gave 141% in 2007—a year it suffered dramatic losses.[224]

As the scale, revenue, and profitability of the firms grew, compensation packages soared for senior executives and other key employees. John Gutfreund, reported to be the highest-paid executive on Wall Street in the late 1980s, received $3.2 million in 1986 as CEO of Salomon Brothers.[225] Stanley O'Neal's package was worth more than $91 million in 2006, the last full year he was CEO of Merrill Lynch.[226] In 2007, Lloyd Blankfein, CEO at Goldman Sachs, received $68.5 million;[227] Richard Fuld, CEO of Lehman Brothers, and Jamie Dimon, CEO of JPMorgan Chase, received about $34 million and $28 million, respectively.[228] That year Wall Street paid workers in New York roughly $33 billion in year-end bonuses alone.[229] Total compensation for the major U.S. banks and securities firms was estimated at $137 billion.[230] (FCIC Report)[231]

---

[224] FCIC Report (2011), Original Footnote 63: Goldman Sachs, 2006 and 2009 10-K; Morgan Stanley, 2008 10-K; Merrill Lynch, 2005 and 2008 10-K.

[225] FCIC Report (2011), Original Footnote 64: "Gutfreund's Pay Is Cut," *New York Times,* December 23, 1987.

[226] FCIC Report (2011), Original Footnote 65: Merrill Lynch, "2007 Proxy Statement," p. 38.

[227] FCIC Report (2011), Original Footnote 66: Goldman Sachs, "Proxy Statement for 2008 Annual Meeting of Shareholders," March 7, 2008, p. 16: Blankfein received $600,000 base salary and a 2007 year-end bonus of $67.9 million.

[228] FCIC Report (2011), Original Footnote 67: Lehman Brothers, "Proxy Statement for Year-end 2007," p. 28; JP Morgan Chase, "2007 Proxy Statement," p. 16.

[229] FCIC Report (2011), Original Footnote 68: New York State Office of the State Comptroller, "New York City Securities Industry Bonus Pool," February 23, 2010. The bonus pool is for securities industry (NAICS 523) employees who work in New York City.

[230] FCIC Report (2011), Original Footnote 69: "Banks Set for Record Pay, Top Firms on Pace to Award $145 Billion for 2009, Up 18%, WSJ Study Finds," WSJ.com, January 14, 2010.

In effect, in all these firms, the focus was on the short-term performance, incentives, and compensation when, in reality, the risks (which existed) were mostly, medium and/or long-term. Of course, the regulator and law and policy-makers sat and watched as compensation soared way beyond acceptable levels and firms started paying as high as 50 percent of their revenues in compensation.

Did not the regulators and policy- and law-makers find it strange that:

a) Goldman Sachs spent between 44 per cent and 49 per cent of its revenue per year on compensation (during the years 2005 to 2008);
b) Morgan Stanley allotted between 46 percent and 59 percent; and
c) Merrill paid out similar percentages in 2005 and 2006, and more importantly, gave as high as 141 percent in 2007 (a year in which it suffered dramatic losses).

What on earth were the regulators and policy and law-makers doing? This is where, again, it is very important for a presidential candidate to forego any close relationships with Wall Street. As the 2008 financial crisis has clearly demonstrated, there is no free lunch.

Eighth Cause

As the FCIC report correctly argues, a lot of this happened because conflicts of interest were at play and they were, in a big measure, responsible for the financial crisis of 2008. While there are innumerable examples from the FCIC report that I could cite as evidence of conflicts of interest that were responsible for the

---

[231] Financial Crisis Inquiry Report, Final Report Of The National Commission On The Causes Of The Financial And Economic Crisis In The United States, The Financial Crisis Inquiry Commission, 2011, http://fcic-static.law.stanford.edu/cdn_media/fcic-reports/fcic_final_report_full.pdf

financial crisis of 2008, one very relevant example from the SEC[232] is given below:

> Another high profile example of conflict of interest in the recent years is the settlement that the SEC reached with Goldman Sachs, in which that firm paid $550 million to settle charges filed by the Commission, and acknowledged that disclosures made in marketing a subprime mortgage product contained incomplete information as they did not disclose the role of a hedge fund client who was taking the opposite side of the trade in the selection of the CDO.[233]

And I quote:

> Goldman acknowledges that the marketing materials for the ABACUS 2007-ACI transaction contained incomplete information. In particular, it was a mistake for the Goldman marketing materials to state that the reference portfolio was "selected by" ACA Management LLC without disclosing the role of Paulson & Co. Inc. in the portfolio selection process and that Paulson's economic interests were adverse to CDO investors. Goldman regrets that the marketing materials did not contain that disclosure.
> (http://www.sec.gov/litigation/litreleases/2010/consent-pr2010-123.pdf , Page 2, point 3)

---

[232] Carlo V. di Florio, 'Conflicts of Interest and Risk Governance', *U.S. Securities and Exchange Commission*, October 22, 2012, https://www.sec.gov/News/Speech/Detail/Speech/1365171491600.
[233] Ibid.

Before I close this chapter, I would like to quote the FCIC report[234] one last time:

> Goldman Sachs Multiplied the Effects of the Collapse in Subprime.
>
> Henry Paulson, the CEO of Goldman Sachs from 1999 until he became secretary of the Treasury in 2006 testified to the FCIC that by the time he became secretary many bad loans already had been issued—"most of the toothpaste was out of the tube"—and that "there really wasn't the proper regulatory apparatus to deal with it."[235] Paulson provided examples: "Subprime mortgages went from accounting for 5 percent of total mortgages in 1994 to 20 percent by 2006. ... Securitization separated originators from the risk of the products they originated." The result, Paulson observed, "was a housing bubble that eventually burst in far more spectacular fashion than most previous bubbles."[236]
>
> Under Paulson's leadership, Goldman Sachs had played a central role in the creation and sale of mortgage securities. From 2004 through 2006, the company provided billions of dollars in loans to mortgage lenders; most went to the subprime lenders Ameriquest, Long Beach, Fremont, New Century, and Countrywide through warehouse lines of credit,

---

[234] Financial Crisis Inquiry Report, Final Report Of The National Commission On The Causes Of The Financial And Economic Crisis In The United States, The Financial Crisis Inquiry Commission, 2011, http://fcic-static.law.stanford.edu/cdn_media/fcic-reports/fcic_final_report_full.pdf

[235] FCIC Report (2011), Original Footnote 96: Henry M. Paulson Jr., testimony before the FCIC, Hearing on the Shadow Banking System, day 2, session 1: Perspective on the Shadow Banking System, May 6, 2010, transcript, p. 22.

[236] FCIC Report (2011), Original Footnote 97: Henry M. Paulson Jr., written testimony for the FCIC, Hearing on the Shadow Banking System, day 2, session 1: Perspective on the Shadow Banking System, May 6, 2010, p. 2.

> often in the form of repos.[237] During the same period, Goldman acquired $ 53 billion of loans from these and other subprime loan originators, which it securitized and sold to investors.[238] From 2004 to 2006 Goldman issued 318 mortgage securitizations totaling $184 billion (about a quarter were subprime), and 63 CDOs totaling $32 billion; Goldman also issued 22 synthetic or hybrid CDOs with a face value of $35 billion between 2004 and June 2006.[239]

To summarize, the FCIC report cites the following as among the key causes for the financial crisis of 2008:

a) the lack of proper regulation and supervision;
b) the lax and laissez-faire attitude of the regulators and law- and policy-makers (due to conflicts of interests);
c) the reckless ride that many Wall Street firms (including investment banks, commercial banks, financial conglomerates etc.) took off on down a highway with no speed limits;
d) the poor operational practices, weak financial condition, and huge compensation packages at many of these Wall Street firms (including investment banks, commercial banks, financial conglomerates etc.);
e) the conflicts of interest that were prevalent in the larger policy, business, and political environment and so on.

Given all of this, the question that begs asking is whether presidential candidates like Hillary Clinton are right in refusing to release speeches made by them to these same Wall Street firms. When a future policy and law-maker, and potential President (i.e., Hillary Clinton) refuses to release her speeches made to Wall Street firms in private, what signals are being sent

---

[237] FCIC Report (2011), Original Footnote 98: Goldman Sachs, 2005 and 2006 10-K (appendix 5a to Goldman's March 8, 2010, letter to the FCIC).
[238] FCIC Report (2011), Original Footnote 99: Appendix 5c to Goldman's March 8, 2010, letter to the FCIC.
[239] FCIC Report (2011), Original Footnote 100: Goldman's March 8, 2010, letter to the FCIC, p. 28 (subprime securities).

to the American people and society at large? Whether Hillary's stance is proper or not is something for the people to decide, but I strongly believe that given the demands of transparency and accountability in public life and electoral politics, Hillary Clinton must come clean on this matter and release her speeches immediately.

Without a doubt, the paid speeches delivered by Hillary Clinton to Wall Street firms create huge areas of conflict of interest. This is especially true given what happened in the late 1990s, when Bill Clinton was President, i.e., unregulated and unmonitored conflicts of interest that directly led to rampant deregulation, thereby resulting in the financial crisis of 2007/2008. Therefore, it is imperative that Hillary Clinton release the transcripts of her speeches immediately and before the general election so that the American people and society at large can make an objective judgment on this hugely important matter once and for all.

In fact, the settlements agreed to be paid by the six large banks with regard to their role in the 2008 financial crisis shows the importance of being transparent about the speeches made to Wall Street firms and the big banks. And as an example, the case of Case of Bank of America/Merrill Lynch clearly illustrates why it is important to know what was told to these big banks and large Wall Street firms in private.

Bank of America/Merrill Lynch (BoA/ML), as evident from the above is a huge favorite of the Clintons. While Hillary gave one speech to BoA/ML, Bill delivered four speeches. While four of these speeches were made during period 2011–2015, one speech was in the pre-financial crisis era (2001–2007). A total of $1,300,000 was received as speaking fees by the Clintons.

In addition, several staff (including senior management) of Bank of America/Merrill Lynch have contributed (individually) to the Hillary Clinton 2016 presidential run for a total of $309,191.[240] Finally, to top it all off, Bank of America Corporation gave

[240] Federal Election Commission (FEC), www.fec.gov

$100,001 to $250,000 to the Clinton Foundation while Bank of America Foundation gave $500,001 to $1,000,000. Huge sums sent to the foundation.

Interestingly, other candidates[241] to whom Bank of America/ Merrill Lynch staff have contributed across the three election cycles include: $94,955 (2016) to Jeb Bush; $40,164 (2016) to Marco Rubio; $1,491,367 (2012) to Mitt Romney; $401,432 (2012) to Barack Obama; $19,112 (2012) to Ron Paul; $669,760 (2008) to Barack Obama; $477,522 (2008) to John S McCain; and $310,072 (2008) to Hillary Clinton.

While Bank of America/Merrill Lynch is one of the largest banks in the United States, it must, however, be remembered that Bank of America reached a settlement of $16.7 billion with the federal and state joint working group formed to investigate wrong doing in the pre-financial crisis mortgage-backed securities market.

In totality, Bank of America has since 2008, "entered into or been subject to 51 major legal settlements, judgments, and regulatory fines. Taken together, they add up to $91.2 billion in monetary and nonmonetary damages."[242]

A list of key settlements by Bank of America reached in 2014 alone are provided in **table 4.6** below, which certainly does not paint a picture of a well-functioning, rule-abiding Wall Street bank by any measure.

Table 4.6: Bank of America Settlements in Year 2014

Date	Issue	Settlement and/or Judgment Amount
Still pending	☞ Sale of toxic mortgage backed securities sold by bank and its legacy	☞ Ambac is reportedly asking is $2.5

[241] See appendix 1 for a list of candidates across election cycles.
[242] John Maxfield, 'The Complete List: Bank of America's Legal Fines and Settlements Since 2008', *The Motley Fool,* October 1, 2014, http://www.fool.com/investing/general/2014/10/01/the-complete-list-bank-of-americas-legal-fines-and.aspx

Table 4.6: Bank of America Settlements in Year 2014		
Date	**Issue**	**Settlement and/or Judgment Amount**
	companies	billion in damages.
September 2014	☞ Over reporting of regulatory capital	☞ SEC fine is $7.65 million
August 2014	☞ Sale of shoddy residential mortgage-backed securities (principally by Countrywide Financial) in the years leading up to the crisis	☞ $16.65 billion settlement with Federal/State agencies
July 2014	☞ Sale of toxic mortgage backed securities sold by bank and its legacy companies	☞ Settlement of $650 million with **American International Group (AIG)**
April 2014	☞ Forcing customers to sign up for extra credit card products	☞ Consumer Financial Protection Bureau fine is $727 million
April 2014	☞ Securities fraud claims	☞ Settles with Allstate amount not known value of securities as per lawsuit is $167 million
April 2014	☞ Securities fraud claims mainly related to Residential Mortgage Backed Securities (RMBS) sold by countrywide financial	☞ Settles with all state amount not known Allstate reportedly asking $700 million
March 2014	☞ Toxic second-lien RMBS	☞ $950 million settlement with Financial Guaranty Insurance Co.

Table 4.6: Bank of America Settlements in Year 2014		
Date	**Issue**	**Settlement and/or Judgment Amount**
March 2014	☞ Defrauding Fannie Mae and Freddie Mac by Bank of America and mainly countrywide financial	☞ $9.5 billion settlement with Federal Housing Finance Agency
March 2014	☞ Security fraud charges associated with Bank of America acquiring Merrill Lynch.	☞ Bank of America and former CEO Ken Lewis settle $25 million
February 2014	☞ Kickback scheme inflating the cost of insurance that homeowners were forced to buy	☞ Settles $228 million (Insurance dispute)
Cross-verified and compiled from several sources including The Fool.com,[243] Bank of America, U.S. Department of Justice, New York Attorney General's Office, Securities and Exchange Commission, Federal Trade Commission, Reuters, Bloomberg, *The New York Times,* and *The Wall Street Journal and other web sources including court documents.*		

Additionally, Merrill Lynch, which has merged with Bank of America, has been charged with the following:

a) The Securities and Exchange Commission … charged Merrill Lynch with making faulty disclosures about collateral selection for two collateralized debt obligations (CDO) that it structured and marketed to investors, and maintaining inaccurate books and records for a third CDO. Merrill Lynch agreed to pay $131.8 million to settle the SEC's charges.[244]

---

[243]Ibid.

[244] 'SEC Charges Merrill Lynch With Misleading Investors in CDOs', *U.S. Securities and Exchange Commission*, December 12, 2013, https://www.sec.gov/News/PressRelease/Detail/PressRelease/1370540492377

b) The Securities and Exchange Commission … charged two Merrill Lynch entities with using inaccurate data in the course of executing short sale orders. Merrill Lynch agreed to admit wrongdoing, pay nearly $11 million, and retain an independent compliance consultant in order to settle the charges.[245]

c) The Financial Industry Regulatory Authority (FINRA) announced … that it has censured and fined Merrill Lynch Professional Clearing Corp. (Merrill Lynch PRO) $3.5 million for violating Regulation SHO, an SEC rule that established a regulatory framework to govern short sales and prevent abusive naked short selling. FINRA also censured and fined its affiliated broker-dealer, Merrill Lynch, Pierce, Fenner & Smith Incorporated (Merrill Lynch), $2.5 million for failing to establish, maintain and enforce supervisory systems and procedures related to Regulation SHO and other areas.[246]

The above clearly shows the kind of wrong doing that Bank of America, Merrill Lynch and its associates engaged in at various times. What is perplexing is the fact that Hillary Clinton/Bill Clinton were delivering paid speeches at Bank of America/Merrill Lynch despite the fraudulent environment prevalent at these institutions. More shockingly, huge donations to the Clinton Foundation, ranging from $100,001 to $250,000 by Bank of America Corporation and $500,001 to $1,000,000 by Bank of America Foundation have been received.

---

[245] 'Merrill Lynch Admits Using Inaccurate Data for Short Sale Orders, Agrees to $11 Million Settlement', *U.S. Securities and Exchange Commission,* June 1, 2015, https://www.sec.gov/news/pressrelease/2015-105.html

[246] 'FINRA Fines Merrill Lynch a Total of $6 Million for Reg. SHO Violations and Supervisory Failures', *FINRA,* October 27, 2014, https://www.finra.org/newsroom/2014/finra-fines-merrill-lynch-total-6-million-reg-sho-violations-and-supervisory-failures

This is yet another example of how *'dirty money'* plays a role in the political process. Given the proximity that Bank of America and Merrill Lynch have with the presidential candidates like Hillary Clinton, and given the kind of issues and problems that these institutions face in their regular operations, what good is any promise or guarantee that Bank of America and Merrill Lynch will not "curry" favors from the White House, if and when their favorite candidate becomes President?

The same applies to Goldman Sachs, Citi Bank, Deutsche Bank, Morgan Stanley, BlackRock, Blackstone and others who have all contributed to various presidential candidates including Hillary Clinton.

Under these circumstances, keeping Wall Street at an arms-length distance from the White House is very critical but is something that is unlikely to happen as long as candidates accept *'dirty money'* from the Wall Street and Big Banks.

Chapter 5

Campaign Finance and Corporate America

If campaign contributions are one way of creating conflicts of interest, accepting paid speaking engagements with organizations could potentially be another. Potentiality may well get converted to actuality when said organizations are involved in corporate crime. This aspect gets further complicated when the concerned organizations are under federal investigation.

It has been long argued that just as donations to presidential PACs and lobbying and campaign contributions could create conflicts of interest, so too can paid speeches given by potential presidential candidates to entities involved in serious corporate crime. This chapter applies the same yardstick to various presidential campaigns and details a series of instances, just as has been done in the case of campaign financing. These cases assume greater significance in the context of Hillary Clinton coming down heavily on President Obama for his perceived softness on corporate crime.[247] Fair point—all the more reason that we should look at the track record of all the candidates on paid speeches to see if any conflicts of interest have been created with regard to corporate crime.

Of all the candidates across the three election cycles of 2016, 2012 and 2008, to the best of my knowledge it appears that the only presidential candidate who has delivered paid speeches to

[247] She has talked of this several times on the campaign trail.

Corporate America is Hillary Clinton. Also, her case is unique, because her spouse, William Jefferson Clinton or Bill Clinton as he is better known, as a former President of the United States, continues to give many speeches to corporations worldwide at fancy rates, after the completion of his two terms as President. Interestingly, many of these speeches were delivered at a time when Hillary Clinton was either a Senator or Secretary of State.

Coming back to Hillary Clinton, she made a total of 91 speeches[248] after she relinquished office as Secretary of State in 2013. It must be noted that Hillary Clinton received a total of $21.14 million from these 91 speeches[249] she gave to various organizations. We will now look at some of the individual cases—that could create a potential conflict of interest—in a sequential manner.

On January 22, 2015, just a few months before she officially announced her 2016 presidential bid, Hillary Clinton reportedly delivered a paid speech at the Canadian Imperial Bank of Commerce (CIBC), Canada. She is said to have been paid $150,000 for her speech.

CIBC is an interesting case in point for a variety of reasons. It has been embroiled with the IRS on issues of abetting tax evasion as espoused by the official communication from the Department of Justice, United States, which noted as follows in a release[250] dated April 30, 2013:

> The Justice Department announced that a federal court in San Francisco entered an order authorizing the Internal Revenue Service (IRS) to serve a John Doe summons

[248] A full listing of all 91 speeches given by Hillary Clinton to 84 organizations (between 2013–2015) is given in the website, http://www.releasethetranscripts.com/

[249] This figure includes her 8 Wall Street speeches for which she received $1.835 million.

[250] *The United States Department of Justice*, April 30, 2013, https://www.justice.gov/opa/pr/court-authorizes-service-john-doe-summons-seeking-identities-us-taxpayers-offshore-accounts

> seeking information about U.S. taxpayers who may hold offshore accounts at 'Canadian Imperial Bank of Commerce First Caribbean International Bank' (CIBC FCIB). The order was signed by Senior District Judge Thelton E. Henderson. The IRS summons seeks records of FCIB's United States correspondent account at Wells Fargo N.A., which will allow the IRS to identify U.S. taxpayers who hold or have held interests in financial accounts at FCIB and other financial institutions that used FCIB's Wells Fargo correspondent[251] account.[252]

The release[253] notes that, according to a statement filed by the IRS Revenue Agent Cheryl R. Kiger in support of the petition, FCIB is based out of Barbados with branches in 18 countries in the Caribbean. While it does not reportedly have any U.S. branches, it has a correspondent account in the United States at Wells Fargo Bank N.A. In addition "as alleged in Agent Kiger's declaration, the IRS learned that U.S. taxpayers were using FCIB to help them keep their offshore accounts undetected by the IRS and not pay U.S. federal income tax on money placed in those offshore accounts."[254]

---

[251] A correspondent account is a bank deposit account maintained by one bank for another bank. Financial transactions involving U.S. dollars flow through U.S. banks. Therefore, foreign banks that do business in U.S. dollars, but have no office in the U.S., obtain a correspondent account at a U.S. bank in order to engage in such transactions. These transactions leave a trail in the U.S. that the IRS can access through the records of the correspondent bank accounts. These correspondent bank accounts have records of money deposited, money paid out through checks and money moved through the correspondent account by wire transfers. All of this information the IRS can obtain through a John Doe summons issued to the U.S. bank holding the correspondent account — https://www.justice.gov/opa/pr/court-authorizes-service-john-doe-summons-seeking-identities-us-taxpayers-offshore-accounts

[252] Ibid.

[253] Ibid

[254] Ibid.

Kiger's declaration is indeed very significant as it describes her review of the information submitted by more than 120 FCIB customers who participated in the IRS's Offshore Voluntary Disclosure Program. It reportedly alleges that many of the FCIB customers in the John Doe class may have been "under-reporting income, evading income taxes, or otherwise violating the internal revenue laws of the United States." [255]

Readers should also note that U.S. tax law "requires U.S. taxpayers to pay taxes on all income earned worldwide. U.S. taxpayers must also report foreign financial accounts if the total value of the accounts exceeds $10,000 at any time during the calendar year. A deliberate failure to report a foreign account can result in a penalty of up to 50 percent of the amount in the account at the time of the violation."[256]

As self evident, the above is a serious matter. Here is an organization that is being pursued by the IRS to release the names of potential U.S. tax evaders. Would not there not be a significant conflict of interest for a potential presidential candidate and a former Secretary of State/Senator to be seen delivering a paid speech to such a tainted organization that the IRS is vigorously following up with.

The above apart, it must be noted that the CIBC has been charged with other infringements as well, including fraud, deception and other violations as shown in the **table 5.1** below.

Table 5.1: Relationship to CIBC Violations and Frauds

Name	Relationship to CIBC	Violations and Frauds
CIHI and World Markets	Subsidiaries of Canadian Imperial Bank of Commerce, Inc.	☞ Participated in a scheme to defraud numerous mutual funds and their shareholders through late trading and deceptive market

[255] Ibid.

[256] Ibid. and: *IRS,* 2012 Offshore Voluntary Disclosure Program, https://www.irs.gov/uac/2012-offshore-voluntary-disclosure-program

Table 5.1: Relationship to CIBC Violations and Frauds		
Name	**Relationship to CIBC**	**Violations and Frauds**
	("CIBC")	timing.
CIHI and World Markets	Subsidiaries of Canadian Imperial Bank of Commerce, Inc. ("CIBC")	☞ Engaged in three types of conduct that violated the federal securities laws: a) CIHI financed hedge fund customers while knowing the hedge funds would use the leverage to late trade and deceptively market time mutual funds; b) CIHI provided, and World Markets arranged, improper financing for market timing hedge fund customers in violation of the margin and extension of credit requirements; and c) a team of World Markets registered representatives ("RR") enabled numerous customers to late trade and deceptively market time mutual funds.
CIHI	Subsidiary of Canadian Imperial Bank of Commerce, Inc. ("CIBC")	☞ With respect to the financing, CIHI provided funds to at least two hedge fund customers knowing those hedge funds would use the leverage to late trade and market time through Security Trust Corporation ("STC"), a Trust Company in Phoenix, Arizona. ☞ A CIHI Managing Director wrote a due diligence memorandum to CIBC's Credit Department in which he explicitly stated that STC's ability to allow late trades provided "significant benefits to our customers." ☞ Moreover, in addition to late

Table 5.1: Relationship to CIBC Violations and Frauds		
Name	**Relationship to CIBC**	**Violations and Frauds**
		trading, numerous CIHI officials understood that the hedge funds they were leveraging, in executing their market timing strategy, had to "hide" their activity, use "stealth" tactics, and otherwise "stay under the radar" of the mutual funds. ☞ By leveraging these entities while knowing they were engaged in deceptive market timing and late trading, CIHI participated in a scheme to defraud mutual funds and their long term shareholders, thus violating the antifraud provisions of the federal securities laws.
CIHI and World Markets	Subsidiaries of Canadian Imperial Bank of Commerce, Inc. ("CIBC")	☞ Moreover, CIHI provided leverage to its hedge fund customers that violated the margin requirements. ☞ CIHI financed market timing hedge funds purportedly through the use of total return swaps ("TRSs"). These TRSs were extensions of credit in excess of 50% of the margin stock's value. Thus, CIHI violated Section 7(d) of the Exchange Act and Regulation U promulgated by the Federal Reserve Board. ☞ In addition, because World Markets helped arrange this financing, World Markets violated Section 7(c) of the Exchange Act and Regulation T

Table 5.1: Relationship to CIBC Violations and Frauds		
Name	**Relationship to CIBC**	**Violations and Frauds**
		promulgated by the Federal Reserve Board. Moreover, because World Markets effected transactions in mutual funds for hedge funds in connection with which it arranged this financing, World Markets violated Section 11(d) of the Exchange Act.
World Markets	Subsidiary of Canadian Imperial Bank of Commerce, Inc. ("CIBC")	☞ From at least 1999 until January 2003, World Markets received over 1,000 letters and emails from mutual funds complaining about abusive trading by a team of RRs at World Markets. ☞ This team of RRs, led by an RR (hereinafter described as "Broker Doe"), used, among other tactics, multiple accounts, multiple RR numbers, and small trade size broken up across related accounts to deceive mutual funds and "stay under the radar" of the mutual funds' internal timing monitors. ☞ Senior World Markets officials knew about this team of RRs' deceptive market timing activities and took steps to assist them, ensuring that this team of significant business producers could continue to facilitate market timing. ☞ In addition, some of these RRs knowingly accepted numerous mutual fund orders from at least one of their timing customers after 4:00 p.m. ET, and processed

Table 5.1: Relationship to CIBC Violations and Frauds		
Name	**Relationship to CIBC**	**Violations and Frauds**
		those orders as though the customer had placed the order prior to 4:00 p.m. ET. ☞ As a result of these acts, World Markets violated the antifraud provisions of the federal securities laws and Rule 22c-1, as adopted under Section 22(c) of the Investment Company Act."
Source: https://www.sec.gov/litigation/admin/33-8592.pdf		

The issues given in table above are indeed serious and one does have to wonder whether or not Hillary Clinton, the former Senator and Secretary of State as well as potential presidential candidate knew of these rather well known and properly documented violations, based on which the Securities and Exchange Commission (SEC) passed the following order:

> A. Respondents shall pay, on a joint and several basis, disgorgement and prejudgment interest in the amount of $100 million, and a civil money penalty in the amount of $25 million, for a total payment of $125 million; ...
>
> D. Respondents shall, within 30 days of the entry of this Order, pay on a joint and several basis, disgorgement and prejudgment interest in the total amount of $100 million, and civil money penalties in the amount of $25 million, for a total payment of $125 million, to the United States Treasury. [257]

[257] United States of America before the Securities Exchange Commission, Canadian Imperial Holding Inc., et al., https://www.sec.gov/litigation/admin/33-8592.pdf

That is not all; there are other issues as well. The SEC also:

> Instituted a settled enforcement proceeding against one of North America's largest financial institutions, Canadian Imperial Bank of Commerce (CIBC), for CIBC's role in Enron Corp.'s manipulation of its financial statements. The SEC also sued three of CIBC's executives, two of whom are settling. The Commission's complaint charges CIBC and the three executives with having helped Enron to mislead its investors through a series of complex structured finance transactions over a period of several years preceding Enron's bankruptcy. The Commission filed a civil injunctive action in U.S. District Court in Texas. CIBC consented to the entry of a final judgment in that action that
>
> i. permanently enjoins CIBC from violating the antifraud, books and records, and internal control provisions of the federal securities laws, and
> ii. orders CIBC to pay $80 million: $37.5 million in disgorgement, a $37.5 million penalty, and $5 million in prejudgment interest.[258]

The Enron case noted above is incredibly famous and needs no introduction. And all of you will be shocked to know that CIBC is not the only case. UBS AG is another example of an organization that—having been pulled up by the I.R.S. on similar tax issues on January 28, 2013—had offered several paid speaking assignments to Bill and Hillary Clinton.

As the Department of Justice, Public Affairs release notes:

> The U.S. District Court for the Southern District of New York entered an order authorizing the IRS to serve a John Doe summons on UBS AG, seeking records of Swiss

---

[258] 'SEC Announces Agreement with Canadian Imperial Bank of Commerce and Two Executives to Settle Charges of Aiding and Abetting Enron Accounting Fraud', Press Release, *Securities and Exchange Commission,* December 22, 2003, https://www.sec.gov/news/press/2003-180.htm

> bank Wegelin & Co.'s United States correspondent account at UBS, which will allow the United States to determine the identity of U.S. taxpayers who hold or held interests in financial accounts at Wegelin and other Swiss financial institutions to evade federal income taxes.[259]

And indeed, as noted above, UBS AG in fact had a very special relationship with Hillary Clinton. Specifically, UBS AG and its affiliates gave Hillary Clinton and her spouse, Bill Clinton, 10 speaking assignments worth $1.915 million between 2011-2015—nine to Bill Clinton and one to Hillary Clinton. Of the nine speeches given to Bill Clinton, five were at a time when Hillary Clinton was the Secretary of State of the United States.

This apart, as shown in **appendix 5.2**, UBS and its affiliates donated substantial amounts to the Clinton Foundation. While UBS AG gave in the range of $50,001—$100,000 to the Clinton Foundation, UBS Wealth Management USA donated in the range of $500,001 to $1,000,000.

A final comment about UBS that describes its character as an organization is in order. It was named in two reports[260] of the Permanent Subcommittee of Investigations, U.S. Senate with regard to abetting 'tax evasion, tax abuse and tax shelter promotion', especially in the case of KPMG, which paid fines in excess of $450 million.[261]

---

[259] *United States Department of Justice,* Office of Public Affairs Release, January 28, 2013, https://www.justice.gov/usao-sdny/pr/court-authorizes-irs-seek-records-ubs-relating-us-taxpayers-swiss-bank-accounts

[260] Tax Haven Abuses: The Enablers, the Tools And Secrecy, Minority & Majority Staff Report, Permanent Subcommittee On investigations, August 1, 2006, and The Role of Professional Firms in the U.S. Tax Shelter Industry Report, Prepared by the Permanent Subcommittee on Investigations Of the Committee on Homeland Security and Governmental Affairs United States Senate, April 13, 2005.

[261] 'KPMG to Pay $456 Million for Criminal Violations', IR-2005-83, *IRS,* August 29, 2005, https://www.irs.gov/uac/kpmg-to-pay-456-million-for-criminal-violations

Given these circumstances, Hillary Clinton's decision to accept a paid speaking assignment to address institutions such as CIBC or UBS certainly comes under a cloud.

At a time when the IRS authorities were using all legal means to obtain information about the use of foreign tax havens by U.S. nationals, and unearth potential tax evaders, it was not appropriate for a former first lady, former Secretary of State and potential presidential candidate to deliver a paid speech at CIBC which—not only had been served with a court order with regard to its subsidiary FCIB but also—had committed several violations in the past.

The same is true of UBS AG where the situation is actually much worse. As noted earlier, Bill and Hillary Clinton delivered a total of 10 speeches between 2011 and 2015 to UBS, when it was embroiled in the IRS tax problem. While Bill Clinton made nine speeches, Hillary Clinton gave one speech. The key point to note here is that five of the speeches delivered by Bill Clinton were at a time when Hillary Clinton served as the Secretary of State. That creates a huge conflict of interest because of the kind of tax issues that UBS was facing with the IRS then.

Thus, given that Hillary and Bill Clinton received large sums of money to the tune of $2.065 million from UBS and CIBC for a total of 11 speeches during the period 2011–15, there is a huge conflict of interest at play. The above events cannot simply be wished away as merely poor judgment as they have occurred several times. In fact, there are more examples of organizations that had perhaps violated the law and had orders passed against them by relevant authorities like the SEC and Federal Agencies. Yet, Bill and Hillary Clinton accepted paid speaking assignments with them. I am not including the details here since the examples provided sufficiently illustrate the degree of conflict already present.

As a former Senator, First Lady, and Secretary of State, what was the rationale behind Hillary Clinton accepting an invitation to speak at the Canadian Imperial Bank of Commerce, especially given that the bank had previously been indicted for several violations including the Canadian Imperial Holdings Inc (CIHI), World Markets, and Enron cases, and against whose Caribbean operations (First Caribbean International Bank) the court had passed an order authorizing service of a John Doe summons seeking the identities of U.S. taxpayers with offshore accounts?

Likewise, what were Hillary and Bill Clinton telling UBS AG in private in their paid speeches after UBS AG had received an IRS "summons requiring UBS AG to produce information about U.S. taxpayers holding accounts at the Swiss bank Wegelin & Co. ("Wegelin") and other banks based in Switzerland with a view to evade federal income taxes?"[262]

These are questions that the American public deserve an answer to prior to their exercising their right to franchise for or against Hillary Clinton in the US presidential elections. Even more so, given that Hillary Clinton has promised the strongest action against offshore accounts and tax evaders.

Now, irrespective of whatever the exact tax situation is with to CIBC or UBS AG, the larger question that becomes relevant is how Clinton can crack down on corporate crime including potential tax evaders(s) or tax shifters (to tax havens), when people supporting her and stakeholders close to her are perhaps guilty of supporting the same thing.

Without a credible explanation, her statements about penalizing tax evaders, especially those who fly away (legally and/or otherwise) to tax havens (like Cayman Islands, Panama etc.) seem to amount to nothing more than mere rhetoric.

---

[262] 'Court Authorizes IRS To Seek Records From UBS Relating To U.S Taxpayers With Swiss Bank Accounts', *United States Department of Justice,* January 28, 2013, https://www.justice.gov/usao-sdny/pr/court-authorizes-irs-seek-records-ubs-relating-us-taxpayers-swiss-bank-accounts

Unfortunately, Hillary Clinton's speaking association with individuals and entities charged with corporate crime does not end here.

Take the case of GE (General Electric) which invited Hillary Clinton for a speech on June 1, 2014, and reportedly paid her $225,000 for the appearance. GE is also said to have donated from $1,000,001 to $5,000,000 to the Clinton Foundation.

In terms of contribution to various candidates[263] across election cycles, key GE staff, mainly senior management, have donated[264]: $112,971 (2016) to Hillary Clinton; $14,825 (2016) to Bernard Sanders; $14,800 (2016) to Lindsey O. Graham; $170,036 (2012) to Mitt Romney; $95,581 (2012) to Barack Obama; $5,250 (2012) to Rick Perry; $123,132 (2008) to Barack Obama; $45,993 (2008) to John S McCain; and $37,257 (2008) to Hillary Clinton.

As a corporation, GE was led by John Francis "Jack" Welch Junior, the legendary CEO (between 1981 and 2001) who catapulted GE to its current standing and fame. GE,[265] which is a classic American multinational conglomerate corporation, is incorporated in New York and headquartered in Fairfield, Connecticut. In 2011, GE figured in the Fortune 500 list as the sixth largest firm in the U.S. by gross revenue, and the fourteenth most profitable.

While all of this reads well with regard to GE, it is also a fact that the SEC charged GE and two of its subsidiaries with FCPA violations as per a release dated 27 July 2010. Specifically:

---

[263] See appendix 1 for a list of candidates across election cycles.

[264] *Federal Election Commission,* www.fec.gov

[265] As of 2015, the company operates in the following sectors: Appliances, Power and Water, Oil and Gas, Energy Management, Aviation, Healthcare, Transportation, and Capital, which cater to the needs of Home Appliances, Financial services, Medical devices, Life Sciences, Pharmaceutical, Automotive, Software Development and Engineering industries.

> The Securities and Exchange Commission charged the General Electric Company with violations of the Foreign Corrupt Practices Act (FCPA) for its involvement in a $3.6 million kickback scheme with Iraqi government agencies to win contracts to supply medical equipment and water purification equipment.[266]

According to the SEC release:

> Two GE subsidiaries—along with two other subsidiaries of public companies that have since been acquired by GE—made illegal kickback payments in the form of cash, computer equipment, medical supplies, and services to the Iraqi Health Ministry or the Iraqi Oil Ministry in order to obtain valuable contracts under the U.N. Oil for Food Program.
>
> GE agreed to pay $23.4 million to settle the SEC's charges against the company as well as the two subsidiaries for which GE assumed liability upon acquiring: Ionics Inc. and Amersham plc. The SEC charged GE, Ionics, and Amersham with violating the books and records and internal controls provisions of the FCPA.[267]
>
> "Bribes and kickbacks are bad business, period," said Robert Khuzami, Director of the SEC's Division of Enforcement,"[268] said Cheryl Scarboro, Chief of SEC's FCPA Enforcement Unit, "GE failed to maintain adequate internal controls to detect and prevent these illicit payments by its two subsidiaries to win Oil for Food contracts, and it failed to properly record the true nature of the payments in its accounting records.[269]

---

[266] 'SEC Charges General Electric and Two Subsidiaries with FCPA Violations', *Securities and Exchange Commission,* July 27, 2010, https://www.sec.gov/news/press/2010/2010-133.htm
[267] Ibid.
[268] Ibid.
[269] Ibid.

And that's not all. As per a release dated August 4, 2009, the SEC also charged GE with accounting fraud and GE agreed to pay $50 million to settle the charges. Specifically:

> The Securities and Exchange Commission filed civil fraud and other charges against General Electric Company (GE), alleging that it misled investors by reporting materially false and misleading results in its financial statements. The SEC alleged that GE used improper accounting methods to increase its reported earnings or revenues and avoid reporting negative financial results. GE quickly agreed to pay the $50 million penalty.
>
> "GE bent the accounting rules beyond the breaking point," said Robert Khuzami, Director of the SEC's Division of Enforcement. "Overly aggressive accounting can distort a company's true financial condition and mislead investors."
>
> David P. Bergers, Director of the SEC's Boston Regional Office, added, "Every accounting decision at a company should be driven by a desire to get it right, not to achieve a particular business objective. GE misapplied the accounting rules to cast its financial results in a better light."
>
> The four accounting violations underlined were:
>
> 1. Beginning in January 2003, an improper application of the accounting standards to GE's commercial paper funding program to avoid unfavorable disclosures and an estimated approximately $200 million pre-tax charge to earnings.
>
> 2. A 2003 failure to correct a misapplication of financial accounting standards to certain GE interest-rate swaps.
>
> 3. In 2002 and 2003, reported end-of-year sales of locomotives that had not yet occurred in order to accelerate more than $370 million in revenue.

> 4. In 2002, an improper change to GE's accounting for sales of commercial aircraft engines' spare parts that increased GE's 2002 net earnings by $585 million.[270]

In effect, GE was charged not only under the FCPA, but also for huge accounting fraud.

Yet another example is Qualcomm Incorporated—a Delaware corporation headquartered in San Diego, California—involved in the design and sale of wireless telecommunication products. Qualcomm invited Hillary Clinton to make a speech that reportedly was delivered in October 2014 and she was paid a fee for $335,000, a huge sum by any standards. Qualcomm has also donated $100,001 to $250,000 to the Clinton Foundation.

In terms of contributions to various candidates[271] across three election cycles (2016, 2012 and 2008), Qualcomm staff, primarily senior management, have given: $36,587 (2016) to Hillary Clinton; $23,889 (2016) to Bernard Sanders; $4,350 (2016) to Donald J. Trump; $110,370 (2012) to Barack Obama; $85,626 (2012) to Mitt Romney; $6,142 (2012) to Ron Paul; $89,011 (2008) to Barack Obama; $56,750 (2008) to John S McCain; and $32,456 (2008) to Hillary Clinton.

Here, it must be mentioned that Qualcomm, way back in the mid-1990s were doing some fantastic and pioneering work related to wireless local loop (WLL). While one really appreciates the value created by Qualcomm to the wireless local loop industry, way back in 1990s, it is again unfortunate to note that Qualcomm is yet another corporation that violated the FCPA.

---

[270] 'SEC Charges General Electric With Accounting Fraud', *U.S. Securities and Exchange Commission,* August 4, 2009, http://www.sec.gov/news/press/2009/2009-178.htm

[271] See appendix 1 for a list of candidates across election cycles.

Specifically, as per the Securities and Exchange Commission release dated March 1, 2016:

> Qualcomm Incorporated agreed to pay $7.5 million to settle charges that it violated the Foreign Corrupt Practices Act (FCPA) by hiring relatives of Chinese government officials deciding whether to select the company's mobile technology products amid increasing competition in the international telecommunications market.[272]

The release said that the, "SEC investigation found that Qualcomm also provided gifts, travel, and entertainment to try to influence officials at government-owned telecom companies in China."[273] It also stated that, "Qualcomm misrepresented in its books and records that the things of value provided to foreign officials were legitimate business expenses."[274]

Said Michele Wein Layne, Director of the SEC's Los Angeles Regional Office, "For more than a decade, Qualcomm went to extraordinary lengths to gain a business advantage with foreign officials deciding between Qualcomm's technology and its competitors."[275]

The above is a very serious statement indeed and given that it occurred for more than a decade, it says a lot about Qualcomm as a company. In fact, the SEC findings, which are very revealing in this regard, note:

> Several violations of the anti-bribery, books and records, and internal controls provisions of the Foreign Corrupt Practices Act ("FCPA") by Qualcomm.

---

[272] 'SEC: Qualcomm Hired Relatives of Chinese Officials to Obtain Business', *U.S. Securities and Exchange Commission,* March 1, 2016, https://www.sec.gov/news/pressrelease/2016-36.html
[273] Ibid
[274] Ibid.
[275] Ibid.

1. From 2002 through 2012, Qualcomm provided things of value to foreign officials—including high-ranking employees of state owned enterprises ("SOEs") and government ministers—to try to influence these decision makers to favor and/or promote Qualcomm-developed technology in an evolving international telecommunications market, thereby providing Qualcomm with a business advantage.

2. Qualcomm's extensive international operations accounted for more than 90% of the company's revenue. Even so, Qualcomm's internal controls were insufficient to prevent or detect improper payments to foreign officials. In several areas of its business operations, including hiring, hospitality planning, and business development, Qualcomm lacked an adequate oversight process to determine whether things of value that it provided to foreign officials were made with the intent to induce those officials to provide a business benefit to Qualcomm.

3. Qualcomm's insufficient internal controls resulted in books and records violations. Qualcomm misrepresented in its books and records that things of value provided to foreign officials were legitimate business expenses.

4. In sum, Qualcomm, through its agents and subsidiaries, violated Section 30A of the Exchange Act by providing things of value to foreign officials to obtain and retain business in China. Qualcomm also violated Section 13(b)(2)(B) of the Exchange Act by failing to devise and maintain internal accounting controls sufficient to provide reasonable assurance of preventing or detecting the authorization or payment of improper payments. Qualcomm violated Section 13(b)(2)(A) of the Exchange Act by having recorded improper payments to foreign officials in its books and records in a manner that failed to

> accurately and fairly reflect the provision of things of value to foreign officials.[276]

As all of the above examples show, here is the case of a presidential candidate who definitely stands compromised by accepting speaking assignments not only from corporations that were under investigation by the IRS but also from those that had violated the FCPA and had been caught paying large and multiple bribes in many foreign countries to further their businesses and thereby make profits.

What was the presidential candidate telling these corporations involved in corporate crime in her speeches? How will the candidate explain to the American public the rationale behind her making frequent paid[277] speeches to large corporations that regularly break the law, offer bribes, and engage in corporate crime?

Given the above serious charges of corruption and bribery, how appropriate is it for candidates to finance their election campaigns with such '*dirty money*'. On the one hand, these candidates, Hillary Clinton included, talk of coming down heavily on corporate crime. On the other hand, they finance their campaigns with such '*dirty money*'. How can this be reconciled? You are either for corruption or against it! You cannot take "corrupt" '*dirty money*' and claim to fight the same money—this is because your money source for the same fight is dirty and I am not sure that stakeholders who dabble in *'dirty money'* will allow the hands that feed to be bitten!

---

[276] United States of America before the Securities and Exchange Commission, In the Matter of QUALCOM Incorporated, https://www.sec.gov/litigation/admin/2016/34-77261.pdf

[277] Almost all the 84 entities including corporations paid hefty fees to Hillary Clinton for her speeches.

Chapter 6

Campaign Finance and Foundations

Just as second chapter discussed aspects related to Donald Trump and his business, this chapter focuses on the 'Clinton Foundation', an important institution in Hillary Clinton's scheme to become President.

Many who have donated to the Clinton Foundation have also contributed to her 2008 and 2016 presidential bid. Likewise, there have been newcomers who have supported her through her election campaign and thereafter hopped on the Clinton Foundation bandwagon as donors.

The Clinton Foundation has been in the news for various issues including its alleged use of Hillary Clinton's position—as Secretary of State—to trade influence and receive (so called) '*dirty money*' for the same.

While conclusive proof on the above is still awaited, it has also been reported that the Internal Revenue Service (IRS) is conducting an audit of the Clinton Foundation's finances with which Hillary Clinton is very closely associated. These are serious matters, especially for a person like Hillary Clinton who is competing for what I call the highest office on the face of this planet—i.e., the office of the President of the United States.

Meanwhile, while we wait for the IRS audit to be completed, I decided to look closely at the strategic core of the Clinton Foundation—its past and present trustees, and examine their antecedents. Part of the reason for this is that the 2016 Panama Papers expose named some Clinton Foundation donors and board directors in its list.

Why look at board members of the Clinton Foundation?

Members of the board represent the strategic core of any organization. From the time of Herbert Simon through Alfred Chandler to Mike Porter, modern day organization behavior theorists and strategic management architects have always emphasized the importance of the board, as it provides the strategic direction for any organization.

The same is true for the Clinton Foundation and therefore I decided to look at its past and present trustees and their antecedents to understand who they are, what they have done and how their profiles impact the Clinton Foundation and its overall image?

Here is what I found and it is indeed shocking:

The first example is that of Vinod Gupta, who as per his *LinkedIn*[278] profile is presently chairman at Everest Group LLC. The profile also mentions that Gupta was former chief executive officer (CEO) and chairman of infoUSA (now infoGroup) apart from serving as a trustee of the Clinton Foundation. Other sources[279] have confirmed the same. He has contributed between

---

[278] Vinod, Gupta, Linkedin, https://www.linkedin.com/in/vinodgupta1 and About Us, Vinod Gupta, *World Education Foundation*, http://worldeducationfoundation.net/about-us/profile/vinod-gupta

[279] Other sources: Deroy Murdoch, 'The Clinton Foundation Reeks of Crooks, Thieves, and Hoods', *National Review,* June 16, 2015, http://www.nationalreview.com/article/419791/clinton-foundation-reeks-crooks-thieves-and-hoods-deroy-murdock and, Warner Todd Huston, Revealed: Four Clinton Foundation Trustees Charged or Convicted of Financial Crimes, *Breitbart,* May 7, 2015,

$1 million – $5 million to the Clinton Foundation as per its own website. He has also donated $33,400 to the Hillary Victory Fund, as part of the 2016 election campaign, besides individually giving $2,700 to Hillary Clinton's presidential run, in 2016 and $2,300 to her 2008 presidential run. In 2016, Gupta also contributed to GOP[280] John R Kasich, the maximum permitted amount of $2,700. The complete details of Vinod Gupta's election contributions are given in **appendix 6.1**.

Interestingly, Vinod Gupta was charged by the Securities and Exchanges Commission (SEC) of fraud and stealing money. "Gupta stole millions of dollars from Info shareholders by treating the company like it was his personal ATM" and "other corporate officers also abused their positions of trust by looking the other way instead of standing up for investors and bringing the scheme to a halt."[281] The SEC complaint filed in the court, noted as follows:

> From 2003 through 2007, Vinod Gupta, the former CEO and Chairman of infoUSA Inc. (now InfoGroup Inc.) ("Info"), engaged in fraud by receiving from Info approximately $9.5 million of unauthorized and undisclosed perquisites, including for the personal use of jets; costs associated with a yacht, homes, automobiles, and life insurance policies; personal credit card expenses; and club memberships and related costs.
>
> For the same period, Info entered into related party transactions totaling approximately $9.3 million with two entities that Gupta controlled, and one entity with which he was affiliated, without disclosing the transactions in Info's public filings with the Commission.

---

http://www.breitbart.com/big-government/2015/05/07/revealed-four-clinton-foundation-trustees-charged-or-convicted-of-financial-crimes/

[280] GOP stands for the Grand Old Party, which is said to represent the Republican Party.

[281] 'SEC Charges Former Executives in Illegal Scheme to Enrich CEO With Perks', Press Release, *U.S. Securities and Exchange Commission,* March 15, 2010, https://www.sec.gov/news/press/2010/2010-39.htm

> Separately, in March and April 2005, Gupta purchased 55,000 shares of Opinion Research Corporation ("ORC") after he had taken steps on behalf of Info to acquire ORC. Info later acquired ORC. In breach of his fiduciary duty to Info, Gupta failed to inform Info's other board members of the material fact that he had purchased ORC shares for his own benefit. Gupta obtained realized and unrealized ill-gotten gains from his ORC trading totaling approximately $240,700, which he has turned over to Info.[282]

He settled with SEC paying $7.4 million and consented to SEC's order that prohibited him from serving as an officer or director of a public company.

The second case is that of Sant Singh Chatwal, which exposes the nexus between politics and corruption even better. Sant Singh Chatwal was trustee of the Clinton Foundation as per his own statement. Other sources[283] also confirm the same. Apart from being a trustee of the Clinton Foundation in the past, Sant Singh Chatwal has donated to the Clinton 2008 presidential run as an individual as did his son, Vikram Chatwal. His company, Hampshire Hotels & Resorts, LLC has donated between $250,001 and $500,000 to the Clinton Foundation as per data given in the Foundation website.[284] The complete details of Chatwal's election contributions are given in **appendix 6.2**.

I came across an interesting piece of information about Sant Singh Chatwal—a court case in the United States District Court,

---

[282] In The United States District Court For The District Of Nebraska, *Securities And Exchange Commission, (Plaintiff) v. Vinod Gupta, Defendant*, https://www.sec.gov/litigation/complaints/2010/comp21451-gupta.pdf

[283] Sant Singh Chatwal, *Wikipedia*, https://en.wikipedia.org/wiki/Sant_Singh_Chatwal and, Sant Singh Chatwal Net Worth, *Born Rich*, http://www.bornrich.com/sant-singh-chatwal.html

[284] Contributor and Granter Information, *Clinton Foundation*, https://www.clintonfoundation.org/contributors?category=%241%2C000%2C001%20to%20%245%2C000%2C000&page=1

Eastern District of New York, Criminal Division. He was charged by the Court of violating the Federal Election Law and creating and reimbursing straw donors for three candidates who were standing for federal office. Some reports even argue that one of the three candidates was Hillary Clinton[285]. Specifically, the case mentions a conspiracy to violate the Election Act by the defendant Sant Singh Chatwal[286] (and others). Here is what was mentioned about Sant Singh Chatwal:

> In or about and between March 2007 and August 2011, both dates being approximate and inclusive, within the Eastern District of New York and elsewhere, the defendant SANT SINGH CHATWAL, together with others, did knowingly and willfully conspire to make, and cause to be made, contributions of money, aggregating $25,000 and more in a calendar year, in the names of others, to the Candidates, all of whom were candidates for federal office, contrary to Title 2, United States Code, Sections 441f and 437g(d) (1) (A) (i). …
>
> In or about September 2008, in New York, New York, CHATWAL, together with others, reimbursed the CI[287] for campaign contributions from the Group A1 Straw Donors and the Group A3 Straw Donors that the CI had previously obtained by reducing by $50,000 the amount of interest that the CI owed on a $2.5 million loan CHATWAL previously made to the CI.

---

[285] Deroy Murdoch, *National Review,* June 16, 2015, http://www.nationalreview.com/article/419791/clinton-foundation-reeks-crooks-thieves-and-hoods-deroy-murdock

[286]United States District Court, Eastern District of New York, Sant Singh Chatwal, Defendant, http://images.politico.com/global/2014/04/17/chatwalinformationlel_signed_1.pdf

[287] A "Cooperating Informant", an individual, whose IDENTITY is known to the United States Attorney (The "CI"), was a business associate of CHATWAL (page 4 of the document given at link http://images.politico.com/global/2014/04/17/chatwalinformationlel_signed_1.pdf, United States District Court.

> On or about October 2, 2010, in New York, New York, CHATWAL and the CI delivered to Candidate B campaign contributions from straw Donors totaling approximately $19,200.
>
> In or about July 2011, from his office in Queens, New York, John Doe #1[288] submitted the July Invoice to Northquay, a company controlled by CHATWAL, in the amount of $129,745, which invoice included approximately $69,000 in reimbursement for campaign contributions that John Doe #1 had raised for Candidate C by reimbursing the Group C Straw Donors.
>
> In or about and between June 2012 and July 2012, both dates being approximate and inclusive, within the Eastern District of New York and elsewhere, the defendant SANT SINGH CHATWAL, together with others, did knowingly and corruptly persuade another person, to wit: John Doe #1, with intent to hinder, delay or prevent the communication to one or more law enforcement officers of the United States: to wit, the Law Enforcement Officers, of information relating to the commission, or possible commission, of one or more federal offenses, to wit: the Federal Offenses.[289]

In fact, Chatwal, was convicted of one count[290] of Conspiracy to Violate the Federal Election Campaign Act and one count of Witness Tampering and subjected to a fine of $500,000, three years' probation, and 1,000 hours of community service.

---

[288] John Doe # 1, an individual whose identity is known to the United States Attorney, was a contractor whose construction company contracted with entities operated by Chatwal to perform millions of dollars in construction work at Chatwal's business properties and at one of Chatwal's personal residences in Old Brookville, New York ("Old Brookville")—page 4 of the document given at link, United States District Court, http://images.politico.com/global/2014/04/17/chatwalinformationlel_signed_1.pdf

[289] Ibid.

[290] Ibid.

According to a source, Chatwal is said to have appeared in Brooklyn's U.S. District Courthouse and reportedly pleaded guilty to "conspiracy, witness tampering, and 'having funnelled more than $180,000 in illegal contributions between 2007 and 2011 to three federal candidates,' including Hillary."[291]

The third case is that of Victor P. Dahdaleh, who lists on his website that he was trustee of the Clinton Foundation. Other sources[292] confirm the same. Victor P. Dahdaleh & The Victor Phillip Dahdaleh Charitable Foundation donated between $1 million – $5 million to the Clinton Foundation.[293]

Interestingly, Victor Dahdaleh is also one of the names that cropped up in the Panama Papers expose. He has been confirmed as the mysterious "Consultant A" named in U.S. court documents. Consultant A is supposed to have given out millions and millions of dollars as inducement to personnel of a Persian Gulf smelting company in return for supplier contracts to one of the world's largest aluminium companies.

Incidentally, Dahdaleh's client, which is a subsidiary of ALCOA, admitted to being on the wrong side of the law as it confessed to a U.S. bribery charge in 2014 in relation to the above scandal. ALCOA and its unit are reported to have together paid one of the largest anti-corruption fines—about $384 million—in the history of the United States.[294]

---

[291] Murdoch, Crooks, 'Thieves, and Hoods, *National Review,* June 16, 2015, http://www.nationalreview.com/article/419791/clinton-foundation-reeks-crooks-thieves-and-hoods-deroy-murdock

[292] Ibid.

[293] Contributor and Grantor Information, *Clinton Foundation,* https://www.clintonfoundation.org/contributors?category=%241%2C000%2C001+to+%245%2C000%2C000

[294]See the CBC article: Zach Dubinsky, 'Panama Papers confirm Canadian billionaire and university benefactor as mystery man in global bribery case,' *CBC News,* May 25, 2016, http://www.cbc.ca/news/business/panama-papers-victor-dahdaleh-alcoa-bribery-case-1.3598527 — "The huge leak of offshore financial

It must also be mentioned that Great Britain's Serious Fraud Office reportedly accused Victor Dahdaleh of giving bribes of £35 million (roughly $52 million) to Bahraini officials to "win sales contracts for ALCOA, the U.S. aluminium giant, with which he was a 'super-agent.'"[295]

Cheryl Saban currently serves as a board member of the Clinton Foundation as per its website[296] and she, her husband (Haim Saban) and the Saban Family Foundation have donated between $10 million – $25 million to the Clinton Foundation. Together, Cheryl and Haim Saban have donated $11.5 million to pro-Clinton PACs and both have also made the maximum permitted individual contributions in the 2016 election run. It must be remembered that Cheryl Saban's husband, Haim Saban, was named in the report of the United States Senate (2006) on 'Tax Abuse and Use of Tax Havens'.

Specifically, Haim Saban was one of the six people named in the Point Transactions case where fake security transactions were created to produce fake capital losses to offset real capital gains—causing losses in hundreds of millions of dollars to the United States Treasury.

Coming to other serving board members, Frank Giustra has been rather controversial and he was also named in the Panama

---

records reveals Dahdaleh, a 72-year-old Jordanian-born metals magnate, is indeed, as long suspected, the mysterious middleman known in U.S. court documents as "Consultant A"—described as having handed out tens of millions of dollars in inducements to officials at a Persian Gulf smelting company in exchange for supplier contracts that went to one of the world's biggest aluminum conglomerates." See: Murdoch, 'Crooks, Thieves, and Hoods', *National Review,* June 16, 2015, http://www.nationalreview.com/article/419791/clinton-foundation-reeks-crooks-thieves-and-hoods-deroy-murdock

[295] 'Murdoch, Crooks, Thieves, and Hoods', *National Review,* June 16, 2015, http://www.nationalreview.com/article/419791/clinton-foundation-reeks-crooks-thieves-and-hoods-deroy-murdock

[296] Board of Directors, *Clinton Foundation,* https://www.clintonfoundation.org/about/board-directors

Papers. He has contributed greater than $25,000,000 to the Clinton Foundation, both in his personal capacity as well as through the Clinton Giustra Enterprise Partnership (Canada).[297]

Cheryl Mills, yet another serving board member,[298] who is one of Hillary Clinton's closest aides, was the Chief of Staff during Hillary Clinton's tenure as Secretary of State. Cheryl Mills, apart from being embroiled in the email controversy, is a board member of the Clinton Foundation—this is solid enough proof of the fact that the lines of activity between the Clinton Foundation and State Department were actually blurred, when Hillary Clinton was the Secretary of State of the United States. And that has turned out to be a key aspect in the 2016 U.S. presidential election. There is an additional issue about Cheryl Mills. It is a fact that she is a member of the board of BlackRock Advisors, which is one of the world's largest asset management firms—this again is a huge conflict of interest for someone who could be very closely associated with the next Clinton Administration.

The above examples do not bode well for the image of the Clinton Foundation, which seems to be the hotbed of '*dirty money*' by way of both its board members and donors being embroiled in various violations and controversies. Association with the Clinton Foundation certainly does not help Hillary Clinton, the Presidential Nominee of the Democratic Party. She would be better advised to keep an appropriate distance from the Clinton Foundation and its activities, especially if she were to become the 45th President of the United States. Whether or not Hillary Clinton does that is an issue that time alone can answer.

---

[297] Contributor and Grantor Information, *Clinton Foundation,* https://www.clintonfoundation.org/contributors
[298] Board of Directors, *Clinton Foundation,* https://www.clintonfoundation.org/about/board-directors

Chapter 7

Campaign Finance and Fracking!

Fracking is the procedure of creating fractures in rocks and rock formations by injecting fluid into cracks to force them further open. The key issue to note here is that the larger the fissures, the greater the oil and gas that can flow out of the formation and into the wellbore from where they can be easily extracted thereafter.[299]

Fracking has become a very significant issue in the 2016 U.S. presidential elections as communities and critics across the United States are pointing to, of course, the potential health and environmental impacts. Most raised concerns include serious contamination of water supplies[300], strong seismic activity caused by the process of fracking[301], and the fears that the enormous glut of gas from fracking may hinder the development of emissions-free renewable sources of power, like wind and

---

[299] Fracking, *Investopedia,* http://www.investopedia.com/terms/f/fracking.asp?layout=orig

[300] Suzanne Goldenberg, 'Drinking water contaminated by shale gas boom in Texas and Pennsylvania', *The Guardian,* September 15, 2014, https://www.theguardian.com/environment/2014/sep/15/drinking-water-contaminated-by-shale-gas-boom-in-texas-and-pennslyvania-study

[301] Oil and gas drilling triggers man-made earthquakes in eight states, USGS finds, *the guardian,* April 23, 2015, https://www.theguardian.com/world/2015/apr/23/oil-gas-drilling-triggers-man-made-earthquakes-usgs

solar[302]. There are other aspects as well—namely, the methane related aspects, rapid industrialization of pristine rural areas, noise pollution from trucks and lorries, among others.[303]

Fracking is therefore a dirty word today and any one, who, by default, has invested in fracking, is a source of '*dirty money*'. That takes us to the Avenue Capital Group run by "fracking-fund billionaire Marc Lasry," who is also a top Clinton advisor and fundraiser.[304]

First, a quick introduction to Marc Lasry is in order. He is the founder and chairman of the Avenue Capital Group. In 2014 he raised $1.3 billion specifically for a fund that supposedly bought debt of distressed energy companies, which later became worthless. Apparently, the Avenue Energy Opportunities Fund used $200 million that belonged to the Pennsylvania Public School Employees' Retirement System. Of course, Lasry has dismissed questions on the losses, arguing that he is sure that the frackers will do well again[305].

In fact, Marc Lasry, his wife Cathy, and son Alex are all top Hillary Clinton fundraisers called Hillblazers. As the Hillblazers site notes, Hillblazers "are individuals who have helped raise $100,000 or more in primary election contributions … We are

---

[302] Fiona Harvey, '"Golden age of gas" threatens renewable energy, IEA warns', *The Guardian,* May 29, 2012, https://www.theguardian.com/environment/2012/may/29/gas-boom-renewables-agency-warns

[303] Adam Vaughan, 'Why is fracking bad?', *The Guardian,* August 19, 2015, https://www.theguardian.com/commentisfree/2015/aug/19/why-is-fracking-bad-google-answer

[304] Hillblazers, https://www.hillaryclinton.com/about/hillblazers/ and, Brad Johnson, 'Fracking-Fund Billionaire Marc Lasry Is a Top Clinton Advisor and Fundraiser', *The Huffington Post,* April 5, 2016, http://www.huffingtonpost.com/entry/frackingfund-billionaire-_b_9611512.html?section=india

[305] Johnson, 'Fracking-Fund Billionaire', *The Huffington Post,* April 5, 2016, http://www.huffingtonpost.com/entry/frackingfund-billionaire-_b_9611512.html?section=india

grateful for their support of Hillary for America."[306] **Appendix 7** provides complete details of Marc Lasry, his family and key staff with regard to their providing campaign finance across the three election cycles—2016, 2012 and 2008.

Not only have Marc Lasry and the Avenue Capital Group raised money for the Hillary Clinton campaign, several of the Avenue Capital Group staff have also contributed individually to the Hillary Clinton campaign (as shown below). Additionally, Marc Lasry's wife, Cathy, and son, Alexander, have also contributed individually to the Hillary Clinton campaign. Further, Marc and Cathy Lasry have given $33,400 each to the super PAC, Hillary Victory Fund. It must also be noted that the Avenue Capital Management II, L.P. has also donated $50,000 to $100,000 to the Clinton Foundation while Marc Lasry has himself donated between $100,001 and $250,000 to the Clinton Foundation.

In fact, it has been reported that in 2015, as soon as Hillary Clinton announced her second presidential run, Lasry is said to have assured that he would raise $270,000 for her in the first week of the campaign.[307] And there is no doubt that he still plays a key, albeit, outsized yet outside role. It must also be noted that Marc Lasry claimed to have invested $1 million in Eaglevale Partners, a hedge fund co-founded by Hillary Clinton's son-in-law Marc Mezvinsky.

Now comes the interesting bit.

Marc Lasry is not just close to Hillary Clinton, the Democratic presidential nominee. He is also reportedly very close to Donald Trump, the Republican presidential nominee as he is reportedly Donald Trump's business partner.

---

[306] Hillblazers, https://www.hillaryclinton.com/about/hillblazers/
[307] Mary Childs, 'Marc Lasry Seeking to Raise $270,000 in Clinton's First Week', *Bloomberg,* April 16, 2015, http://www.bloomberg.com/politics/articles/2015-04-15/lasry-seeking-to-raise-270-000-in-clinton-s-first-week

Trump Entertainment Resorts and its predecessors reportedly filed for Chapter 11 bankruptcy protection four times—first, in 1991, following construction of the $1 billion Trump Taj Mahal, and subsequently, in 2004, 2009 and 2014.

It is said that when the casino group filed for bankruptcy in February 2009, owing almost $1.2 billion, two sets of debt holders eventually proposed reorganization plans for the group in the U.S. bankruptcy court.

Initially, Trump is said to have preferred banker/high-stakes poker player Andrew Beal, owner of Beal Bank, which supposedly held $500 million in the group's debt, to take over the resorts.

However, Trump apparently cited concerns about Beal Bank's experience with gaming and brought in Avenue Capital. This plan was reportedly supported by other bond-holders as well.

As per Trump's agreement with Avenue Capital, he was to receive 5 percent stock in the reorganized company with another 5 percent stock to be granted for the use of his name and likeness in perpetuity.

In 2011, it was reported that The New Jersey Casino Control Commission officially gave Marc Lasry and the hedge fund Avenue Capital Group (ACG) oversight of the three Trump properties in Atlantic City. Lasry supposedly became chairman of Trump Entertainment Resorts, Inc. **Thus, Marc Lasry is reportedly Donald Trump's business partner.**[308]

---

[308] 'Trump, Clinton And The Marc Lasry Connection', *Wide Awake Gentile,* February 26, 2016, https://wideawakegentile.wordpress.com/2016/02/26/trump-clinton-and-the-marc-lasry-connection/

That is not all.

Marc Lasry seems to be well connected everywhere and he was reportedly President Obama's pick for being the U.S. Ambassador to France. But, while Lasry dropped out, citing official work at Avenue Capital, it has been said that he primarily dropped out fearing the backlash of his closeness with "a 27-year-old Russian who was among the 34 people charged …in connection to a high-stakes poker game at the Carlyle Hotel with alleged mob ties."[309]

Several issues have been put forth in this chapter with regard to the case of the fracking fund billionaire Marc Lasry.

Therefore, accepting campaign finance or having a business partnership with Marc Lasry cannot be seen as anything but involvement with '*dirty money*', given the dirty word that fracking is today and also given the above information on Lasry's reported closeness with people recently charged in connection to a high-stakes poker game at the Carlyle Hotel with alleged ties to the mob world.

Truly, the case stands out because of Lasry's closeness not only to Hillary Clinton but also Donald Trump as shown in **figure 7.1**.

---

[309] Joe Coscarelli, 'Obama's French Ambassador Pick May Have Been Sunk by Carlyle Hotel Poker Bust', *New York,* April 26, 2013, http://nymag.com/daily/intelligencer/2013/04/marc-lasry-tied-to-carlyle-hotel-poker-bust.html

Figure 7.1: Marc Lasry, The True Hedge Fund Manager

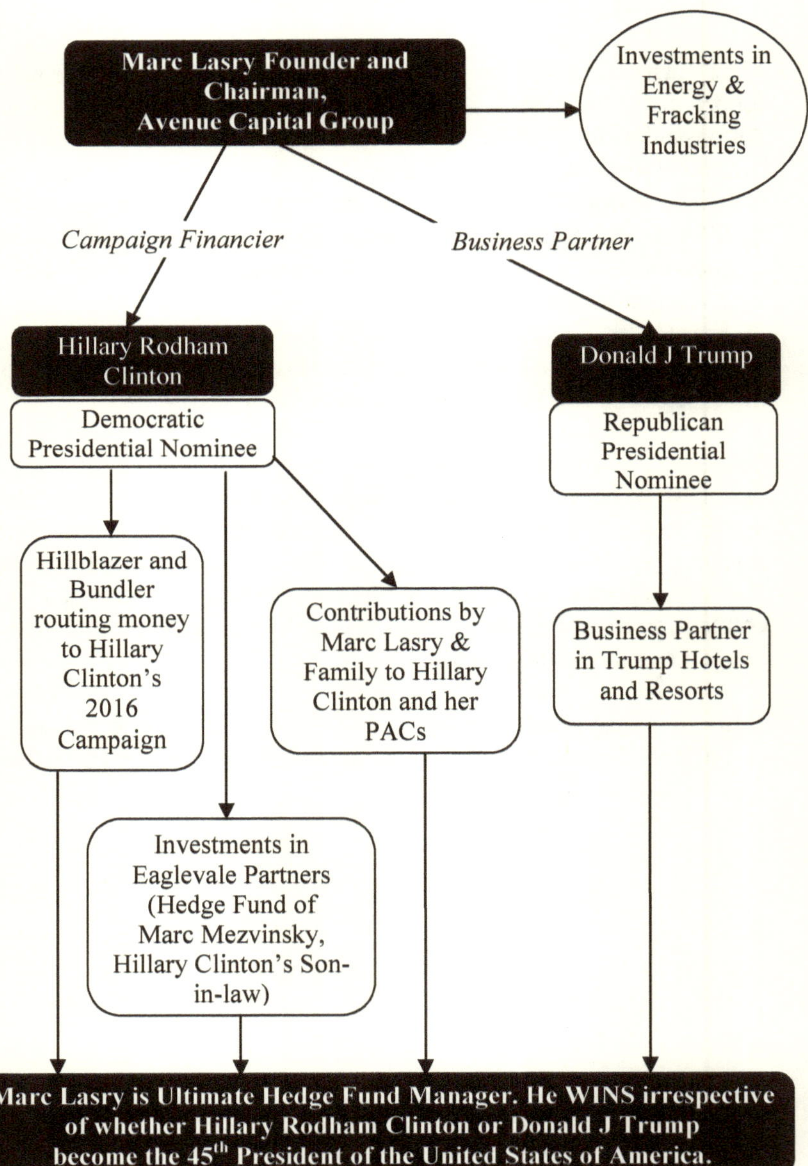

To recapitulate, as an ardent supporter of Hillary Clinton, Lasry has helped funnel significant contributions to her campaign. At the same time, Lasry is Trump's business partner and is reportedly close to him as well.

Indeed, as shown above in **figure 7.1,** Lasry is a true hedge fund manager as he wins, irrespective of whether Hillary Clinton or Donald Trump becomes the 45th President of the United States.

Look at it this way. Marc Lasry and the Avenue Capital Group are heavily invested in the energy, fossil fuel, and fracking industries.

The fortunes of the companies where they have invested money and as well as their own future would, in many ways, depend on how well these industries do, which, in turn, will also depend on the regulatory environment in the future.

Therefore, there is no doubt that, the 45th President of the United States, whether Hillary Clinton or Donald Trump, will have to decide on a range of urgent climate change issues that could put these very industries at huge risk. The question is can and will they do that fairly and objectively?

The positive answer becomes even more doubtful considering the fact that both candidates have close ties to these industries and also given that one of their strongest and closest Wall Street backers[310], Marc Lasry, has deep-rooted ties to these industries and more importantly, his fortunes and that of his hedge fund, Avenue Capital Group, depend on these industries.

In fact, the key issue here is, in the event of Hillary Clinton or Donald Trump becoming the 45th President of the United States, will they look to support their campaign financier or business partner or alternatively, save mother Earth? Without a doubt, looking at the past record of both Hillary Clinton and Donald Trump, the question does seem an extremely pertinent and legitimate one that time alone will answer.

---

[310] It has also been reported that, among several others with close Clinton ties, Marc Lasry and Goldman Sachs CEO Lloyd Blankfein invested in Eaglevale Partners, the hedge fund set up by Marc Mezvinsky, Chelsea Clinton's husband. Lasry claimed to have invested $1 million. That the fund "underperformed" is another matter. Hillary Clinton thus has another linkage that reinforces the inherent conflicts of interest that she has with the Avenue Capital Group and Marc Lasry. See: Matthew Goldstein and Steve Eder, 'For Clintons, a Hedge Fund in the Family', *The New York Times,* March 22, 2015, http://www.nytimes.com/2015/03/23/business/dealbook/for-clintons-a-hedge-fund-in-the-family.html. Trump, is perhaps closer to Marc Lasry as Lasry is his business partner as noted in the text. See: 'Trump, Clinton and The Marc Lasry Connection', *The Wide Awake Gentile,* February 26, 2016, https://wideawakegentile.wordpress.com/2016/02/26/trump-clinton-and-the-marc-lasry-connection/

Chapter 8

Conclusion

"Over a fourteen-year period from 1999 to 2013, one hedge fund carried out an investment strategy utilizing hundreds of millions of trades, virtually all of which lasted less than 12 months, and characterized the vast majority of the resulting $34 billion in trading profits as long-term capital gains ... resulting in estimated tax avoidance of more than $6 billion."

— Permanent Subcommittee on Investigations, United States Senate, 2014

This publicly recorded statement exposes the shocking truth about how Wall Street, and the billionaire class, have continued to manipulate and exploit the financial system, taking advantage of loop holes to pull the wool over the eyes of the Internal Revenue Service (IRS). Routing some of this '*dirty money*' into the election campaign coffers of various presidential candidates provides them with access to the levers of power 'inside the beltway'.

The Financial Crisis Inquiry Commission (FCIC), that looked into the causes and consequences of the 2008 financial crisis in America – which had its impact worldwide - famously remarked in its final report that the power and ability of Wall Street to lobby 'Washington' should not be underestimated. The FCIC noted in its final report[311] and I quote,

---

[311] Final Report Of The National Commission On The Causes Of The Financial And Economic Crisis In The United States, The Financial Crisis Inquiry Commission, http://fcic-

> It did not surprise the Commission that an industry of such wealth and power would exert pressure on policy makers and regulators. From 1998 to 2008 the financial sector expended $2.7 billion in reported federal lobbying expenses; individuals and political action committees in the sector made more than $1 billion in campaign contributions. What troubled us was the extent to which the nation was deprived of the necessary strength and independence of the oversight necessary to safeguard financial stability. (FCIC Report, 2011)

What is really sad is that despite the financial crisis that has crippled America and the world since 2008, campaign finance in the United States of America is no different in 2016 – simply because many candidates for the office of the President of the United States across election cycles and the major political parties[312] are ready to accept '*dirty money*' from Wall Street and the billionaire class. Indeed, today, '*dirty money*' flows through the campaign finance system perhaps much more than before, and this book has attempted to provide numerous examples of the same.

Take the case of James Harris Simons (founder, present chair and former CEO) and Robert Mercer (Co-CEO), both of whom are closely associated with Renaissance Technologies (RenTec). Both Simons and Mercer have played a very important role in shaping RenTec's strategy, growth and operations—over the last two decades—making it one of the world leading hedge funds. Yet, interestingly, RenTec, has been named in a report by the U.S. Senate (Permanent Subcommittee on Investigations) for tax evasion of around $6.46 billion—which is very serious. Indeed, both Simons and Mercer are reportedly fighting the biggest tax cases[313] with IRS.

---

static.law.stanford.edu/cdn_media/fcic-reports/fcic_final_report_full.pdf

[312] The Democratic and Republican Parties.

[313] Noam Scheiber and Patricia Cohen, 'For the Wealthiest, a Private Tax System That Saves Them Billions', *The New York Times,*

To give a bit of background, the IRS identified the "basket options strategy" used by RenTec and other hedge funds as tax abusive in a public memorandum in 2010. This was followed by the final report of the United States Senate Permanent Subcommittee on Investigations in 2014, whose quote is given above. That being the case, when the IRS was trying to do everything possible, as per the law, to recoup the loss to the United States Exchequer, why did the candidates for the Presidential election of 2012 and 2016, accept '*dirty money*' from James Simons and Robert Mercer of RenTec? Clearly, Simons and Mercer derive their wealth from RenTec, whose operational practices have been called out by not only the IRS but also the United States Senate Permanent Subcommittee on Investigations.

Interestingly, together James Simons and Robert Mercer have contributed[314] over $50 million across three election cycles (2016, 2012 and 2008) to various presidential and down ballot candidates in America. For example, in the present 2016 cycle, James Simons has given about $7 million to Priorities USA Action, a political action committee (PAC) supporting Hillary Clinton, while Robert Mercer donated around $13.5 million to a PAC supporting Ted Cruz (*Keep the Promise I*) which has subsequently converted itself to a PAC supporting Donald Trump (*Make America Number I*). In 2012, Simons gave liberally to PACs supporting President Obama (2012 – $5 million) while Mercer contributed handsomely to Republican Mitt Romney (2012 – $3 million).

Indeed, if you look at what Mercer and Simons have spent on campaign finance in the last three cycles (cost = $50 million) to what they have *notionally* gained (benefit = $6.46 billion), it is unbelievable—for every $ 1 spent, they have (notionally) gained almost $129, which signifies a return of about 12,800%—

December 29, 2015, http://www.nytimes.com/2015/12/30/business/economy/for-the-wealthiest-private-tax-system-saves-them-billions.html

[314] Federal Election Commission, www.fec.gov

something that is unheard of. And to top it off, the U.S. Senate database shows that RenTec lobbied the federal government close to 80 times over the last several years. Clearly, there is no free lunch ever and campaign finance from staff of entities like RenTec will always have a *quid pro quo.* Given the above, any money from entities such as RenTec is undoubtedly '*dirty money*' and it is clear that the aforementioned candidates have accepted this '*dirty money*' for their campaigns.

Moving on, let us look at the case of Haim Saban and Cheryl Saban, one of the top contributors in the 2016 presidential election. Haim and his wife Cheryl Saban have given over $11 million to various pro-Clinton PACs. Additionally, Haim and Cheryl Saban and the Saban Family Foundation have together donated in the range of $10 million – $25 million to the Clinton Foundation as per its website[315]. Interestingly, Haim Saban was named along with six others in a United States Senate Permanent Subcommittee report[316] with regard to tax abuses. This Senate report remarked that fake security transactions were created to post fake capital losses to offset real capital gains that had accrued—thereby costing the United States Treasury millions of dollars in taxes.

That is not all. The facilitator of the "POINT" tax shelter transactions for Haim Saban – Quellos was also cited[317] as having been closely involved in similar dubious and dirty

---

[315]Contributor and Grantor Information, *Clinton Foundation,* https://www.clintonfoundation.org/contributors?category=%2410%2C000%2C001+to+%2425%2C000%2C000.

[316] 'Tax Haven Abuses: The Enablers, the Tools And Secrecy', Minority & Majority Staff Report, Permanent Subcommittee On Investigations, August 1, 2006.

[317] 'Tax Haven Abuses: The Enablers, the Tools And Secrecy', Minority & Majority Staff Report, Permanent Subcommittee On Investigations, August 1, 2006 and 'The Role of Professional Firms in the U.S. Tax Shelter Industry Report', Prepared by the Permanent Subcommittee on Investigations Of the Committee on Homeland Security and Governmental Affairs United States Senate, April 13, 2005.

transactions with regard to a tax shelter product called "FLIP" in the famous KPMG tax scam of the early 2000's. To refresh peoples' memory, the KPMG tax criminal case led to around $456 million being paid in fines, restitution and penalties to various stakeholders.[318]

Two other major donors, George Soros (who has contributed over $7 million to pro-Clinton PACs) and Donald Sussman (who donated over $9.5 million to pro-Clinton PACs) have been named in the Panama Papers expose which deals with the use of tax shelters and tax havens. Besides, George Soros was convicted of insider trading in France. And both Donald Sussman and George Soros have donated to the Clinton Foundation—while the Sussman Family Foundation gave between $50,000 -$100,000 to the Clinton Foundation, the Soros Foundation donated between $500,001 – $1,000,000.

The icing on the cake is, however, Donald Trump, because of several issues related to his campaign finance and its structure. The key point to note is that while his campaign has, by and large, been self-funded, people like Robert Mercer, Co-CEO of Renaissance Technologies (RenTec) are supporting him now[319]. As noted earlier, RenTec was named in a United States Senate Permanent Subcommittee report for evading taxes to the tune of

---

[318] 'KPMG to Pay $456 Million for Criminal Violations', IR-2005-83, *IRS,* August 29, 2005, https://www.irs.gov/uac/kpmg-to-pay-456-million-for-criminal-violations

[319] See: Nicholas Confessore, 'How One Family's Deep Pockets Helped Reshape Donald Trump's Campaign', *The New York Times,* August 18, 2016, http://www.nytimes.com/2016/08/19/us/politics/robert-mercer-donald-trump-donor.html?hpw&rref=politics&action=click&pgtype=Homepage&module=well-region®ion=bottom-well&WT.nav=bottom-well&_r=0 and, Theodore Schleifer, 'Yet another Donald Trump super PAC launches, this one with a link to Ted Cruz', *CNN Politics,* June 23, 2016, http://edition.cnn.com/2016/06/23/politics/donald-trump-super-pac-fundraising/

$6.46 billion[320]. Donald Trump has no moral right what-so-ever to criticize Hillary Clinton because he and Hillary Clinton represent two sides of the same coin. While Hillary Clinton has been heavily funded by Rentec's former CEO and present chair, James Harris Simons, Donald Trump is being supported by Robert Mercer, the present Co-CEO[321] of RenTec. That is not all, as **chapter 7** has revealed. Both Hillary Clinton and Donald Trump are extremely close to the fracking fund billionaire, Marc Lasry, who is not only a major fund raiser for Hillary Clinton but also a key business partner of Donald Trump.

This again proves that Hillary Clinton and Donald Trump as two sides of the same coin. Incidentally, as the *New York Times*[322] noted, James Harris Simons and Robert Mercer are fighting huge tax cases with the IRS and by taking money from both Robert Mercer and James Simons, Donald Trump and Hillary Clinton have, without a doubt, accepted '*dirty money*'.

A further issue with Donald Trump is that he has not released his tax returns as yet—this is not appropriate behavior of a candidate running for office of the President of the United States. To the best of my knowledge, Donald Trump appears to have no legal basis for claiming that '*because his taxes are being audited, they cannot be released*'—the law is crystal clear and it does not prohibit anyone from releasing their tax returns, even if they are being audited. Even assuming Trump's statement to be true, the next question is why is he not releasing his tax returns for the

---

320 Report: Abuse Of Structured Financial Products: Misusing Basket Options to Avoid Taxes and Leverage Limits, *Homeland Security and Government Affairs,* July 22, 2014, http://www.hsgac.senate.gov/subcommittees/investigations/hearings/abuse-of-structured-financial-products_misusing-basket-options-to-avoid-taxes-and-leverage-limits

321 https://en.wikipedia.org/wiki/Robert_Mercer_(businessman)

322 Scheiber and Cohen, 'For the Wealthiest, a Private Tax System That Saves Them Billions', *The New York Times,* December 29, 2015, **http://www.nytimes.com/2015/12/30/business/economy/for-the-wealthiest-private-tax-system-saves-them-billions.html**

years that are not under audit? Donald Trump seems to have no explanation for that!

From the above, it appears that Donald Trump has something to hide with regard to his taxes, and a couple of articles in the press in the run up to the 2016 election suggest that all may not be clean with Donald Trump and his taxes. This argument becomes stronger when you consider the fact that Donald Trump received almost $885 million in tax breaks (using inside connections) to support his real estate ventures.[323] Reportedly, Donald Trump and his children have also been named in a $250 million tax scam.[324] Besides, apparently, there is new evidence that Donald Trump didn't pay taxes.[325] In fact, another recent *New York Times* article[326] claims that Donald Trump reportedly declared "a $916 million loss on his 1995 income tax returns". The article goes on to argue that this huge tax deduction may have helped him to legally avoid paying any (federal) income taxes for up to 18 years. Imagine, what would happen if you or I did that. It is indeed sad that businessmen like Donald Trump are able to get away with this and more – what is worse is that they are also

[323] Charles V. Bagli, 'A Trump Empire Built on Inside Connections and $885 Million in Tax Breaks', *The New York Times,* September 17, 2016, http://mobile.nytimes.com/2016/09/18/nyregion/donald-trump-tax-breaks-real-estate.html?emc=edit_th_20160918&nl=todaysheadlines&nlid=73858581&referer=

[324] See: David Cay Johnston, 'Donald Trump and Kids Named in $250M Tax Scam', *The Daily Beast,* July 15, 2016, http://www.thedailybeast.com/articles/2016/07/14/donald-trump-junior-and-ivanka-material-witnesses-in-huge-tax-scam-case.html

[325] David Cay Johnston, 'New Evidence Donald Trump Didn't Pay Taxes', *The Daily Beast,* June 15, 2016, http://www.thedailybeast.com/articles/2016/06/15/new-evidence-donald-trump-didn-t-pay-taxes.html

[326] David Barstow et al, 'Trump Tax Records Obtained by The Times Reveal He Could Have Avoided Paying Taxes for Nearly Two Decades' *The New York Times*, October 1, 2016, http://www.nytimes.com/2016/10/02/us/politics/donald-trump-taxes.html?_r=0

able to run for the highest office on the face of this planet – the President of the United States.

These are serious issues and coming from organizations like the *New York Times* and other well known news agencies, they ought not to be taken lightly—especially given the transparency expected of a presidential candidate. And given Donald Trump's refusal to release his tax returns, one is naturally tempted to ask as to what is Donald Trump really hiding? Besides, it must be noted here that there are other serious issues pertaining to Donald Trump as claimed in articles[327] by *The Washington Post* and *The Wall Street Journal*—while the former deals with aspects pertaining to Trump's Foundation claiming that the 'Trump Foundation' did not have the certification to receive public donations, the latter deals with the issue of how Donald Trump reportedly pleaded for leniency during an SEC fraud probe, post 9/11—these are not issues that flatter the Republican presidential nominee in any measure what-so-ever.

Thus, the above again goes to show that billionaires like Robert Mercer, James Simons and Donald Trump, are able to use various means to avoid paying taxes whereas the ordinary average American has his taxes deducted first and has to claim any excess deductions back subsequently. This indeed has been a central issue in this 2016 U.S. presidential election and I am not sure that Donald Trump or, for that matter, Hillary Clinton perform well in terms of not using '*dirty money*'—in this case,

---

[327] David A Fahrenthold, Trump Foundation lacks the certification required for charities that solicit money, *The Washington Post,* September 29, 2016, https://www.washingtonpost.com/politics/trump-foundation-lacks-the-certification-required-for-charities-that-solicit-money/2016/09/29/7dac6a68-8658-11e6-ac72-a29979381495_story.html?postshare=8291475225419946&tid=ss_tw Reid J. Epstein and Dave Michaels, Donald Trump Pointed to 9/11 Attacks in Asking SEC for Leniency During Fraud Probe, *The Wall Street Journal,* September 29, 2016, http://www.wsj.com/articles/donald-trump-pointed-to-9-11-attacks-in-asking-sec-for-leniency-during-fraud-probe-1475186563

money tainted by tax evasion, tax abuse, use of tax shelters/havens and tax breaks. Indeed, many other presidential candidates like Ted Cruz (2016 primary cycle) and those in the previous cycles (2012)—e.g., Mitt Romney and Barack Obama—have accepted and used '*dirty money*' in their election campaigns.

Tax evasion and abuse are just one aspect of corporate crime with regard to Wall Street and the billionaire class.

Others have been charged with serious violations including fraud by the Securities and Exchanges Commission (SEC). The case of Blackstone which settled with the SEC, paying over $38 million is one example. Specifically, the SEC ruled[328] that "*Blackstone breached its fiduciary duty ... in violation of Section 206(2) of the Advisers Act and also violated Section 206(4) of the Advisers Act and Rule 206(4)-8 there under. ... Section 206(2) of the Advisers Act prohibits investment advisers from directly or indirectly engaging 'in any transaction, practice, or course of business which operates as a fraud or deceit upon any client or prospective client.'*" It has been reported that Blackstone's President held a fundraiser[329] for Clinton and the money is said to have been donated to Hillary Clinton's 2016 campaign. Additionally, the Blackstone Group has also donated in the range of $250,001 – $500,000 to the Clinton Foundation as per its website.[330]

---

[328] United States of America, before the Securities and Exchange Commission, In the Matter of Blackstone et al., October 7, 2015, https://www.sec.gov/litigation/admin/2015/ia-4219.pdf

[329] David Sirota and Andrew Perez, 'Hillary Clinton Denounces Corporate Crime While Accepting Cash From Blackstone, Firm Sanctioned by SEC', *International Business Times,* December 16, 2015, http://www.ibtimes.com/political-capital/hillary-clinton-denounces-corporate-crime-while-accepting-cash-blackstone-firm

[330] Contributor and Grantor Information, *Clinton Foundation,* https://www.clintonfoundation.org/contributors?category=%2410%2C000%2C001+to+%2425%2C000%2C000

Vinod Gupta, a former trustee of the Clinton Foundation and close associate of the Clintons, settled[331] with the SEC, paying about $7.4 million, after it brought charges of fraud[332] against him for "receiving ... approximately $9.5 million of unauthorized and undisclosed perquisites". He has contributed between $1 million – $5 million to the Clinton Foundation and given $33,400 to the Clinton campaign (Hillary Victory Fund).[333]

There are other Clinton "associates" who have been plucked from the bunch as examples by the Internal Revenue Service (IRS) and the Department of Justice (DoJ). The case of UBS is still fresh in memory. UBS, when it was tackling the "IRS problem", paid $1.915 million for a total of 10 speeches to the Clintons—nine by Bill Clinton (five of them when Hillary Clinton was Secretary of State) and one by Hillary Clinton. The question is whether conflicts of interest were at play, especially because several of the above speeches were made when UBS was 'tackling' the IRS problem. The issue gets further compounded when one considers the fact that UBS AG donated between $50,000 – $100,000 and UBS Wealth Management, USA contributed in the range of $500,001 – $1,000,000 to the Clinton Foundation. Clearly, this is not the best example of governance in practice.

Yet others have been charged with violations under the Foreign Corrupt Practices Act (FCPA), having bribed their way to profits and business overseas. The case of Stryker Corporation, which is part owned by Pat and Jon Stryker, who are both big time Clinton donors, is a great example. Pat and Jon Stryker have together contributed in excess of $6 million to the Clinton campaign and pro-Clinton PACs. It is pertinent to note that the

---

[331] 'SEC Charges Former Executives in Illegal Scheme to Enrich CEO with Perks', *U.S. Securities and Exchange Commission,* March 15, 2010, https://www.sec.gov/news/press/2010/2010-39.htm

[332] In the United States District Court for the District of Nebraska, Vinod Gupta, Defendant, https://www.sec.gov/litigation/complaints/2010/comp21451-gupta.pdf

[333] Federal Election Commission, www.fec.gov

Stryker Corporation paid a fine of more than $13.2 million to settle[334] with SEC for "violating the Foreign Corrupt Practices Act (FCPA)" because its "subsidiaries in five different countries bribed doctors, health care professionals, and other government-employed officials in order to obtain or retain business".

Indeed, as the RenTec, Haim Saban, George Soros, Donald Sussman, Pat and Jon Stryker, D. E. Shaw, Blackstone and BlackRock cases as well as the recent **Wells Fargo episode** clearly demonstrate, Wall Street and the billionaire class have always taken advantage of the financial system and to safeguard their interests, they have not only lobbied Washington but also contributed '*dirty money*' handsomely to the various candidates across the political spectrum, through a corrupt campaign finance system.

The 2016 U.S. presidential election has seen a lot of attention focused on this 'corrupt' political campaign finance system and it is time the real truth emerged. Indeed, using this watershed 2016 election as the context, this book has offered a candid analysis of the campaign contributions to various presidential candidates across three presidential election cycles (2008, 2012 and 2016) to trace the total flow of '*dirty money*' from its source to those presidential campaigns.

While America had typically been allowed to see just the tip of iceberg so far, '*Dirty Money*,' has revealed the '*dirty money*' trail it in its entirety, making available previously hidden information on the key top donors in each presidential election cycle, and the beneficiaries of their vast and corrupt contributions. And this corruption within the United States is indeed a global issue, given the huge inter-linkages that the U.S. economy has with rest of the world. As the only super power of this century, the United States of America simply cannot afford to have a corrupt campaign finance system that not only breeds domestic corruption but also enables its spread globally, as has been

[334] United States of America before the Securities and Exchange Commission, In the Matter of Stryker Corporation, October 24, 2013, https://www.sec.gov/litigation/admin/2013/34-70751.pdf

demonstrated earlier in this book. Corruption cannot exist without conflict of interest and therefore, any system like the campaign finance system that exacerbates conflicts of interests must be reformed unequivocally so that nothing is left to chance.

Just as Bernie Sanders has often remarked (through the Democratic Primaries), this book has clearly demonstrated that the campaign finance system in the United States actively fosters an environment where conflicts of interests and corruption thrive. This has already led to the undermining of democratic values,[335] governance and public accountability and facilitated all kinds of criminal activity within and across borders, including legal, paralegal and illegal trafficking of money and associated aspects.[336] The use of tax shelters, tax havens, tax breaks and basket options as well as payment of bribes are good examples of such trafficking in '*dirty money*' and this year has been replete with large scale evidence of this, thanks to the Panama Papers expose.[337]

While '*dirty money*' and a corrupt campaign finance system impede the ability to promote freedom and democracy, fight poverty, and tackle crime and terrorism, more importantly, they prevent the establishment of a '*government by the people, for the people and of the people.*' Therefore, it is my fervent plea that the 45th President of the United States—whosoever it may be—must urgently undertake to reform the corrupt campaign finance system that is strongly in the grasp of Wall Street and the billionaire class and weed out the *'dirty money'* from the same. Only that will facilitate President Lincoln's dreams—of having '*a government by the people, for the people and of the people*'—to come true. Whether the 45th President has the political and administrative will to do this and whether Wall Street and the

[335] I am referring to what happened in the Democratic primaries in 2016. These are serious issues and least expected in a developed country, least of all, The United States of America.
[336] It is noteworthy that the Panama Papers expose occurred in 2016 and during the Democratic primaries.
[337] The Panama Papers, *ICIJ,* https://panamapapers.icij.org/

billionaire class will permit him/her to do so, is a question that time alone can answer.

Appendix 1

Presidential Candidates in the 2016 U.S. General Election

- Hillary Clinton (Democratic Party)
- Donald Trump (Republican Party)
- Jill Stein (Green Party)
- Gary Johnson (Libertarian Party)

Presidential Candidates in the 2016 U.S. Primaries

- Hillary Clinton (Democratic Party)
- Bernie Sanders (Democratic Party)
- Donald Trump (Republican Party)
- Ted Cruz (Republican Party)
- Marco Rubio (Republican Party)
- John Kasich (Republican Party)

Presidential Candidates in the 2012 U.S. General Election

- Barack Obama (Democratic Party)
- Mitt Romney (Republican Party)

Presidential Candidates in the 2008 U.S. General Election[338]

- Barack Obama (Democratic Party)
- John McCain (Republican Party)

Please note that all Federal Election Commission (FEC) data accessed is dated July 31, 2016, unless otherwise noted – this is because as at the time of writing the book, that was the last available data. It is also believed that subsequent data will not make any material difference as the bulk of the campaign finance data is used in this book for analysis. The primary source of data is www.fec.gov. Some data has also been taken from Open Secrets Database (https://www.opensecrets.org/).

[338] Hillary Clinton contested the 2008 U.S primaries as a Democrat.

Appendix 2

Appendix 2.1: James Harris Simons

Table 2.1.1: Contributions to Presidential Campaigns (2016, 2012 and 2008)			
Year	**2016 Presidential Elections**	**2012 Presidential Elections**	**2008 Presidential Elections**
Whether James Simons Contributed to **PACs Related to Presidential Candidates?**	• $7,000,000 to Priorities USA Action, PAC supporting Hillary Clinton • $1,000,000 to House Majority PAC • $1,600,000 to Senate Majority PAC • $5,000 to Common Ground PAC	• $5,000,000 to Priorities USA Action, PAC supporting Obama • $1,500,000 House Majority PAC • $3,000,000 Majority PAC	• Nil
Whether James Simons Contributed Individually to Presidential Candidates?	• $2,700 to Hillary Clinton	• Nil	• $2,300 to Hillary Clinton • $2,300 to Hillary Clinton • $2,300 to Barack Obama • $2,300 to Barack Obama • $2,100 to Christopher J Dodd • $200 to Christopher J Dodd

Table 2.1.1: Contributions to Presidential Campaigns (2016, 2012 and 2008)			
Year	**2016 Presidential Elections**	**2012 Presidential Elections**	**2008 Presidential Elections**
Total Contributions	**$9,607,700**	**$9,500,000**	**$11,500**
Grand Total Contribution – All Years	**$26,119,200**		
Grand Total Contribution Includes House and Senate Majority PACs 2014 as Shown Below • $2,000,000 to House Majority PAC • $5,000,000 to Senate Majority PAC			
Source:	http://www.fec.gov/		

Table 2.1.2: Company/Entity Staff Contributions to Presidential Campaigns (2016, 2012 and 2008)			
Year	**2016 Presidential Elections**	**2012 Presidential Elections**	**2008 Presidential Elections**
Whether James Simons Company /Entity Staff Contributed to PACs Related to Presidential Candidates Companies - RenTec and Euclidean Capital etc	• Laufer, Henry $1,000,000 to Senate Majority PAC • Dellapietra, Vincent $2,700 to Hillary Victory Fund	• Robert, Stephen $1,000,000 to Priorities USA Action, PAC supporting Obama	• Nil
Whether James Simons Company/Entity Staff Contributed Individually to Presidential Candidates Companies – RenTec and	• $8,220 to Hillary Clinton • $5,400 to Jeb Bush • $5,400 to Marco Rubio • $2,700 to John R. Kasich	• $29,500 to Mitt Romney • $26,968 to Barack Obama • $2500 to Rick Santorum	• $44,145 to Hillary Clinton • $40,605 to Barack Obama • $10,350 to C J Dodd

Table 2.1.2: Company/Entity Staff Contributions to Presidential Campaigns (2016, 2012 and 2008)			
Year	**2016 Presidential Elections**	**2012 Presidential Elections**	**2008 Presidential Elections**
Euclidean Capital etc	• $434 to Bernard Sanders	• $2,500 to Ron Paul	• $5,100 to John S McCain • $2,550 to Rudolph W Giuliani • $500 to Ron Paul
Total Contributions	**$1,024,854**	**$1,061,468**	**$102,750**
Grand Total Contribution – All Years	**$2,189,072**		
Source:	http://www.fec.gov/		

Table 2.1.3: Family Members' Contributions to Presidential Campaigns (2016, 2012 and 2008)			
Year	**2016 Presidential Elections**	**2012 Presidential Elections**	**2008 Presidential Elections**
Whether James Simons' Family Members Contributed Individually and/or to PACs Related to Presidential Candidates	• Simons, Marilyn Hawrys $2,700 to Hillary Clinton • Simons, Barbara $1,700 to Hillary Clinton • Simons, Barbara $1,000 to Hillary Clinton • Simons, Barbara $250 to Hillary	• Simons, Marilyn Hawrys $2,500 to Barack Obama • Simons, Marilyn Hawrys $2,500 to Barack Obama • Simons, Barbara $2,500 to Barack	• Simons, Marilyn Hawrys $2,300 to Barack Obama • Simons, Marilyn Hawrys $2,300 to Barack Obama • Simons, Marilyn Hawrys $2,300 to

Table 2.1.3: Family Members' Contributions to Presidential Campaigns (2016, 2012 and 2008)			
Year	**2016 Presidential Elections**	**2012 Presidential Elections**	**2008 Presidential Elections**
	Clinton • Simons, Marilyn $500,000 to Women Vote! PAC • Simons, Nat $2,700 to Lindsey Graham 2016 PAC	Obama • Simons, Nathaniel $2,500 to Barack Obama • Simons, Nathaniel $2500 to Barack Obama • Simons, Marilyn $75,000 to Planned Parenthood Votes PAC	Hillary Clinton • Simons, Marilyn Hawrys $2300 to Hillary Clinton • Simons, Nat $2,300 to Barack Obama • Simons, Nat $1000 to Barack Obama • Simons, Nat $700 to Barack Obama • Simons, Nat $250 to Barack Obama • Simons, Nat $250 to Barack Obama • Simons, Nat $100 to Barack Obama
Total Contributions	**$508,250**	**$87,500**	**$13,800**
Grand Total Contribution – All Years	**$609,550**		
Source:	http://www.fec.gov/		

Table 2.1.4: Contributions to Foundations Related to 'Presidential Candidates'	
Whether James Simons and/or his Companies/ Foundations/ Family Members Contributed to Foundations Related to Presidential Candidates	• Nat Simons has also donated between $10,001 to $25,000 to the Clinton Foundation • Henry and Marsha Laufer (RenTec) also donated between $250,001 to $500,000 to the Clinton Foundation

Table 2.1.5: Contributions Via Paid Speeches/Assignments to 'Presidential Candidates', Within Three Years of Candidacy Announcement	
Whether James Simons and/or his Companies/ Foundations/ Family Members Gave Speaking and Advisory Assignments to Presidential candidates	• Nil

Appendix 2.2: Robert Leroy Mercer

Table 2.2.1: Company/Entity Staff Contributions to Presidential Campaigns (2016, 2012 and 2008)

Year	2016 Presidential Elections	2012 Presidential Elections	2008 Presidential Elections
Whether Robert Leroy Mercer Contributed to **PACs Related to Presidential Candidates?**	• Mercer, Robert L $13,500,000 to Keep The Promise I, PAC supporting Ted Cruz which transformed into a new super PAC supporting Donald Trump, "Make America Number I" • Mercer, Robert L $2,000,000 to John Bolton Super PAC • Mercer, Robert L $500,000 to	• Mercer, Robert L, $2,500,000 to Freedom Partners Action Fund Inc PAC • Mercer, Robert L, $2,000,000 to American Crossroads, PAC supporting Mitt Romney • Mercer, Robert L $1,000,000 to	• Nil

Table 2.2.1: Company/Entity Staff Contributions to Presidential Campaigns (2016, 2012 and 2008)			
Year	**2016 Presidential Elections**	**2012 Presidential Elections**	**2008 Presidential Elections**
	Fighting For Ohio Fund PAC • Mercer, Robert L $500,000 to New York Wins PAC • Mercer, Robert L $425,500 to Black Americans For A Better Future • Mercer, Robert L $250,000 to Club For Growth Action • Mercer, Robert L $200,000 to Fighting For Florida Fund • Mercer, Robert L $50,000 to Defend Rural Arizona PAC • Mercer, Robert L $10,000 to Make DC Listen, PAC supporting Ted Cruz	Restore Our Future, PAC supporting Mitt Romney • Mercer, Robert L $600,000 to Club For Growth Action	
Whether Robert Leroy Mercer Contributed Individually to Presidential Candidates?	• $8,100 to Carly Fiorina • $5,400 to Donald J Trump • $2,700 to Bobby Jindal	• $5,000 to Mitt Romney • $2,500 to Rick Santorum • $2,500 to Ron Paul	• $1700 to C J Dodd
Total	**$17,451,700**	**$6,110,000**	**$1,700**

Table 2.2.1: Company/Entity Staff Contributions to Presidential Campaigns (2016, 2012 and 2008)			
Year	**2016 Presidential Elections**	**2012 Presidential Elections**	**2008 Presidential Elections**
Contributions			
Grand Total Contribution – All Years	**$25,713,400**		
Grand Total Contribution Includes House and Senate Majority PACs 2014 as Shown Below • Mercer, Robert L $1,150,000 to Club For Growth Action • Mercer, Robert L $1,000,000 to John Bolton Super PAC			
Source:	http://www.fec.gov/		

Appendix 2.3: George Soros

Table 2.3.1: Contributions to Presidential Campaigns (2016, 2012 and 2008)			
Year	**2016 Presidential Elections**	**2012 Presidential Elections**	**2008 Presidential Elections**
Whether George Soros Contributed to **PACs Related to Presidential Candidates?**	• $7,000,000 to Priorities USA Action, PAC supporting Hillary Clinton • $1,000,000 to Senate Majority PAC • $343,400 to Hillary Victory Fund • $25,000 to Hillary Ready PAC • $2,000,000 to American Bridge 21st Century	• $1,000,000 to Priorities USA Action, PAC supporting Obama • $675,000 to House Majority PAC • $100,000 to Majority PAC • $1,000,000 to American Bridge 21st Century	• Nil

Table 2.3.1: Contributions to Presidential Campaigns (2016, 2012 and 2008)			
Year	**2016 Presidential Elections**	**2012 Presidential Elections**	**2008 Presidential Elections**
Whether George Soros Contributed Individually to Presidential Candidates?	• $2,700 to Hillary Clinton	• $2,500 to Barack Obama • $2,500 to Barack Obama	• $2,300 to Hillary Clinton • $2,300 to Barack Obama • $2100 to Barack Obama
Total Contributions	**$10,371,100**	**$2,780,000**	**$6,700**
Grand Total Contribution – All Years	**$15,657,800**		
Grand Total Contribution Includes House and Senate Majority PACs 2014 as Shown Below • $500,000 to House Majority PAC • $500,000 to Senate Majority PAC • $500,000 to Planned Parenthood Votes • $1,000,000 to American Bridge 21st Century			
Source:	http://www.fec.gov/		

Table 2.3.2: Company/Entity Staff Contributions to Presidential Campaigns (2016, 2012 and 2008)			
Year	**2016 Presidential Elections**	**2012 Presidential Elections**	**2008 Presidential Elections**
Whether George Soros Company/Entity Staff Contributed to PACs Related to Presidential	• Rubin, Howard A. $25,000 to Right To Rise USA, PAC supporting Jeb Bush • Bessent, Scott $5,000 to Right To Rise USA, PAC	• Nil	• Nil

Table 2.3.2: Company/Entity Staff Contributions to Presidential Campaigns (2016, 2012 and 2008)			
Year	**2016 Presidential Elections**	**2012 Presidential Elections**	**2008 Presidential Elections**
Candidates Companies - Soros Fund Management, Open Society Foundations and Quantum Fund Capital etc	supporting Jeb Bush • Cohen, Alexander Z $2,000 to Lindsey Graham 2016 • Canavan, Terence $1,700 to Hillary Victory Fund • Bessent, Scott $1,500 to Lindsey Graham 2016 • Wassong, David $500 to Right To Rise USA, PAC supporting Jeb Bush • Taylor, Greg $250 to Hillary Victory Fund		
Whether George Soros Company/Entity Staff Contributed Individually to Presidential Candidates. Companies - Soros Fund Management, Open Society Foundations and Quantum Fund Capital etc	• $12,047 to Hillary Clinton • $4,500 to Jeb Bush • $2,700 to John R. Kasich • $2,700 to Marco Rubio • $3,500 to Lindsey O. Graham • $1,124 to Bernard Sanders	• $27,023 to Barack Obama • $18,000 to Mitt Romney	• $8,950 to Barack Obama • $3,380 to Hillary Clinton • $2300 to John S McCain
Total Contributions	**$61,521**	**$45,023**	**$14,630**
Grand Total Contribution – All Years	**$121,174**		
Source:	http://www.fec.gov/		

Table 2.3.3: Family Members' Contributions to Presidential Campaigns (2016, 2012 and 2008)			
Year	**2016 Presidential Elections**	**2012 Presidential Elections**	**2008 Presidential Elections**
Whether George Soros Family Members Contributed Individually and/or to PACs Related to Presidential Candidates	• Soros, Alexander G. $2,700 to Hillary Clinton • Soros, Gregory $2,700 to Bernard Sanders • Soros, Gregory $2,700 to Hillary Clinton • Soros, Jonathan $2,700 to Hillary Clinton • Soros, Jonathan $2,700 to Martin Joseph O'Malley • Soros, Jonathan $2,700 to Lawrence Lessig • Soros, Alex $1,000,000 to Priorities USA Action, PAC	• Soros, Jonathan A $2,500 to Barack Obama • Soros, Jonathan A $2,500 to Barack Obama • Soros, Jonathan Allan $2,100 to Barack Obama • Soros, Alexander $2,500 to Barack Obama • Soros, Alexander $2,500 to Barack Obama • Soros, Andrea $2,500 to Barack Obama • Soros, Andrea $2,500 to Barack Obama • Soros, Jennifer $2,500 to Barack Obama • Soros, Jennifer $2,500 to Barack Obama • Allan Soros, Jonathan $250,000 to Planned Parenthood Votes PAC	• Soros, Jonathan $2,300 to Barack Obama • Soros, Jonathan Allan $2,100 to Barack Obama • Soros, Melissa S $2,300 to Barack Obama • Soros, Melissa S $2,300 to Barack Obama • Soros, Robert $2,300 to Barack Obama • Soros, Robert $2,300 to Barack Obama • Soros, Andrea $2,300 to Barack Obama • Soros,

Table 2.3.3: Family Members' Contributions to Presidential Campaigns (2016, 2012 and 2008)			
Year	**2016 Presidential Elections**	**2012 Presidential Elections**	**2008 Presidential Elections**
	supporting Hillary Clinton • Soros, Alexander G. $350,000 to Hillary Victory Fund • Allan Soros, Jonathan $1,000,000 to Planned Parenthood Votes PAC • Allan Soros, Jennifer $1,000,000 to Planned Parenthood Votes PAC • Soros Colombel, Andrea $250,000 to Planned Parenthood Votes PAC	• Soros, Melissa $100,000 to Planned Parenthood Votes PAC • Soros, Melissa $500,000 to Planned Parenthood Votes PAC	Annaliese $2,300 to Barack Obama • Soros, Annaliese $2,300 to Hillary Clinton • Soros, Jennifer Allan $2300 to Hillary Clinton • Soros, Andrea $2,000 to Hillary Clinton
Total Contributions	**$3,616,200**	**$872,100**	**$24,800**
Grand Total Contribution – All Years	**$4,763,100**		
Grand Total Contribution Includes House and Senate Majority PACs 2014 as Shown Below • Soros Colombel, Andrea $250,000 to Planned Parenthood Votes PAC			
Source:	http://www.fec.gov/		

Table 2.3.4: Contributions to Foundations Related to 'Presidential Candidates'	
Whether George Soros and/or his Companies/ Foundations/ Family Members Contributed to Foundations Related to Presidential Candidates	• Soros Foundation has also donated between $500,001 to $1,000,000 to the Clinton Foundation

Table 2.3.5: Contributions Via Paid Speeches/Assignments to 'Presidential Candidates', Within Three Years of Candidacy Announcement	
Whether George Soros or his Entities/Family Members Gave Speaking Assignments to Presidential candidates	• Nil

Appendix 2.4: Haim and Cheryl Saban

Table 2.4.1: Contributions to Presidential Campaigns (2016, 2012 and 2008)			
Year	**2016 Presidential Elections**	**2012 Presidential Elections**	**2008 Presidential Elections**
Whether Haim and Cheryl Saban Contributed to **PACs Related to Presidential Candidates?**	• Saban, Haim $5,000,000 to Priorities USA Action, PAC supporting Hillary Clinton • Saban, Haim $1,000,000 to Senate Majority PAC • Saban, Haim $696,800 to Hillary Victory Fund • Saban, Haim $100,000 to Committee For Maryland's Progress • Saban, Cheryl $5,000,000 to Priorities USA Action, PAC supporting Hillary Clinton • Saban, Cheryl $706,800 to Hillary Victory Fund	• Nil	• Nil
Whether Haim and Cheryl Saban Contributed Individually to Presidential Candidates?	• Saban, Haim $2,700 to Hillary Clinton • Saban, Haim $2,700 to Hillary Clinton	• Saban, Haim $2,500 to Barack Obama • Saban, Haim $2,500 to Barack Obama	• Saban, Haim $2,300 to Hillary Clinton

Table 2.4.1: Contributions to Presidential Campaigns (2016, 2012 and 2008)			
Year	2016 Presidential Elections	2012 Presidential Elections	2008 Presidential Elections
	• Saban, Cheryl $2,700 to Hillary Clinton • Saban, Cheryl $2,700 to Hillary Clinton	• Saban, Cheryl $2,500 to Barack Obama • Saban, Cheryl $2,500 to Barack Obama	• Saban, Haim $2300 to Hillary Clinton
Total Contributions	**$12,514,400**	**$10,000**	**$4,600**
Grand Total Contribution – All Years	**$12,779,000**		
Grand Total Contribution Includes House and Senate Majority PACs 2014 as Shown Below ❖ Saban, Haim $250,000 to Senate Majority PAC			
Source:	http://www.fec.gov/		

Table 2.4.2: Company/Entity Staff Contributions to Presidential Campaigns (2016, 2012 and 2008)			
Year	2016 Presidential Elections	2012 Presidential Elections	2008 Presidential Elections
Whether Haim Saban Company/ Entity Staff Contributed to PACs Related to Presidential Candidates Company - Saban Entertainment and Saban Capital Group etc	• $193 to Hillary Victory Fund	• Nil	• Nil
Whether Haim Saban Company/Entity Staff Contributed	• $20,947 to Hillary Clinton	• $1,000 to Mitt Romney	• $29,900 to Hillary Clinton

Table 2.4.2: Company/Entity Staff Contributions to Presidential Campaigns (2016, 2012 and 2008)			
Year	**2016 Presidential Elections**	**2012 Presidential Elections**	**2008 Presidential Elections**
Individually to Presidential Candidates Companies - Saban Entertainment and Saban Capital Group etc		• $319 to Barack Obama	• $500 to Barack Obama
Total Contributions	**$21,140**	**$319**	**$30,400**
Grand Total Contribution – All Years	**$51,859**		
Source:	http://www.fec.gov/		

Table 2.4.3: Family Members' Contributions to Presidential Campaigns (2016, 2012 and 2008)			
Year	**2016 Presidential Elections**	**2012 Presidential Elections**	**2008 Presidential Elections**
Whether Haim Saban Family Members Contributed Individually and/or to PACs Related to Presidential Candidates	• Saban, Ness $2,700 to Hillary Clinton • Saban, Tanya $2,700 to Hillary Clinton	• Nil	• Nil
Total Contributions	**$5,400**	-	-
Grand Total Contribution – All Years	**$5,400**		
Source:	http://www.fec.gov/		

Table 2.4.4: Contributions to Foundations Related to 'Presidential Candidates'	
Whether Haim Saban and/or his Companies/ Foundations/ Family Members Contributed to Foundations Related to Presidential Candidates	• Cheryl and Haim Saban & The Saban Family Foundation has also donated between $10,000,001 to $25,000,000 to the Clinton Foundation

Table 2.4.5: Contributions Via Paid Speeches/Assignments to 'Presidential Candidates', Within Three Years of Candidacy Announcement	
Whether Haim Saban and/or his Companies/ Foundations/ Family Members Gave Speaking and Advisory Assignments to Presidential candidates	• Nil

Appendix 2.5: Donald Sussman

Table 2.5.1: Contributions to Presidential Campaigns (2016, 2012 and 2008)			
Year	**2016 Presidential Elections**	**2012 Presidential Elections**	**2008 Presidential Elections**
Whether Donald Sussman Contributed to **PACs Related to Presidential Candidates?**	• $8,000,000 to Priorities USA Action, PAC supporting Hillary Clinton • $2,000,000 to Women Vote PAC • $2,000,000 to House Majority PAC • $1,100,000 to Working for Us PAC • $686,800 to Hillary Victory Fund	• $1,150,000 to House Majority PAC • $100,000 to Women Vote PAC	• Nil

Table 2.5.1: Contributions to Presidential Campaigns (2016, 2012 and 2008)			
Year	**2016 Presidential Elections**	**2012 Presidential Elections**	**2008 Presidential Elections**
	• $100,000 to Correct the Record supporting Hillary Clinton • $20,000 to 21st Century Leaders		
Whether Donald Sussman Contributed Individually to Presidential Candidates?	• $2,700 to Hillary Clinton	• $2,500 to Barack Obama • $2,500 to Barack Obama	• $2,300 to Hillary Clinton • $2,300 to Hillary Clinton • $2,300 to Barack Obama • $2,300 to Bill Richardson
Total Contributions	**$13,909,500**	**$1,255,000**	**$9,200**
Grand Total Contribution – All Years	**$17,523,700**		
Grand Total Contribution Includes House and Senate Majority PACs 2014 as Shown Below: • $1,750,000 to House Majority PAC • $500,000 to Women Vote PAC • $100,000 to Senate Majority PAC			
Source:	http://www.fec.gov/		

Table 2.5.2: Company/Entity Staff Contributions to Presidential Campaigns (2016, 2012 and 2008)			
Year	**2016 Presidential Elections**	**2012 Presidential Elections**	**2008 Presidential Elections**
Whether Donald Sussman Company/Entity Staff Contributed to PACs Related to Presidential Candidates Company - Paloma Partners and Trust Asset Management	• Nil	• Nil	• Nil
Whether Donald Sussman Company/Entity Staff Contributed Individually to Presidential Candidates Companies - Paloma Partners and Trust Asset Management	• $3,200 to Hillary Clinton • $2,700 to Christopher J. Christie • $600 to Carly Fiorina • $100 to Bernard Sanders	• $4,360 to Mitt Romney	• Nil
Total Contributions	**$6,600**	**$4,360**	**-**
Grand Total Contribution – All Years	**$10,960**		
Source:	http://www.fec.gov/		

Table 2.5.3: Family Members' Contributions to Presidential Campaigns (2016, 2012 and 2008)			
Year	**2016 Presidential Elections**	**2012 Presidential Elections**	**2008 Presidential Elections**
Whether Donald Sussman Family Members Contributed Individually and/or to PACs Related to Presidential Candidates	• Sussman, Emily Tisch $2,700 to Hillary Clinton • Sussman, Emily Tisch $2,638 to Hillary Clinton	• Nil	• Nil
Total Contributions	**$5,338**	-	-
Grand Total Contribution – All Years	**$5,338**		
Source:	http://www.fec.gov/		

Table 2.5.4: Contributions to Foundations Related to 'Presidential Candidates'	
Whether Donald Sussman and/or his Companies/Foundations/ Family Members Contributed to Foundations Related to Presidential Candidates	• Sussman Family Foundation has also donated between $50,000 to $100,000 to the Clinton Foundation

Table 2.5.5: Contributions Via Paid Speeches/Assignments to 'Presidential Candidates', Within Three Years of Candidacy Announcement	
Whether Donald Sussman and/or his Entities/Family Members Gave Speaking and Advisory Assignments to Presidential candidates	Nil

Appendix 3

Appendix 3.1: Pat Stryker

Table 3.1.1: Contributions to Presidential Campaigns (2016, 2012 and 2008)			
Year	**2016 Presidential Elections**	**2012 Presidential Elections**	**2008 Presidential Elections**
Whether Pat Stryker Contributed to **PACs Related to Presidential Candidates?**	• $1,500,000 to Priorities USA Action, PAC supporting Hillary Clinton • $666,800 to Hillary Victory Fund • $500,000 to Correct The Record PAC supporting Hillary Clinton • $50,000 to Women Vote! PAC	• Nil	• Nil
Whether Pat Stryker Contributed Individually to Presidential Candidates?	• $2,700 to Hillary Clinton • $2,700 to Hillary Clinton	• $2,500 to Barack Obama • $2,500 to Barack Obama	• $2,300 to Barack Obama • $2,300 to Barack Obama • $2,300 to Hillary Clinton • $2,300 to John Edwards
Total Contributions	**$2,722,200**	**$5,000**	**$9,200**

Table 3.1.1: Contributions to Presidential Campaigns (2016, 2012 and 2008)			
Year	**2016 Presidential Elections**	**2012 Presidential Elections**	**2008 Presidential Elections**
Grand Total Contribution – All Years	**$3,536,400**		
Grand Total Contribution Includes House and Senate Majority PACs 2014 as Shown Below • $500,000 to NEXTGEN Climate Action Committee PAC • $300,000 to Mayday PAC			
Source:	http://www.fec.gov/		

Table 3.1.2: Company/Entity Staff Contributions to Presidential Campaigns (2016, 2012 and 2008)			
Year	**2016 Presidential Elections**	**2012 Presidential Elections**	**2008 Presidential Elections**
Whether Pat Stryker Company/Entity Staff Contributed to PACs Related to Presidential Candidates Companies – Stryker Corporation and Bohemian Foundation etc	• Nil	• Evans, James A $200 to American Crossroads PAC	• Nil
Whether Pat Stryker Company/Entity Staff Contributed Individually to Presidential Candidates Companies - Stryker Corporation and	• $2,700 to Hillary Clinton • $500 to John R Kasich • $500 to Marco Rubio • $250 to Rafael Edward 'Ted' Cruz	• $5,704 to Barack Obama • $4,360 Mitt Romney • $2,500 to Rick Perry	• $2,970 to Barack Obama • $850 Mitt Romney

Table 3.1.2: Company/Entity Staff Contributions to Presidential Campaigns (2016, 2012 and 2008)			
Year	**2016 Presidential Elections**	**2012 Presidential Elections**	**2008 Presidential Elections**
Bohemian Foundation etc			
Total Contributions	**$3,950**	**$12,764**	**$3,820**
Grand Total Contribution – All Years	**$20,534**		
Source:	http://www.fec.gov/		

Table 3.1.3: Contributions to Foundations Related to 'Presidential Candidates'	
Whether Pat Stryker and/or her Companies/ Foundations/ Family Members Contributed to Foundations Related to Presidential Candidates	• Nil

Table 3.1.4: Contributions Via Paid Speeches/Assignments to 'Presidential Candidates', Within Three Years of Candidacy Announcement	
Whether Pat Stryker and/or her Companies/ Foundations/ Family Members Gave Speaking and Advisory Assignments to Presidential candidates	• Nil

Appendix 3.2: Jon Stryker

Table 3.2.1: Contributions to Presidential Campaigns (2016, 2012 and 2008)			
Year	**2016 Presidential Elections**	**2012 Presidential Elections**	**2008 Presidential Elections**
Whether Jon Stryker Contributed to **PACs Related**	• Jon Stryker $2,000,000 to Priorities USA Action, PAC	• $2,000,000 to Priorities USA Action, PAC	• Nil

Table 3.2.1: Contributions to Presidential Campaigns (2016, 2012 and 2008)			
Year	**2016 Presidential Elections**	**2012 Presidential Elections**	**2008 Presidential Elections**
to Presidential Candidates?	supporting Hillary Clinton • Jon Stryker $1,100,000 to House Majority PAC • Jon Stryker $581,500 to Hillary Victory Fund • Jon Stryker $550,000 to Senate Majority PAC • Jon Stryker $150,000 to American Bridge 21st Century • Jon Stryker $100,000 to Correct The Record PAC supporting Hillary Clinton • Jon Stryker $100,000 to Planned Parenthood Votes PAC • Jon Stryker $100,000 to American Bridge 21st Century • Jon Stryker $75,000 to Women Vote! PAC • Jon Stryker	supporting Obama • Jon Stryker $500,000 to House Majority PAC	

Table 3.2.1: Contributions to Presidential Campaigns (2016, 2012 and 2008)			
Year	**2016 Presidential Elections**	**2012 Presidential Elections**	**2008 Presidential Elections**
	$5,000 to Humane Society Legislative Fund Political Action Committee		
Whether Jon Stryker Contributed Individually to Presidential Candidates?	• Jon Stryker $2,700 to Hillary Clinton	• Jon Stryker $2,500 to Barack Obama • Jon Stryker $2,500 to Barack Obama	• Jon Stryker $2,300 to Barack Obama
Total Contributions	**$4,764,200**	**$2,505,000**	**$2,300**
Grand Total Contribution – All Years	**$8,871,500**		
Grand Total Contribution Includes House and Senate Majority PACs 2014 as Shown Below • Jon Stryker $1,200,000 to House Majority PAC • Jon Stryker $400,000 to Senate Majority PAC			
Source:	http://www.fec.gov/		

Table 3.2.2: Contributions to Foundations Related to 'Presidential Candidates'	
Whether Jon Stryker and/or his Companies/ Foundations/ Family Members Contributed to Foundations Related to Presidential Candidates	• Jon L Stryker & Slobodan Randjelovic has also donated between $250,001 to $500,000 to the Clinton Foundation • Arcus Foundation has also donated between $25,001 to $50,000 to the Clinton Foundation

Table 3.2.3: Stryker Violations Under FCPA			
Dates	**Subsidiary**	**What Happened?**	**Remarks**
Between March 2004 and January 2007	Stryker's wholly-owned subsidiary in Mexico ("Stryker Mexico")	Stryker Mexico made three payments totaling more than $76,000 to foreign officials employed by a Mexican governmental agency responsible for providing social security for government employees	Stryker made these payments to win bids to sell its medical products to certain public hospitals in Mexico. These payments were made at the direction of Stryker Mexico employees, including country level management, and paid to the foreign officials through third party agents. Stryker Mexico earned more than $2.1 million in profits as a result of these illicit payments
Between August 2003 and November 2006	Stryker's wholly-owned subsidiary in Poland ("Stryker Poland")	Stryker Poland made 32 improper payments to foreign officials in Poland for the purpose of obtaining or retaining business at public hospitals. In total, Stryker Poland made approximately $460,000 in unlawful payments	These improper payments were recorded in Stryker's books and records as legitimate expenses, including reimbursement for business travel, consulting and service contract payments, and charitable donations. Stryker Poland earned more than $2.4 million of illicit profits
From at least 2003 through	Stryker's wholly-owned	Stryker Romania made 192 improper	Stryker Romania recorded these payments as legitimate

Table 3.2.3: Stryker Violations Under FCPA			
Dates	**Subsidiary**	**What Happened?**	**Remarks**
July 2007	subsidiary in Romania ("Stryker Romania")	payments to foreign officials totaling approximately $500,000 in order to obtain or retain business with affiliated public hospitals	sponsorships of foreign officials' attendance, travel and lodging at conferences, and medical events, when in reality they were illicit payments made to obtain or retain business. As a result of these, Stryker Romania earned more than $1.7 million in illicit profits
Between 2005 and 2008	Stryker's wholly-owned subsidiary in Argentina ("Stryker Argentina")	Stryker Argentina made 392 commission payments, or "honoraria," to physicians employed in the public healthcare system in order to obtain or retain business with affiliated public hospitals	Stryker Argentina routinely made these payments by check to doctors at rates between 20% and 25% of the related sale. Stryker Argentina booked these payments as commission expenses in an account entitled "Honorarios Medicos," when in fact they were unlawful payments made to compensate doctors for purchasing Stryker products. In total, Stryker Argentina made more than $966,500 in improper honoraria payments during the relevant period, causing

Table 3.2.3: Stryker Violations Under FCPA			
Dates	**Subsidiary**	**What Happened?**	**Remarks**
			Stryker Argentina to earn more than $1.04 million in profits from the public hospitals with which the doctors were associated.
In 2007	Stryker's wholly-owned subsidiary in Greece ("Stryker Greece")	Made a sizeable and atypical donation of $197,055 to a public university (the "Greek University") to fund a laboratory, pursuant to a quid pro quo arrangement whereby Stryker Greece understood it would obtain and retain business from the public hospitals	Stryker Greece made the donation to the Greek University in three installments, each of which was improperly booked as a legitimate marketing expense in an account entitled "Donations and Grants". As a result of this, Stryker Greece earned a total of $183000 in illicit profits

Appendix 3.3: D. E. Shaw

Table 3.3.1: Contributions to Presidential Campaigns (2016, 2012 and 2008)			
Year	**2016 Presidential Elections**	**2012 Presidential Elections**	**2008 Presidential Elections**
Whether D. E. Shaw Contributed to **PACs Related to Presidential Candidates?**	• $3,000,000 to Priorities USA Action, PAC supporting Hillary Clinton • $66,800 to Hillary Victory Fund • $50,000 to Ready PAC supporting Hillary Clinton • $225,000 to Senate Majority PAC	• $1,375,000 to Priorities USA Action, PAC supporting Obama	• Nil
Whether D. E. Shaw Contributed Individually to Presidential Candidates?	• $2,700 to Hillary Clinton	• Nil	• $2,300 to Joseph R Biden
Total Contributions	**$3,344,500**	**$1,375,000**	**$2,300**
Grand Total Contribution – All Years	**$5,371,800**		
Grand Total Contribution Includes House and Senate Majority PACs 2014 as Shown Below • $200,000 to House Majority PAC • $450,000 to Senate Majority PAC			
Source:	http://www.fec.gov/		

Table 3.3.2: Company/Entity Staff Contributions to Presidential Campaigns (2016, 2012 and 2008)			
Year	**2016 Presidential Elections**	**2012 Presidential Elections**	**2008 Presidential Elections**
Whether D. E. Shaw Company/ Entity Staff Contributed to PACs Related to Presidential Candidates Companies - D. E. Shaw & Co. and D. E. Shaw Research etc	• Beck, Andrew E. III $25,000 to Priorities USA Action, PAC supporting Hillary Clinton • Reff, Jeremy $3,316 to Hillary Victory Fund • Lehner, Marina $250 to Hillary Victory Fund	• Beck, Andrew E. $100,000 to Priorities USA Action, PAC supporting Obama	• Edwards, Michael $2,500 to AMERIPAC
Whether D. E. Shaw Company/Entity Staff Contributed Individually to Presidential Candidates Companies - D. E. Shaw & Co. and D. E. Shaw Research etc	• $21,267 to Hillary Clinton • $2,700 to Christopher J. Christie • $2,700 to Jeb Bush • $510 to Rafael Edward 'Ted' Cruz • $300 to Bernard Sanders	• $36,979 to Barack Obama • $16,990 to Mitt Romney	• $58,678 to Barack Obama • $13,723 to Hillary Clinton • $500 to John Edwards
Total Contributions	**$56,043**	**$153,969**	**$72,901**
Grand Total Contribution – All Years	**$382,913**		

Table 3.3.2: Company/Entity Staff Contributions to Presidential Campaigns (2016, 2012 and 2008)			
Year	**2016 Presidential Elections**	**2012 Presidential Elections**	**2008 Presidential Elections**
Grand Total Contribution Includes House and Senate Majority PACs 2014 as Shown Below • Beck, Andrew III $50,000 to Senate Majority PAC • Beck, Andrew III $50,000 to Majority PAC			
Source:	http://www.fec.gov/		

Table 3.3.3: Family Members' Contributions to Presidential Campaigns (2016, 2012 and 2008)			
Year	**2016 Presidential Elections**	**2012 Presidential Elections**	**2008 Presidential Elections**
Whether D. E. Shaw Family Members Contributed Individually and/or to PACs Related to Presidential Candidates	• Nil	• Shaw, Beth Kobliner $2,500 to Barack Obama • Shaw, Beth Kobliner $2,500 to Barack Obama	• Shaw, Beth Kobliner $2,300 to Hillary Clinton • Shaw, Beth Kobliner $2,300 to Hillary Clinton
Total Contributions	-	**$5,000**	**$4,600**
Grand Total Contribution – All Years	**$9,600**		
Source:	http://www.fec.gov/		

Table 3.3.4: Contributions to Foundations Related to 'Presidential Candidates'	
Whether D. E. Shaw and/or his Companies/ Foundations/ Family Members Contributed to Foundations Related to Presidential Candidates	• Beth and David Shaw has also donated between $500,001 to $1,000,000 to the Clinton Foundation

Table 3.3.5: Contributions Via Paid Speeches/Assignments to 'Presidential Candidates', Within Three Years of Candidacy Announcement	
Whether D. E. Shaw and/or his Companies/ Foundations/Family Members Gave Speaking and Advisory Assignments to Presidential candidates	• Nil

Table 3.3.6: D. E. Shaw's Short Selling, Specific instances along with the associated antecedents and consequences			
When it Happened?	**What D. E. Shaw Did?**	**What Happened Thereafter?**	**D. E. Shaw's Gain Because of Short Selling and Violations!**
From April 29 through May 4, 2010	D. E. Shaw sold short 103,560 shares of Radian Group Inc. ("RDN") during the restricted period at a weighted average price of $14.4586 per share	On May 5, 2010, RDN announced the pricing of a follow-on offering of its common stock at $11.00 per share. D. E. Shaw received an allocation of 1,250,000 shares in that offering. The difference between D. E. Shaw's proceeds from the restricted period short sales of RDN shares and the price paid for the 103,560 shares received in the offering was $358,172.62	Thus, D. E. Shaw's participation in the RDN offering netted total profits of $358,172.62
On March	D. E. Shaw sold	On March 1,	Thus, D. E.

Table 3.3.6: D. E. Shaw's Short Selling, Specific instances along with the associated antecedents and consequences			
When it Happened?	**What D. E. Shaw Did?**	**What Happened Thereafter?**	**D. E. Shaw's Gain Because of Short Selling and Violations!**
1, 2011	short 2,200 shares of DDR Corp. ("DDR") during the restricted period at a weighted average price of $14.1005 per share	2011, DDR announced the pricing of a follow-on offering of its common stock at $13.80 per share. D. E. Shaw received an allocation of 700,000 shares in that offering. The difference between D. E. Shaw's proceeds from the restricted period short sales of DDR shares and the price paid for the 2,200 shares received in the offering was $661.10	Shaw's participation in the DDR offering netted total profits of $661.10
From March 30 through March 31, 2011	D. E. Shaw sold short 400 shares of Kraton Performance Polymers Inc. ("KRA") during the restricted period at a weighted average price of $ 39.7775 per share	On March 31, 2011, KRA announced the pricing of a follow-on offering of its common stock at $37.75 per share. D. E. Shaw received an allocation of 100,000 shares in	Thus, D. E. Shaw's participation in the KRA offering netted total profits of $4,366.72

Table 3.3.6: D. E. Shaw's Short Selling, Specific instances along with the associated antecedents and consequences			
When it Happened?	**What D. E. Shaw Did?**	**What Happened Thereafter?**	**D. E. Shaw's Gain Because of Short Selling and Violations!**
		that offering The difference between D. E. Shaw's proceeds from the restricted period short sales of KRA shares and the price paid for the 400 shares received in the offering was $811.00. D. E Shaw also improperly obtained a benefit of $3,555.72 by purchasing the remaining 99,600 shares at a discount from KRA's market price	
On January 3, 2012	D. E. Shaw sold short 4,878 shares of Vical Incorporated ("VICL") during the restricted period at a weighted average price of $ 4.47 per share	On January 6, 2012, VICL announced the pricing of a follow-on offering of its common stock at $3.75 per share. D. E. Shaw received an allocation of 50,000 shares in that offering. The difference	Thus, D. E. Shaw's participation in the VICL offering netted total profits of $3,561.79

Table 3.3.6: D. E. Shaw's Short Selling, Specific instances along with the associated antecedents and consequences			
When it Happened?	**What D. E. Shaw Did?**	**What Happened Thereafter?**	**D. E. Shaw's Gain Because of Short Selling and Violations!**
		between D. E. Shaw's proceeds from the restricted period short sales of VICL shares and the price paid for the 4,878 shares received in the offering was $3,512.16. D. E Shaw also improperly obtained a benefit of $49.63 by purchasing the remaining 45,122 shares at a discount from VICL's market price	
On March 21, 2012	D. E. Shaw sold short 14,263 shares of Hercules Offshore, Inc. ("HERO") during the restricted period at a weighted average price of $5.4110 per share	On March 22, 2012, HERO announced the pricing of a follow-on offering of its common stock at $5.10 per share. D. E. Shaw received an allocation of 700,000 shares in that offering. The difference between D. E. Shaw's proceeds	Thus, D. E. Shaw's participation in the HERO offering netted total profits of $81,032.61

Table 3.3.6: D. E. Shaw's Short Selling, Specific instances along with the associated antecedents and consequences			
When it Happened?	**What D. E. Shaw Did?**	**What Happened Thereafter?**	**D. E. Shaw's Gain Because of Short Selling and Violations!**
		from the restricted period short sales of HERO shares and the price paid for the 14,263 shares received in the offering was $4,435.79. D. E Shaw also improperly obtained a benefit of $76,596.82 by purchasing the remaining 685,737 shares at a discount from HERO's market price	

Appendix 3.4: Blackstone

Table 3.4.1: Contributions to Presidential Campaigns (2016, 2012 and 2008)			
Year	**2016 Presidential Elections**	**2012 Presidential Elections**	**2008 Presidential Elections**
Whether Blackstone Staff and Senior Management Contributed to **PACs Related to Presidential**	• Chae, Michael S (Sr. Managing Director of Private Equity) $150,000 to Right to Rise USA, PAC supporting Jeb	• Melwani, Prakash (Senior Managing Director) $100,000 to Restore Our Future Inc. supporting	• Nil

Table 3.4.1: Contributions to Presidential Campaigns (2016, 2012 and 2008)			
Year	**2016 Presidential Elections**	**2012 Presidential Elections**	**2008 Presidential Elections**
Candidates?	Bush • Schwarzman, Stephen A (Chairman & CEO) $100,000 to Right to Rise USA, PAC supporting Jeb Bush • Wien, Byron (Vice Chairman) $33,400 to Hillary Victory Fund • James, Hamilton (President) $16,700 to Hillary Victory Fund • Agarwal, AJ (Senior. Managing Director) $16,700 to Hillary Victory Fund • Schwarzman, Stephen A (Chairman & CEO) $5,000 to Country First PAC	Mitt Romney	
Whether Blackstone Staff and Senior	• Schwarzman, Stephen A (Founder & CEO) $2,800 to	• Schwarzman, Stephen A (CEO & Founder)	• Schwarzman, Stephen A (Investment Banker)

Table 3.4.1: Contributions to Presidential Campaigns (2016, 2012 and 2008)			
Year	**2016 Presidential Elections**	**2012 Presidential Elections**	**2008 Presidential Elections**
Management Contributed Individually to Presidential Candidates?	Marco Rubio • Schwarzman, Steve A. (Chairman CEO Co-Founder) $2,700 to Marco Rubio • Schwarzman, Stephen A (Founder & CEO) $2,700 to Jeb Bush • Agarwal, AJ $2,700 to Hillary Clinton	$2,500 to Mitt Romney • Schwarzman, Stephen A (CEO & Founder) $2,500 to Mitt Romney • Coleman, Timothy (Senior Managing Director) $2,500 to Barack Obama • Coleman, Timothy (Senior Managing Director) $2,500 to Barack Obama • Lee, Miyoung (Senior Managing Director) $2,500 to Barack Obama • Lee, Miyoung (Senior Managing Director) $2,500 to Barack Obama	$2,300 to Mitt Romney • Guffey, Lawrence H (Partner Sr Mgr Dir) $2,300 to Barack Obama • Nathoo, Raffiq A (Managing Director) $2,300 to Barack Obama • Rose, Clifton Peter (Managing Director) $2,300 to Barack Obama • Peterson, Peter G (Senior Chairman & Co Founder) $1,000 to Bill Richardson • Moran, Garrett M (Senior Managing Director) $2,300 to Christopher J

Table 3.4.1: Contributions to Presidential Campaigns (2016, 2012 and 2008)			
Year	2016 Presidential Elections	2012 Presidential Elections	2008 Presidential Elections
		• Mulrow, William J (Senior Managing Director) $2,500 to Barack Obama • Mulrow, William J (Senior Managing Director) $2,500 to Barack Obama • Nathoo, Raffiq A. (Managing Director) $2,500 to Barack Obama • Quigley, Matthew (Senior Managing Director) $2,500 to Barack Obama • Quigley, Matthew (Senior Managing Director) $2,500 to Barack	Dodd • Peterson, Peter G (Sr. Chairman) $2,000 to Christopher J Dodd • James, Hamilton E (President) $2,000 to Christopher J Dodd • Long, Scott A. (Managing Director) $1,000 to Christopher J Dodd • Huffard, Paul (Senior Managing Director) $1,000 to Christopher J Dodd • Liao, Arthur (Managing Director) $1,000 to Christopher J Dodd • Blitzer, David Scott (Senior Managing Director)

Table 3.4.1: Contributions to Presidential Campaigns (2016, 2012 and 2008)			
Year	**2016 Presidential Elections**	**2012 Presidential Elections**	**2008 Presidential Elections**
		Obama • Rose, Clifton Peter (Managing Director) $2,500 to Barack Obama • Rose, Clifton Peter (Managing Director) $2,500 to Barack Obama • Wien, Byron R (Vice Chairman) $2,500 to Barack Obama • Wien, Byron R (Vice Chairman) $2,500 to Barack Obama • Beutler, Gregory S. (Executive Director) $2,500 to Mitt Romney • Blitzer, David S. (Senior Managing Director) $2,500 to	$2,300 to John S McCain • Chu, Chinh (Senior Managing Director) $2,300 to John S McCain • Findley, Marshall K (Managing Director) $2,300 to John S McCain • Hill, James Tomilson III (Sr. Managing Director) $2,300 to John S McCain • Puglisi, Michael a. (Senior Managing Director) $2,300 to John S McCain • Schorr, Paul C. IV (Senior Managing Director-

Table 3.4.1: Contributions to Presidential Campaigns (2016, 2012 and 2008)			
Year	**2016 Presidential Elections**	**2012 Presidential Elections**	**2008 Presidential Elections**
		Mitt Romney • Blitzer, David S. (Senior Managing Director) $2,500 to Mitt Romney • Chu, Chinh (Senior Managing Director) $2,500 to Mitt Romney • Chu, Chinh (Senior Managing Director) $2,500 to Mitt Romney • Chu, Chinh (Senior Managing Director) $2,500 to Mitt Romney • Guffey, Lawrence H. (Senior Managing Director) $2,500 to Mitt Romney • Guffey, Lawrence H. (Senior Managing Director) $2,500 to	Private Equity) $4,600 to John S McCain • Sztejnberg, Xavier (Managing Director) $2,300 to Mitt Romney • Guffey, Lawrence H. (Senior Managing Director) $2,300 to Rudolph W Giuliani • Hill, J. Tomilsen III (Vice Chairman) $2,300 to Rudolph W Giuliani

Table 3.4.1: Contributions to Presidential Campaigns (2016, 2012 and 2008)			
Year	**2016 Presidential Elections**	**2012 Presidential Elections**	**2008 Presidential Elections**
		Mitt Romney • Quella, James A (Senior Managing Director) $2,500 to Mitt Romney • Quella, James A (Senior Managing Director) $2,500 to Mitt Romney	
	$332,700	**$162,500**	**$42,500**
Grand Total Contribution – All Years	**$542,700**		
• Schwarzman, Stephen A (Chairman & CEO) $5,000 to Country First PAC			
Source:	http://www.fec.gov/		

Table 3.4.2: Company/Entity Staff Contributions to Presidential Campaigns (2016, 2012 and 2008)			
Year	**2016 Presidential Elections**	**2012 Presidential Elections**	**2008 Presidential Elections**
Whether Blackstone and/or Related Entity Staff Contributed to PACs Related to Presidential Candidates	• Zelin, Steve $33,400 to Hillary Victory Fund • Shelby, Bryan $2,700 to Hillary Victory Fund • Berman, Wayne L. $2,500 to	• Oglesby, William $25,000 to Restore Our Future Inc. supporting Mitt Romney	• Nil

Table 3.4.2: Company/Entity Staff Contributions to Presidential Campaigns (2016, 2012 and 2008)			
Year	**2016 Presidential Elections**	**2012 Presidential Elections**	**2008 Presidential Elections**
	Lindsey Graham 2016 • Kaden, David $1,000 to Hillary Victory Fund • Pieper, Jeanette $500 to Hillary Victory Fund		
Whether Blackstone and/or Related Entity Staff Contributed Individually to Presidential Candidates	• $21,000 to Hillary Clinton • $7,452 to Marco Rubio	• $151,406 to Mitt Romney • $28,936 to Barack Obama • $4,500 to Newt Gingrich • $201 to Ron Paul	• $60,650 to John S McCain • $51,678 to Barack Obama • $34,200 to Christopher J Dodd • $19,050 to Hillary Clinton • $9,900 to Mitt Romney • $9,400 to Rudolph W Giuliani • $3,300 to Bill Richardson

Table 3.4.2: Company/Entity Staff Contributions to Presidential Campaigns (2016, 2012 and 2008)			
Year	**2016 Presidential Elections**	**2012 Presidential Elections**	**2008 Presidential Elections**
			• $2,300 to Mike Huckabee • $1,000 to Ron Paul
Total Contributions	**$68,552**	**$210,043**	**$191,478**
Grand Total Contribution – All Years	**$475,073**		
Grand Total Contribution Includes House and Senate Majority PACs 2014 as Shown Below • Berman, Wayne L. $5,000 to Country First PAC			
Source:	http://www.fec.gov/		

Table 3.4.3: Contributions to Foundations Related to 'Presidential Candidates'	
Whether Blackstone Group and/or Related Companies/Foundations and/or Family Members of Senior Management Contributed to Foundations Related to Presidential Candidates	• The Blackstone Group L.P. has also donated between $250,001 to $500,000 to the Clinton Foundation

Table 3.4.4: Contributions Via Paid Speeches/Assignments to 'Presidential Candidates', Within Three Years of Candidacy Announcement	
Whether Blackstone Group and/or Related Companies/ Foundations and/or Family Members of Senior Management Gave Speaking and Advisory Assignments to Presidential candidates	• Nil

Appendix 3.5: BlackRock

Table 3.5.1: Contributions to Presidential Campaigns (2016, 2012 and 2008)			
Year	**2016 Presidential Elections**	**2012 Presidential Elections**	**2008 Presidential Elections**
Whether BlackRock Staff and Senior Management Contributed to **PACs Related to Presidential Candidates?**	• Nil	• Nil	• Nil
Whether BlackRock Staff and Senior Management Contributed Individually to Presidential Candidates?	• Buchwald, Zach (Managing Director) $2,700 to Hillary Clinton • Hill, Joseph (Managing Director) $2,700 to Hillary Clinton • Larsen, Eric Paul (Manager) $2,700 to Hillary Clinton • Mallow, Matthew (Lawyer) $2,700 to Hillary Clinton • Mallow, Matthew Jonothan (Lawyer) $2,700 to Hillary Clinton	• Magnus, Jabari (Managing Director) $2,500 to Barack Obama • Magnus, Jabari (Managing Director) $2,500 to Barack Obama • Pearl, Morris B (Managing Director) $2,500 to Barack Obama • Pearl, Morris B (Managing Director) $2,500 to Barack Obama • Shuping Russell, Sallie Shuping (Managing Director) $2,500 to	• Fink, Lawrence (Chairman & CEO) $2,300 to Barack Obama • Beard, Anson H (Managing Director) $2,300 to Barack Obama • Larsen, Eric (Manager) $2,300 to Barack Obama • Walker, Shari (Director) $2,300 to Barack Obama

Table 3.5.1: Contributions to Presidential Campaigns (2016, 2012 and 2008)			
Year	**2016 Presidential Elections**	**2012 Presidential Elections**	**2008 Presidential Elections**
	• Ramji, Salim (Senior Managing Director) $2,700 to Hillary Clinton • Winshel, Deborah (Global Head Of Impact Investing) $2,700 to Hillary Clinton • Rieder, Rick (Managing Director) $2,700 to Jeb Bush • Wiedman, Mark (Manager) $2,700 to John R. Kasich • Kommareddi, Madhuri (Vice President) $300 to Hillary Clinton	Barack Obama • Shuping Russell, Sallie Shuping (Managing Director) $2,500 to Barack Obama • Lint, Milan (Chief Operating Officer) $2,500 to Barack Obama • Lint, Milan (Chief Operating Officer) $1,500 to Barack Obama • Derry, Hanna (Managing Director) $2,500 to Mitt Romney • Derry, Hanna (Managing Director) $2,500 to Mitt Romney • Keeley, Terrence R (Manager/ Director) $2,500 to Mitt Romney • Keeley, Terrence R	• Schlosstein, Ralph (President) $2,500 to Christopher J Dodd • Russell, Sallie Shuping (Managing Director) $2,300 to John Edwards • Steenberg, Russell W. (Managing Director) $4,600 to John S McCain • Miller, Tyler (Director) $2,037 to Barack Obama • Buchwald, Zach (Managing Director) $1,000 to Barack Obama

Table 3.5.1: Contributions to Presidential Campaigns (2016, 2012 and 2008)			
Year	**2016 Presidential Elections**	**2012 Presidential Elections**	**2008 Presidential Elections**
		(Manager/ Director) $2,500 to Mitt Romney • Keeley, Terrence R(Manager/ Director) $2,500 to Mitt Romney • Palumbo, Lawrence (Director), $2,500 to Mitt Romney • Palumbo, Lawrence (Director), $2,500 to Mitt Romney • Palumbo, Lawrence (Director), $2,500 to Mitt Romney • Porcelli, Frank M (Managing Director) $2,500 to Mitt Romney • Porcelli, Frank M (Managing Director) $2,500 to Mitt Romney • Porcelli, Frank M. (Managing Director)	

Table 3.5.1: Contributions to Presidential Campaigns (2016, 2012 and 2008)			
Year	**2016 Presidential Elections**	**2012 Presidential Elections**	**2008 Presidential Elections**
		$3,000 to Mitt Romney • Mallow, Matthew J(Lawyer) $2,500 to Barack Obama • Mallow, Matthew J (Lawyer) $1,500 to Barack Obama	
Total Contributions	**$24,600**	**$51,000**	**$23,037**
Grand Total Contribution – All Years	**$98,637**		
Source:	http://www.fec.gov/		

Table 3.5.2: Company/Entity Staff Contributions to Presidential Campaigns (2016, 2012 and 2008)			
Year	**2016 Presidential Elections**	**2012 Presidential Elections**	**2008 Presidential Elections**
Whether BlackRock and/or Related Entity Staff Contributed to PACs Related to Presidential Candidates Company is BlackRock	• $40,319 to Hillary Victory Fund	• Nil	• Nil
Whether BlackRock and/or Related	• $60,191 to Hillary Clinton	• $76,444 to Mitt Romney	• $32,229 to Barack Obama

Table 3.5.2: Company/Entity Staff Contributions to Presidential Campaigns (2016, 2012 and 2008)			
Year	**2016 Presidential Elections**	**2012 Presidential Elections**	**2008 Presidential Elections**
Entity Staff Contributed Individually to Presidential Candidates Company is BlackRock	• $6,400 to Jeb Bush • $3,034 to Bernard Sanders • $580 to Donald J. Trump • $549 to Benjamin S. Carson • $500 to Marco Rubio and Martin Joseph O'Malley • $250 to John R. Kasich	• $31,221 to Barack Obama • $5,500 to Jon Huntsman • $1000 to Ron Paul	• $15,700 to John S McCain • $16,475 to Hillary Clinton • $6,700 to Christophe r J Dodd • $2,500 to Bill Richardson
Total Contributions	**$137,223**	**$165,165**	**$95,766**
Grand Total Contribution – All Years	**$398,154**		
Source:	http://www.fec.gov/		

Table 3.5.3: Contributions to Foundations Related to 'Presidential Candidates'	
Whether BlackRock and/or Related Companies/ Foundations/ and/or Family Members of Senior Management Contributed to Foundations Related to Presidential Candidates	• Joshua A Fink has also donated between $10,001 to $25,000 to the Clinton Foundation

Appendix 4

Appendix 4.1: Bank of America and Merrill Lynch

Table 4.1.1: Contributions to Presidential Campaigns (2016, 2012 and 2008)			
Year	**2016 Presidential Elections**	**2012 Presidential Elections**	**2008 Presidential Elections**
Whether Bank of America/ Merrill Lynch Staff and Senior Management Contributed to **PACs Related to Presidential Candidates?**	• Johnston, Nelinda (Senior Financial Advisor) $20,250 to Hillary Victory Fund • Campbell, Laurie (Managing Partner) $10,000 to Hillary Victory Fund • Garrido, Paul (Senior Vice President-Wealth Management) $1,000 to Lindsey Graham 2016	• Bank of America/Merrill Lynch $25,092 to Women Vote!	• Nil
Whether Bank of America/ Merrill Lynch Staff and Senior Management Contributed Individually to Presidential Candidates?	• Von Savage, Jackson (Senior VP) $2,700 to Christopher J. Christie • Murray, Terrence (Chairman & CEO) $2,700	• Finucane, Anne M (CMO) $2,500 to Barack Obama • Finucane, Anne M (CMO) $2,500 to	• Baldwin, Tracy (SR Change Manager) $2,447 to Barack Obama • Zimpfer, Cindy J (Treasury

Table 4.1.1: Contributions to Presidential Campaigns (2016, 2012 and 2008)			
Year	**2016 Presidential Elections**	**2012 Presidential Elections**	**2008 Presidential Elections**
	to Hillary Clinton • Bowman, Charles (Market President) $2,700 to Hillary Clinton • Campbell, Laurie (Managing Partner) $2,700 to Hillary Clinton • Campbell, Laurie (Managing Partner) $2,700 to Hillary Clinton • Celenza, Matthew (Director Of Private Wealth Management) $2,700 to Hillary Clinton • Finucane, Anne M. (Vice Chairman) $2,700 to Hillary Clinton • Malik, Omeed (Managing Director) $2,700 to Hillary Clinton • Delen, Sonia	Barack Obama • Meyer, Lorna (Managing Director/ Investments) $2,500 to Barack Obama • Meyer, Lorna (Managing Director/ Investments) $2,500 to Barack Obama • Nadel, Mitchell (Manager), $2,500 to Barack Obama • Atwood, James (Senior Vice President) $2,500 to Mitt Romney • Atwood, James (Senior Vice President) $2,500 to Mitt Romney • Banks, Keith (President U.S. Trust) $2,500 to Mitt	Manager) $2,300 to Barack Obama • Busch, William JR (Accounts Manager) $2,300 to Barack Obama • Cambell, Laurie (MGR Director) $2,300 to Barack Obama • Hawyer-Scott, Khristian (Bank Executive) $2,000 to Barack Obama • Cockrell, Serena P (Executive VP) $1,750 to Barack Obama • Carbone, Frank Mr (Senior Vice President) $700 to

Table 4.1.1: Contributions to Presidential Campaigns (2016, 2012 and 2008)			
Year	**2016 Presidential Elections**	**2012 Presidential Elections**	**2008 Presidential Elections**
	(Senior Vice President) $2,695 to Hillary Clinton • Petras, AJ (Senior Vice President) $2,650 to Hillary Clinton • Darnell, David C (Vice Chairman) $2,700 to Jeb Bush • Mccarthy, Brian (Vice Chairman) to $2,700 to Jeb Bush • Montag, Thomas K (COO) to $2,700 to Jeb Bush • Rowen, Howard (Managing Director) $2,700 to Donald J Trump • Rowen, Howard (Managing Director) $2,700 to Donald J Trump	Romney • Banks, Keith (President U.S. Trust) $2,500 to Mitt Romney • Banks, Keith (President U.S. Trust) $2,500 to Mitt Romney • Brookfield, Mark (Senior Vice President) $2,500 to Mitt Romney • Callahan, Brian (Managing Director) $2,500 to Mitt Romney • Fuszard, Joseph T. (Bank Executive) $2,500 to Mitt Romney • Hyzy, Christopher M (Chief Investment Officer) $2,000 to Mitt Romney • Sieg, Andrew M.	Barack Obama • Ashkinos, Mark (VP) $730 to Barack Obama • Connelly, Cristian (Vice President) $500 to Barack Obama • Debnam, Henry (Sr. Vice President) $250 to Barack Obama • Finucane, Anne (Executive) $2,300 to Christopher J Dodd • Moynihan, Brian T (Executive) $2,300 to Christopher J Dodd • Quick, Christopher (Executive) $2,300 to Christopher

Table 4.1.1: Contributions to Presidential Campaigns (2016, 2012 and 2008)			
Year	**2016 Presidential Elections**	**2012 Presidential Elections**	**2008 Presidential Elections**
	• Fernon, Michael (Senior Vice President) $2,700 to Hillary Clinton • Nelson, Dawn (Senior Vice President) $2,900 to Hillary Clinton	(Managing Director) $2,500 to Mitt Romney • Sieg, Andrew M (Managing Director) $2,500 to Mitt Romney • Sieg, Andrew M (Managing Director) $2,500 to Mitt Romney • Stokes, Miranda (Director) $2,500 to Mitt Romney • Stokes, Miranda (Director) $2,500 to Mitt Romney • Warrender, Scott (Managing Director) $2,000 to Mitt Romney • Welsh, Rick (Senior Vice President) $2,000 to Mitt Romney • Heartfield, Edward (Managing	J Dodd • Robinson, Floyd (Executive) $2,300 to Christopher J Dodd • Gifford, Charles (Board of Directors) $2,100 to Christopher J Dodd • Taylor, Roger (Executive) $2,100 to Christopher J Dodd • Mahoney, James E. (Executive) $2,000 to Christopher J Dodd • Silverman, Richard (Executive) $2,000 to Christopher J Dodd • Richter, Todd B (Managing Director) $1,000 to Christopher

Table 4.1.1: Contributions to Presidential Campaigns (2016, 2012 and 2008)			
Year	2016 Presidential Elections	2012 Presidential Elections	2008 Presidential Elections
		Director) to $2,500 to Timothy Pawlenty	J Dodd • Bessant, Catherine (President) $2,300 to Hillary Clinton • Mccaffrey, Steven M (Senior Vice President) $2,300 to Hillary Clinton • Mccaffrey, Steven M (Senior Vice President) $2,300 to Hillary Clinton • Mercurio, Patricia L (President) $2,300 to Hillary Clinton • Rappaport, Alan H (Family Wealth Advisors President) $2,300 to Hillary Clinton

Table 4.1.1: Contributions to Presidential Campaigns (2016, 2012 and 2008)			
Year	**2016 Presidential Elections**	**2012 Presidential Elections**	**2008 Presidential Elections**
			• Boylan, Marti (Manager) $2,076 to Hillary Clinton • Harris - Shipman, Anna Katherine (Senior Vice President) $1,000 to Hillary Clinton • Brille, Brian J (Managing Director) $4,600 to John S McCain • Lewis, Daniel N (Senior Vice President) $2,300 to John S McCain • Malhotra, Rajesh D (MD Senior Trader) $4,600 to John S McCain

Table 4.1.1: Contributions to Presidential Campaigns (2016, 2012 and 2008)			
Year	2016 Presidential Elections	2012 Presidential Elections	2008 Presidential Elections
			• Cochran, John R (COO) $2,300 to Joseph R Jr Biden • Freeh, Louis J. (Executive) $3,300 to Joseph R Jr Biden • Gifford, Charles (Chairman Emeritus) $2,300 to Joseph R Jr Biden • Hammonds, Bruce L (President & CEO) $4,600 to Joseph R Jr Biden • Braz, Daniel (Vice President) $2,300 to Mitt Romney • Quick, Christopher C (Vice Chairman) $2,300 to

Table 4.1.1: Contributions to Presidential Campaigns (2016, 2012 and 2008)			
Year	**2016 Presidential Elections**	**2012 Presidential Elections**	**2008 Presidential Elections**
			Rudolph W Giuliani
Total Contributions	**$77,295**	**$78,592**	**$76,853**
Grand Total Contribution – All Years	**$232,740**		
Source:	http://www.fec.gov/		

Table 4.1.2: Company/Entity Staff Contributions to Presidential Campaigns (2016, 2012 and 2008)			
Year	**2016 Presidential Elections**	**2012 Presidential Elections**	**2008 Presidential Elections**
Whether Bank of America/ Merrill Lynch and/or Related Entity Staff Contributed to PACs Related to Presidential Candidates	• $12,239 to Hillary Victory Fund	• Campbell, Laurie $2,500 to Planned Parenthood Votes • Vanderpluym, David $800 to Freedom Works For America	• Nil
Whether Bank of America/ Merrill Lynch and/or Related Entity Staff Contributed Individually to Presidential Candidates	• $236,857 to Hillary Clinton • $86,855 to Jeb Bush • $40,164 to Marco Rubio • $36,966 to Bernard Sanders • $32,695 to Rafael Edward 'Ted' Cruz • $23,506 to	• $1,452,867 to Mitt Romney • $388,932 to Barack Obama • $19,112 to Ron Paul • $7,430 to Newt Gingrich • $6,600 to Jon Huntsman • $6,225 to Rick Santorum	• $654,183 to Barack Obama • $463,722 to John S McCain • $295,496 to Hillary Clinton • $233,800 to Rudolph W Giuliani

Table 4.1.2: Company/Entity Staff Contributions to Presidential Campaigns (2016, 2012 and 2008)			
Year	**2016 Presidential Elections**	**2012 Presidential Elections**	**2008 Presidential Elections**
	Donald J. Trump • $19,431 to John R. Kasich • $15,195 to Christopher J. Christie • $12,228 to Carly Fiorina • $11,975 to Benjamin S. Carson • $2,950 to Lawrence Lessig • $2,750 to Martin Joseph O'Malley • $2,000 to Lindsey O. Graham • $500 to Richard J Santorum • $500 to George E Pataki • $300 to James Henry Jr Webb • $250 to James R (Rick) Perry • $250 to Mike Huckabee • $126 to Rand Paul	• $5,600 to Rick Perry • $5,250 to Timothy Pawlenty • $1,270 to Herman Cain • $1,000 to Gary Earl Johnson • $540 to Michele Bachmann • $225 to Charles E. 'Buddy' III Roemer	• $193,330 to Mitt Romney • $99,900 to C J Dodd • $32,150 to Joseph R Jr Biden • $28,003 to John Edwards • $20,585 to Ron Paul • $13,837 to Mike Huckabee • $13,100 to Bill Richardson • $9,725 to Fred Dalton Thompson • $1,000 to Samuel Dale Brownback • $300 to Dennis J Kucinich
Total Contributions	**$537,737**	**$1,898,351**	**$2,059,131**
Grand Total Contribution – All Years	**$4,495,219**		

Table 4.1.2: Company/Entity Staff Contributions to Presidential Campaigns (2016, 2012 and 2008)			
Year	**2016 Presidential Elections**	**2012 Presidential Elections**	**2008 Presidential Elections**
Source:	http://www.fec.gov/		

Table 4.1.3: Contributions to Foundations Related to 'Presidential Candidates'	
Whether Bank of America/Merrill Lynch Senior Management and/or Related Companies/Foundations/ Family Members Contributed to Foundations Related to Presidential Candidates	• Bank of America Foundation has also donated between \$500,001 to \$1,000,000 to the Clinton Foundation • Bank of America Corporation has also donated between \$100,001 to \$250,000 to the Clinton Foundation • Merrill Lynch & Company Foundation, Inc. has also donated between \$100,001 to \$250,000 to the Clinton Foundation

Table 4.1.4: Contributions Via Paid Speeches/Assignments to 'Presidential Candidates', Within Three Years of Candidacy Announcement	
Whether Bank of America/ Merrill Lynch and Senior Management and/or Related Companies/ Foundations/ Family Members Gave Speaking and Advisory Assignments to Presidential candidates	**Bill Clinton** • 30 November, 2007 – \$175,000 • 1 December, 2011 – \$200,000 • 13 November, 2012 – \$200,000 • 6 March, 2014 – \$500,000 **Hillary Clinton** • 13 November 2013 – \$225,000

Appendix 4.2: UBS and Its Affiliates

Table 4.2.1: Contributions to Presidential Campaigns (2016, 2012 and 2008)			
Year	**2016 Presidential Elections**	**2012 Presidential Elections**	**2008 Presidential Elections**
Whether UBS AG Staff and Senior Management Contributed to **PACs Related to Presidential Candidates?**	• Nil	• Nil	• Nil
Whether UBS AG Staff and Senior Management Contributed Individually to Presidential Candidates?	• Nil	• Rego, Mariana (Associate Director) $250 to Barack Obama • Pulkkinen, Peter (Managing Director) $2,000 to Mitt Romney	• Kroll, Roxanne (Associate Director) $575 to Barack Obama • Valluru, Sateesh (Director) $500 to Barack Obama
Total Contributions	-	**$2,250**	**$1,075**
Grand Total Contribution – All Years	**$3,325**		
Source:	http://www.fec.gov/		

Table 4.2.2: Company/Entity Staff Contributions to Presidential Campaigns (2016, 2012 and 2008)			
Year	**2016 Presidential Elections**	**2012 Presidential Elections**	**2008 Presidential Elections**
Whether UBS AG and/or	• Nil	• Nil	• Nil

Table 4.2.2: Company/Entity Staff Contributions to Presidential Campaigns (2016, 2012 and 2008)			
Year	**2016 Presidential Elections**	**2012 Presidential Elections**	**2008 Presidential Elections**
Related Entity Staff Contributed to PACs Related to Presidential Candidates			
Whether UBS AG and/or Related Entity Staff Contributed Individually to Presidential Candidates	• $819 to Bernard Sanders	• $5,265 to Barack Obama • $4,874 to Mitt Romney	• $17,600 to Barack Obama • $4,350 to Hillary Clinton • $2,300 to Christopher J Dodd • $2,200 to Mitt Romney • $550 to John S McCain
Total Contributions	**$819**	**$10,139**	**$27,000**
Grand Total Contribution – All Years	**$37,958**		
Source:	http://www.fec.gov/		

Table 4.2.3: Contributions to Foundations Related to 'Presidential Candidates'	
Whether UBS AG and Senior Management and/or Related Companies/ Foundations/Family Members Contributed to Foundations Related to Presidential Candidates	• UBS AG has also donated between $50,000 to $100,000 to the Clinton Foundation • UBS Wealth Management USA has also donated between $500,001 to $1,000,000 to the Clinton Foundation

Table 4.2.4: Contributions Via Paid Speeches/Assignments to 'Presidential Candidates', Within Three Years of Candidacy Announcement	
Whether UBS AG and Senior Management and/or Related Companies/ Foundations/ Family Members Gave Speaking and Advisory Assignments to Presidential Candidates	**Bill Clinton (When Hillary Clinton was Secretary of State)** • 1 August, 2011 – $165,000 • 17 October, 2011 – $150,000 • 21 February, 2012 – $175,000 • 17 April 2012 – $175,000 • 18 October, 2012 – $175,000 **Bill Clinton (When Hillary Clinton was NOT Secretary of State)** • 9 May, 2013 – $175,000 • 19 May, 2014 – $225,000 • 14 October, 2014 – $225,000 • 19 February, 2015 - $225,000 **Hillary Clinton (When She was NOT Secretary of State)** • 11 July, 2013 – $225,000

Table 4.2.5: Hillary Clinton Wall Street Speeches

Name of Financial Institution and Bank	Amount in US $	Number of Speeches by Hillary Clinton	Percentage
Morgan Stanley	225,000	1	12.26%
Goldman Sachs	675,000	3	36.78%
Bank of America/Merrill Lynch	225,000	1	12.26%
Deutsch Bank	485,000	2	26.43%
UBS	225,000	1	12.26%
Total	**1,835,000**	**8**	**100.00%**
Compiled from: http://edition.cnn.com/2016/02/05/politics/hillary-clinton-bill-clinton-paid-speeches/			

Table 4.2.5: Bill Clinton Wall Street Speeches			
Name of Financial Institution and Bank	**Amount in US $**	**Number of Speeches by Bill Clinton**	**Percentage**
2001-2007			
Morgan Stanley	125,000	1	5.56%
Goldman Sachs	950,000	6	42.22%
Bank of America and Merrill Lynch	175,000	1	7.78%
Deutsch Bank	300,000	2	13.33%
City Group	700,000	4	31.11%
Total	2,250,000	14	100.00%
2011-2015			
UBS	1,690,000	9	46.17%
Goldman Sachs	600,000	3	16.39%
Bank of America/Merrill Lynch	900,000	3	24.59%
Deutsch Bank	470,000	2	12.84%
Total II	3,660,000	17	100.00%
Compiled and analyzed using data from: http://edition.cnn.com/2016/02/05/politics/hillary-clinton-bill-clinton-paid-speeches/			

Appendix 5

Appendix 5.1: Canadian Imperial Bank of Commerce (CIBC)

Table 5.1.1: Contributions to Presidential Campaigns (2016, 2012 and 2008)			
Year	**2016 Presidential Elections**	**2012 Presidential Elections**	**2008 Presidential Elections**
Whether CIBC and its Senior Management Contributed to **PACs Related to Presidential Candidates?**	• Nil	• Nil	• Nil
Whether CIBC and its Senior Management Contributed Individually to Presidential Candidates?	• Nil	• Nil	• O'connell, David (Director) $3,050 to Barack Obama
Total Contributions	-	-	**$3,050**
Grand Total Contribution – All Years	**$3,050**		
Source:	http://www.fec.gov/		

Table 5.1.2: Company/Entity Staff Contributions to Presidential Campaigns (2016, 2012 and 2008)			
Year	**2016 Presidential Elections**	**2012 Presidential Elections**	**2008 Presidential Elections**
Whether CIBC and/or related Entity Staff Contributed to PACs Related to Presidential Candidates	• Nil	• Nil	• Nil

Table 5.1.2: Company/Entity Staff Contributions to Presidential Campaigns (2016, 2012 and 2008)			
Year	**2016 Presidential Elections**	**2012 Presidential Elections**	**2008 Presidential Elections**
Whether CIBC and/or related Entity Staff Contributed Individually to Presidential Candidates	• $2,700 to John R Kasich • $536 to Hillary Clinton • $250 to Marco Rubio • $250 to Bernard Sanders • $200 to Donald J Trump	• $9,000 to Mitt Romney • $500 to Barack Obama • $138 to Ron Paul	• $5,480 to Barack Obama • $2,300 to Bill Richardson • $2,300 to Dennis J Kucinich • $1,750 to Hillary Clinton • $1,750 to John S McCain • $750 to Rudolph W Giuliani • $350 to Ron Paul
Total Contributions	**$3,936**	**$9,638**	**$14,680**
Grand Total Contribution – All Years	**$28,254**		
Source:	http://www.fec.gov/		

Table 5.1.3: Contributions to Foundations Related to 'Presidential Candidates'	
Whether CIBC and its Senior Management and/or related Companies/ Foundations/	• Nil

Table 5.1.3: Contributions to Foundations Related to 'Presidential Candidates'	
Family Members Contributed to Foundations Related to Presidential Candidates	

Table 5.1.4: Contributions Via Paid Speeches/Assignments to 'Presidential Candidates', Within Three Years of Candidacy Announcement	
Whether CIBC and its Senior Management and/or related Companies/ Foundations/ Family Members Gave Speaking and Advisory Assignments to Presidential candidates	• 22 January, 2015 – $150,000 to Hillary Rodhan Clinton

Appendix 5.2: UBS and Its Affiliates

Table 5.2.1: Contributions to Presidential Campaigns (2016, 2012 and 2008)			
Year	**2016 Presidential Elections**	**2012 Presidential Elections**	**2008 Presidential Elections**
Whether UBS AG and its Senior Management Contributed to **PACs Related to Presidential Candidates?**	• Nil	• Nil	• Nil
Whether UBS AG and its Senior Management Contributed Individually to Presidential Candidates?	• Nil	• Rego, Mariana (Associate Director) $250 to Barack Obama • Pulkkinen, Peter (Managing	• Kroll, Roxanne (Associate Director) $575 to Barack Obama • Valluru,

Table 5.2.1: Contributions to Presidential Campaigns (2016, 2012 and 2008)			
Year	**2016 Presidential Elections**	**2012 Presidential Elections**	**2008 Presidential Elections**
		Director) $2,000 to Mitt Romney	Sateesh (Director) $500 to Barack Obama
Total Contributions	-	**$2,250**	**$1,075**
Grand Total Contribution – All Years	**$3,325**		
Source:	http://www.fec.gov/		

Table 5.2.2: Company/Entity Staff Contributions to Presidential Campaigns (2016, 2012 and 2008)			
Year	**2016 Presidential Elections**	**2012 Presidential Elections**	**2008 Presidential Elections**
Whether UBS AG and/or Entity Staff Contributed to PACs Related to Presidential Candidates	• Nil	• Nil	• Nil
Whether UBS AG and/or related Entity Staff Contributed Individually to Presidential Candidates	• $819 to Bernard Sanders	• $5,265 to Barack Obama • $4,874 to Mitt Romney	• $17,600 to Barack Obama • $4,350 to Hillary Clinton • $2,300 to Christopher J Dodd • $2,200 to Mitt Romney • $550 to John S McCain

Table 5.2.2: Company/Entity Staff Contributions to Presidential Campaigns (2016, 2012 and 2008)			
Year	**2016 Presidential Elections**	**2012 Presidential Elections**	**2008 Presidential Elections**
Total Contributions	**$819**	**$10,139**	**$27,000**
Grand Total Contribution – All Years	**$37,958**		
Source:	http://www.fec.gov/		

Table 5.2.3: Contributions to Foundations Related to 'Presidential Candidates'	
Whether UBS AG and its Senior Management and/or their Companies/ Foundations/ Family Members Contributed to Foundations Related to Presidential Candidates	• UBS AG has also donated between $50,000 to $100,000 to the Clinton Foundation • UBS Wealth Management USA has also donated between $500,001 to $1,000,000 to the Clinton Foundation

Table 5.2.4: Contributions Via Paid Speeches/Assignments to 'Presidential Candidates', Within Three Years of Candidacy Announcement	
Whether UBS AG and its Senior Management and/or their Companies/ Foundations/ Family Members Gave Speaking and Advisory Assignments to Presidential Candidates	**Bill Clinton (When Hillary Clinton was Secretary of State)** • 1 August, 2011 – $165,000 • 17 October, 2011 – $150,000 • 21 February, 2012- $175,000 • 17 April 2012 - $175,000 • 18 October, 2012 - $175,000 **Bill Clinton (When Hillary Clinton was NOT Secretary of State)** • 9 May, 2013 – $175,000 • 19 May, 2014 – $225,000 • 14 October, 2014 – $225,000 • 19 February, 2015 – $225,000 **Hillary Clinton (When She was NOT secretary of State)** • 11th July, 2013 - $225,000

Appendix 5.3: General Electric Company

Table 5.3.1: Contributions to Presidential Campaigns (2016, 2012 and 2008)			
Year	**2016 Presidential Elections**	**2012 Presidential Elections**	**2008 Presidential Elections**
Whether GE and Senior Management Contributed to **PACs Related to Presidential Candidates?**	• Immelt, Jeffrey R (Chairman & CEO) $25,000 Security Is Strength PAC	• Nil	• Nil
Whether GE and Senior Management Contributed Individually to Presidential Candidates?	• Immelt, Jeffrey R (Chairman & CEO) $2,700 to Lindsey O Graham • Comstock, Elizabeth (Senior Vice President) $2,700 to Hillary Clinton • Comstock, Elizabeth (Senior Vice President) $2,700 to Hillary Clinton • Frenkel, Orit (Senior Manager) $2,700 to Hillary Clinton • Frenkel, Orit (Senior Manager)	• Daley, Pamela (Senior Vice President) $2,500 to Barack Obama • Daley, Pamela (Senior Vice President) $2,500 to Barack Obama • Bhatia, Karan (Vice President) $2,500 to Mitt Romney • Bhatia, Karan (Vice President) $2,500 to Mitt Romney • Hajdarovic, Margaret Keane (President & CEO Capital	• Immelt, Jeffrey R. (Chairman & CEO) $2,300 to Rudolph W Giuliani • Rice, John G (Chairman & CEO GE Energy) $2,300 to Rudolph W Giuliani • Daley, Pamela (Senior Vice President) $2,300 to Barack Obama • Amirghahari, Zhazeh (VP) $1,000 to Hillary Clinton • Begor, Mark W (CEO-GE Money Americas)

Table 5.3.1: Contributions to Presidential Campaigns (2016, 2012 and 2008)			
Year	**2016 Presidential Elections**	**2012 Presidential Elections**	**2008 Presidential Elections**
	$2,700 to Hillary Clinton • Hartwell, Olga (Vice President) $2,700 to Hillary Clinton • Miller, Jamie (Business Leader) $2,700 to Hillary Clinton • Al-Lamadani, Muhammad (General Manager) $1,350 to Hillary Clinton	Retail) $2,500 to Mitt Romney • Kekedjian, Aris (Vice-President) $1,000 to Mitt Romney • Molnar, John (General Manager) $2,402 to Mitt Romney • Neal, Michael A (Vice Chairman) $2,500 to Mitt Romney	$2,300 to Mitt Romney • Campbell, James P (Chief Executive Officer) $2,300 to Rudolph W Giuliani • Dorn, Nancy P (Vice President Corporate Government) $2,000 to Rudolph W Giuliani • Begor, Mark W. (CEO) $1,000 to Rudolph W Giuliani • Campbell, Karen H (CEO) $1,000 to Rudolph W Giuliani
Total Contributions	**$45,250**	**$18,402**	**$16,500**
Grand Total Contribution – All Years	**$80,152**		
Source:	http://www.fec.gov/		

Table 5.3.2: Company/Entity Staff Contributions to Presidential Campaigns (2016, 2012 and 2008)			
Year	2016 Presidential Elections	2012 Presidential Elections	2008 Presidential Elections
Whether GE or related Entity Staff Contributed to PACs Related to Presidential Candidates	• $12,299 to Hillary Victory Fund	• Nil	• Nil
Whether GE or related Entity Staff Contributed Individually to Presidential Candidates	• $83,122 to Hillary Clinton • $14,825 to Bernard Sanders • $14,800 to Lindsey O. Graham • $8,263 to Rafael Edward 'Ted' Cruz • $4,175 to Marco Rubio • $3,325 to John R. Kasich • $2,700 to Martin Joseph O'Malley • $2,461 to Donald JTrump • $1,000 to Gary Johnson • $1,000 to Jeb Bush • $955 to Benjamin S Carson • $270 to Rand Paul	• $156,634 to Mitt Romney • $90,581 to Barack Obama • $5,250 to Rick Perry • $5,212 to Ron Paul • $1,023 to Rick Santorum • $1,000 to Jon Huntsman • $500 to Herman Cain • $375 to Michele Bachmann • $250 to Newt Gingrich • $150 to Charles E 'Buddy' III Roemer	• $120,832 to Barack Obama • $45,993 to John S McCain • $36,257 to Hillary Clinton • $14,650 to Rudolph W Giuliani • $7,123 to Ron Paul • $6,360 to Mitt Romney • $3,600 to Bill Richardson • $3,470 to John Edwards • $2,300 to Christopher J Dodd • $500 to Mike Huckabee • $300 to Joseph R

Table 5.3.2: Company/Entity Staff Contributions to Presidential Campaigns (2016, 2012 and 2008)			
Year	**2016 Presidential Elections**	**2012 Presidential Elections**	**2008 Presidential Elections**
	• $250 to Carly Fiorina • $25 to Mike Huckabee		Biden Jr • $150 to Dennis J Kucinich • $100 to Duncan Hunter
Total Contributions	**$149,470**	**$260,975**	**$241,635**
Grand Total Contribution – All Years	**$652,080**		
Source:	http://www.fec.gov/		

Table 5.3.3: Contributions to Foundations Related to 'Presidential Candidates'	
Whether GE and Senior Management and/or related Companies/Foundations/ Family Members Contributed to Foundations Related to Presidential Candidates	• General Electric has also donated between $1,000,001 to $5,000,000 to the Clinton Foundation • The GE Foundation has also donated between $10,001 to $25,000 to the Clinton Foundation

Table 5.3.4: Contributions Via Paid Speeches/Assignments to 'Presidential Candidates', Within Three Years of Candidacy Announcement	
Whether GE and Senior Management and/or related Companies/ Foundations / Family Members Gave Speaking and Advisory Assignments to Presidential candidates	• 1 June, 2014 – $225,500

Appendix 5.4: Qualcomm

Table 5.4.1: Contributions to Presidential Campaigns (2016, 2012 and 2008)			
Year	**2016 Presidential Elections**	**2012 Presidential Elections**	**2008 Presidential Elections**
Whether Qualcomm and Senior Management Contributed to **PACs Related to Presidential Candidates?**	• Nil	• Nil	• Nil
Whether Qualcomm and Senior Management Contributed Individually to Presidential Candidates?	• Jacobs, Paul (President) $2,700 to Hillary Clinton • Tibbits, Nathan (Senior Vice President) $2,700 to Hillary Clinton • Tibbits, Nathan (Senior Vice President) $2,700 to Hillary Clinton • Covell, Shawn (Vice President) $2,700 to Hillary	• Jacobs, Paul E (Chairman & CEO) $2,500 to Barack Obama • Jacobs, Paul E (Chairman & CEO) $2,500 to Barack Obama • Jacobs, Irwin Mark (Co-Founder) $2,500 to Barack Obama • Jacobs, Irwin Mark (Co-Founder) $2,500 to Barack Obama • Covell, Shawn (Vice President) $2,000 to Barack Obama	• Jacobs, Irwin (Chairman Of The Board) $2,550 to Barack Obama • Jacobs, Stacy R (CEO) $2,550 to Barack Obama • Jacobs, Stacy R (CEO) $2,550 to Barack Obama • Altman, Steven (President) $2,300 to Hillary Clinton • Altman, Steven (President) $1,700 to Hillary Clinton

Table 5.4.1: Contributions to Presidential Campaigns (2016, 2012 and 2008)			
Year	**2016 Presidential Elections**	**2012 Presidential Elections**	**2008 Presidential Elections**
	Clinton • Rosenberg, Donald (Executive Vice President) $2,663 to Hillary Clinton • Wasilewski, Tom (Vice President) $250 to Hillary Clinton	• Blecker, Marvin (Sr. Vice President) $2,500 to Mitt Romney • Blecker, Marvin (Sr. Vice President) $2,500 to Mitt Romney • Blecker, Marvin (Sr. Vice President) $2,500 to Mitt Romney • Blecker, Marvin (Sr. Vice President) $2,500 to Mitt Romney	• Covell, Shawna (Senior Director-Govnt Affairs) $2,300 to Hillary Clinton • Covell, Shawna (Senior Director-Govnt Affairs) $2,300 to Hillary Clinton • Jacobs, Irwin Mark (Chairman & CEO) $2,300 to Hillary Clinton • Jacobs, Irwin Mark (Chairman & CEO) $1,000 to Hillary Clinton • Blecker, Marvin (Executive Vice President) $2,300 to John S McCain • Blecker, Marvin (Executive

Table 5.4.1: Contributions to Presidential Campaigns (2016, 2012 and 2008)			
Year	**2016 Presidential Elections**	**2012 Presidential Elections**	**2008 Presidential Elections**
			Vice President) $1,000 to John S McCain • Bold, William (VP) $2,300 to John S McCain • Grajski, Kamil Dr. (Vice President Engineering) $2,300 to John S McCain • Grajski, Kamil Dr. (Vice President Engineering) $2,300 to John S McCain • Jacobs, Paul E (CEO) $2,300 to John S McCain • Jones, Donald John (Vice President) $1,000 to John S McCain • Lauer, Len J (Executive Vice President) $4,300 to John S McCain • Lupin, Louis

Table 5.4.1: Contributions to Presidential Campaigns (2016, 2012 and 2008)			
Year	**2016 Presidential Elections**	**2012 Presidential Elections**	**2008 Presidential Elections**
			M. (Executive Vice President) $2,300 to John S McCain • Neihardt, Jonas E (Executive Vice President) $2,300 to John S McCain • Neihardt, Jonas E. (Executive Vice President) $1,000 to John S McCain • Sullivan, Daniel L (Executive Vice President) $2,300 to John S McCain • Waltman, Joan Mrs. (President) $2,300 to John S McCain
Total Contributions	**$13,713**	**$22,000**	**$47,550**
Grand Total Contribution – All Years	**$83,263**		
Source:	http://www.fec.gov/		

Table 5.4.2: Company/Entity Staff Contributions to Presidential Campaigns (2016, 2012 and 2008)			
Year	**2016 Presidential Elections**	**2012 Presidential Elections**	**2008 Presidential Elections**
Whether Qualcomm and/or related Entity Staff Contributed to PACs Related to Presidential Candidates	• $1,332 to Hillary Victory Fund	• Nil	• Nil
Whether Qualcomm and/or related Entity Staff Contributed Individually to Presidential Candidates	• $23,889 to Bernard Sanders • $21,542 to Hillary Clinton • $4,350 to Donald J. Trump • $3,210 to Rafael Edward 'Ted' Cruz • $1,700 to Marco Rubio • $1,000 to Jeb Bush • $500 to James Henry Jr. Webb • $300 to John R. Kasich • $200 to Benjamin S. Carson • $150 to Jill	• $98,370 to Barack Obama • $75,626 to Mitt Romney • $6,142 to Ron Paul • $400 to Jon Huntsman • $400 to Michele Bachmann	• $81,361 to Barack Obama • $27,450 to John S McCain • $20,556 to Hillary Clinton • $4,850 to Rudolph W Giuliani • $3,325 to Ron Paul • $950 to Dennis J Kucinich • $550 to Mike Huckabee • $450 to Fred Dalton Thompson • $400 to Bill Richardson • $250 to John Edwards

Table 5.4.2: Company/Entity Staff Contributions to Presidential Campaigns (2016, 2012 and 2008)			
Year	**2016 Presidential Elections**	**2012 Presidential Elections**	**2008 Presidential Elections**
	Stein		
Total Contributions	**$58,173**	**$180,938**	**$140,142**
Grand Total Contribution – All Years	**$379,253**		
Source:	http://www.fec.gov/		

Table 5.4.3: Contributions to Foundations Related to 'Presidential Candidates'	
Whether Qualcomm and Senior Management and/or related Companies/ Foundations/ Family Members Contributed to Foundations Related to Presidential Candidates	• Qualcomm Incorporated has also donated between $100,001 to $250,000 to the Clinton Foundation

Table 5.4.4: Contributions Via Paid Speeches/Assignments to 'Presidential Candidates', Within Three Years of Candidacy Announcement	
Whether Qualcomm and Senior Management and/or related Companies/ Foundations/ Family Members Gave Speaking and Advisory Assignments to Presidential candidates	• 14 October 2014 - $335,000

Table 5.4.5: Hillary Clinton Speeches to Wall Street and Corporate America			
Date	**Entity**	**Location**	**Amount Received for Speech (in US$)**
18th April 2013	Morgan Stanley	Washington, DC	2,25,000
24th April 2013	Deutsche Bank	Washington, DC	2,25,000
24th April 2013	National Multi Housing Council	Dallas, TX	2,25,000
30th April 2013	Fidelity Investments	Naples, FL	2,25,000
5th August 2013	Gap, Inc.	San Francisco, CA	2,25,000
14th May 2013	Apollo Management Holdings, LP	New York, NY	2,25,000
16th May 2013	Itau BBA USA Securities	New York, NY	2,25,000
21st May 2013	Verizon Communications, Inc.	Washington, DC	2,25,000
29th May 2013	Sanford C. Bernstein and Co., LLC	New York, NY	2,25,000
6th April 2013	The Goldman Sachs Group	Palmetto Bluffs, SC	2,25,000
6th June 2013	Spencer Stuart	New York, NY	2,25,000
16th June 2013	Society for Human Resource Management	Chicago, IL	2,85,000
17th June 2013	Economic Club of Grand Rapids	Grand Rapids, MI	2,25,000
20th June 2013	Boston Consulting Group, Inc.	Boston, MA	2,25,000
20th June 2013	Let's Talk Entertainment, Inc.	Toronto, Canada	2,50,000
24th June 2013	American Jewish University	University City, CA	2,25,000
24th June 2013	Kohlberg Kravis Roberts and	Palos Verdes, CA	2,25,000

Table 5.4.5: Hillary Clinton Speeches to Wall Street and Corporate America			
Date	**Entity**	**Location**	**Amount Received for Speech (in US$)**
	Company, LP		
7th November 2013	UBS Wealth Management	New York, NY	2,25,000
8th July 2013	Global Business Travel Association	San Diego, CA	2,25,000
8th December 2013	National Association of Chain Drug Stores	Las Vegas, NV	2,25,000
18th September 2013	American Society for Clinical Pathology	Chicago, IL	2,25,000
19th September 2013	American Society of Travel Agents, Inc.	Miami, FL	2,25,000
10th April 2013	Long Island Association	Long Island, NY	2,25,000
15th October 2013	National Association of Convenience Stores	Atlanta, GA	2,65,000
23rd October 2013	SAP Global Marketing, Inc.	New York, NY	2,25,000
24th October 2013	Accenture	New York, NY	2,25,000
24th October 2013	The Goldman Sachs Group	New York, NY	2,25,000
27th October 2013	Beth El Synagogue	Minneapolis, MN	2,25,000
28th October 2013	Jewish United Fund/Jewish Federation of Metropolitan Chicago	Chicago, IL	4,00,000
29th October 2013	The Goldman Sachs Group	Tuscon, AZ	2,25,000
11th April	Mase Productions,	Orlando, FL	

Table 5.4.5: Hillary Clinton Speeches to Wall Street and Corporate America			
Date	**Entity**	**Location**	**Amount Received for Speech (in US$)**
2013	Inc.		2,25,000
11th April 2013	London Drugs, Ltd.	Mississauga, ON	2,25,000
11th June 2013	Beaumont Health System	Troy, MI	3,05,000
11th July 2013	Golden Tree Asset Management	New York, NY	2,75,000
11th September 2013	National Association of Realtors	San Francisco, CA	2,25,000
13th November 2013	Mediacorp Canada, Inc.	Toronto, Canada	2,25,000
14th November 2013	CB Richard Ellis, Inc.	New York, NY	2,50,000
18th November 2013	CME Group	Naples, FL	2,25,000
18th November 2013	Press Ganey	Orlando, FL	2,25,000
21st November 2013	U.S. Green Building Council	Philadelphia, PA	2,25,000
1st June 2014	GE	Boca Raton, FL	2,25,500
27th January 2014	National Automobile Dealers Association	New Orleans, LA	3,25,500
27th January 2014	Premier Health Alliance	Miami, FL	2,25,500
2nd June 2014	Salesforce.com	Las Vegas, NV	2,25,500
17th February 2014	Novo Nordisk A/S	Mexico City, Mexico	1,25,000

Table 5.4.5: Hillary Clinton Speeches to Wall Street and Corporate America			
Date	**Entity**	**Location**	**Amount Received for Speech (in US$)**
26th February 2014	Healthcare Information and Management Systems Society	Orlando, FL	2,25,500
27th February 2014	A&E Television Networks	New York, NY	2,80,000
3rd April 2014	Association of Corporate Counsel - Southern California	Los Angeles, CA	2,25,500
3rd May 2014	The Vancouver Board of Trade	Vancouver, Canada	2,75,500
3rd June 2014	tinePublic Inc.	Calgary, Canada	2,25,500
13th March 2014	Pharmaceutical Care Management Association	Orlando, FL	2,25,500
13th March 2014	Drug Chemical and Associated Technologies	New York, NY	2,50,000
18th March 2014	Xerox Corporation	New York, NY	2,25,000
18th March 2014	Board of Trade of Metropolitan Montreal	Montreal, Canada	2,75,000
24th March 2014	Academic Partnerships	Dallas, TX	2,25,500
4th August 2014	Marketo, Inc.	San Francisco, CA	2,25,500
4th August 2014	World Affairs Council	Portland, OR	2,50,500
4th October 2014	Institute of Scrap Recycling Industries, Inc.	Las Vegas, NV	2,25,500
4th October 2014	Let's Talk Entertainment	San Jose, CA	2,65,000

Table 5.4.5: Hillary Clinton Speeches to Wall Street and Corporate America			
Date	**Entity**	**Location**	**Amount Received for Speech (in US$)**
4th November 2014	California Medical Association (via Satellite)	San Diego, CA	1,00,000
5th June 2014	National Council for Behavorial Healthcare	Washington, DC	2,25,500
6th February 2014	International Deli-Dairy-Bakery Association	Denver, CO	2,25,500
6th February 2014	Let's Talk Entertainment	Denver, CO	2,65,000
6th October 2014	United Fresh Produce Association	Chicago, IL	2,25,000
18th June 2014	tinePublic Inc.	Toronto, Canada	1,50,000
18th June 2014	tinePublic Inc.	Edmonton, Canada	1,00,000
20th June 2014	Innovation Arts and Entertainment	Austin, TX	1,50,000
25th June 2014	Biotechnology Industry Organization	San Diego, CA	3,35,000
25th June 2014	Innovation Arts and Entertainment	San Francisco, CA	1,50,000
26th June 2014	GTCR	Chicago, IL	2,80,000
22nd July 2014	Knewton, Inc.	San Francisco, CA	2,25,500
26th July 2014	Ameriprise	Boston, MA	2,25,500
29th July 2014	Corning, Inc.	Corning, NY	2,25,500
28th August 2014	Nexenta System, Inc.	San Francisco, CA	3,00,000
28th August 2014	Cisco	Las Vegas, NV	3,25,000

Table 5.4.5: Hillary Clinton Speeches to Wall Street and Corporate America			
Date	**Entity**	**Location**	**Amount Received for Speech (in US$)**
9th April 2014	Robbins Geller Rudman & Dowd, LLP	San Diego, CA	2,25,500
15th September 2014	Cardiovascular Research Foundation	Washington, DC	2,75,000
10th February 2014	Commercial Real Estate Women Network	Miami Beach, FL	2,25,500
10th June 2014	Canada 2020	Ottawa, Canada	2,15,500
10th July 2014	Deutsche Bank AG	New York, NY	2,80,000
10th August 2014	Advanced Medical Technology Association (AdvaMed)	Chicago, IL	2,65,000
13th October 2014	Council of Insurance Agents and Brokers	Colorado Springs, CO	2,25,500
14th October 2014	Salesforce.com	San Francisco, CA	2,25,500
14th October 2014	Qualcomm Incorporated	San Diego, CA	3,35,000
12th April 2014	Massachusetts Conference for Women	Boston, MA	2,05,500
21st January 2015	tinePublic Inc.	Winnipeg, Canada	2,62,000
21st January 2015	tinePublic Inc.	Saskatoon, Canada	2,62,500
22nd January 2015	Canadian Imperial Bank of Commerce	Whistler, Canada	1,50,000
24th February 2015	Watermark Silicon Valley Conference for Women	Santa Clara, CA	2,25,500
3rd November	eBay Inc.	San Jose, CA	3,15,000

Table 5.4.5: Hillary Clinton Speeches to Wall Street and Corporate America			
Date	**Entity**	**Location**	**Amount Received for Speech (in US$)**
2015			
19th March 2015	American Camping Association	Atlantic City, NJ	2,60,000
	TOTAL FEES RECEIVED		21,442,000
Compiled from http://www.releasethetranscripts.com/			

Appendix 6

Appendix 6.1: Vinod Gupta

Table 6.1.1: Contributions to Presidential Campaigns (2016, 2012 and 2008)			
Year	**2016 Presidential Elections**	**2012 Presidential Elections**	**2008 Presidential Elections**
Whether Vinod Gupta Contributed to **PACs Related to Presidential Candidates?**	• $33,000 to Hillary Victory Fund	• $1,000 to Priorities USA Action, PAC supporting Obama • $15,000 to End The Gridlock	• Nil
Whether Vinod Gupta Contributed Individually to Presidential Candidates?	• $2,700 to Hillary Clinton • $2,700 to Hillary Clinton • $2,700 to John RKasich	• $505 to Barack Obama	• $2,300 to Hillary Clinton • $2,300 to John S McCain
Total Contributions	**$41,100**	**$16,505**	**$4,600**
Grand Total Contribution – All Years	**$62,205**		
Source:	http://www.fec.gov/		

Table 6.1.2: Company/Entity Staff Contributions to Presidential Campaigns (2016, 2012 and 2008)			
Year	**2016 Presidential Elections**	**2012 Presidential Elections**	**2008 Presidential Elections**
Whether Vinod Gupta Company/ Entity Staff Contributed to PACs Related to Presidential Candidates Company – infoGROUP and Everest Group	• Nil	• Nil	• Nil
Whether Vinod Gupta Company/ Entity Staff Contributed Individually to Presidential Candidates Company - infoGROUP and Everest Group	• $15,146 to Hillary Clinton • $2,275 to Rafael Edward 'Ted' Cruz • $1,321 to Bernard Sanders	• $5,123 to Barack Obama • $500 to Mitt Romney • $450 to Ron Paul	• $3,680 to Barack Obama • $3,250 to Hillary Clinton • $164 to John S McCain
Total Contributions	**$18,742**	**$6,073**	**$7,094**
Grand Total Contribution – All Years	**$31,909**		
Source:	http://www.fec.gov/		

Table 6.1.3: Family Members' Contributions to Presidential Campaigns (2016, 2012 and 2008)			
Year	**2016 Presidential Elections**	**2012 Presidential Elections**	**2008 Presidential Elections**
Whether Vinod Gupta Family Members Contributed Individually and/or to PACs Related to Presidential Candidates	• Nil	• Gupta, Jess $2,500 to Barack Obama	• Gupta, Alexander A $2,300 to Hillary Clinton • Gupta, Jess $2,300 to Hillary Clinton • Gupta, Jess $2,300 to Hillary Clinton
Total Contributions	-	**$2,500**	**$6,900**
Grand Total Contribution – All Years	**$9,400**		
Source:	http://www.fec.gov/		

Table 6.1.4: Contributions to Foundations Related to 'Presidential Candidates'	
Whether Vinod Gupta and/or his Companies/ Foundations/ Family Members Contributed to Foundations Related to Presidential Candidates	• Vinod Gupta has also donated between $1,000,001 to $5,000,000 to the Clinton Foundation • InfoGROUP has also donated between $250,001 to $500,000 to the Clinton Foundation

Appendix 6.2: Sant Singh Chatwal

Table 6.2.1: Contributions to Presidential Campaigns (2016, 2012 and 2008)			
Year	**2016 Presidential Elections**	**2012 Presidential Elections**	**2008 Presidential Elections**
Whether Sant Singh Chatwal Contributed to **PACs Related to Presidential Candidates?**	• Nil	• Nil	• Nil
Whether Sant Singh Chatwal Contributed Individually to Presidential Candidates?	• Nil	• Nil	• $2,300 to Hillary Clinton
Total Contributions	**-**	**-**	**$2,300**
Grand Total Contribution – All Years	**$2,300**		
Source:	http://www.fec.gov/		

Table 6.2.2: Family Members' Contributions to Presidential Campaigns (2016, 2012 and 2008)			
Year	**2016 Presidential Elections**	**2012 Presidential Elections**	**2008 Presidential Elections**
Whether Sant Singh Chatwal Family Members Contributed Individually and/or to PACs Related to Presidential Candidates	• Nil	• Nil	• Chatwal, Vikram $2,300 to Hillary Clinton • Chatwal, Vivek $2,300 to Hillary Clinton • Chatwal, Vikram

Table 6.2.2: Family Members' Contributions to Presidential Campaigns (2016, 2012 and 2008)			
Year	**2016 Presidential Elections**	**2012 Presidential Elections**	**2008 Presidential Elections**
			$5,000 to National Leadership PAC
Total Contributions	-	-	**$9,600**
Grand Total Contribution – All Years	**$9,600**		
Source:	http://www.fec.gov/		

Table 6.2.3: Contributions to Foundations Related to 'Presidential Candidates'	
Whether Sant Singh Chatwal and/or his Companies/Foundations/ Family Members Contributed to Foundations Related to Presidential Candidates	• Hampshire Hotels & Resorts, LLC has also donated between $250,001 to $500,000 to the Clinton Foundation

Appendix 6.3: Victor P. Dahdaleh

Table 6.3.1: Contributions to Foundations Related to 'Presidential Candidates'	
Whether Victor Dahdaleh and/or his Companies/Foundations/ Family Members Contributed to Foundations Related to Presidential Candidates	• Victor P Dahdaleh & The Victor Phillip Dahdaleh Charitable Foundation has also donated between $1,000,001 to $5,000,000 to the Clinton Foundation

Appendix 7: Marc Lasry

Table 7.1: Contributions to Presidential Campaigns (2016, 2012 and 2008)			
Year	**2016 Presidential Elections**	**2012 Presidential Elections**	**2008 Presidential Elections**
Whether Marc Lasry Contributed to **PACs Related to Presidential Candidates?**	• $33,400 to Hillary Victory Fund	• Nil	• Nil
Whether Marc Lasry Contributed Individually to Presidential Candidates?	• $2,700 to Hillary Clinton • $2,700 to Hillary Clinton	• $2,500 to Barack Obama • $2,500 to Barack Obama	• $2,300 to Barack Obama • $2,300 to Barack Obama
Total Contributions	**$38,800**	**$5,000**	**$4,600**
Grand Total Contribution – All Years	**$48,400**		
Source:	http://www.fec.gov/		

Table 7.2: Company/Entity Staff Contributions to Presidential Campaigns (2016, 2012 and 2008)			
Year	**2016 Presidential Elections**	**2012 Presidential Elections**	**2008 Presidential Elections**
Whether Marc Lasry Company/ Entity Staff Contributed to PACs Related to Presidential Candidates Company -	• Nil	• Nil	• Nil

Table 7.2: Company/Entity Staff Contributions to Presidential Campaigns (2016, 2012 and 2008)			
Year	**2016 Presidential Elections**	**2012 Presidential Elections**	**2008 Presidential Elections**
Avenue Capital Group			
Whether Marc Lasry Company/ Entity Staff Contributed Individually to Presidential Candidates Company - Avenue Capital Group	• $37,129 to Hillary Clinton	• $6,520 to Barack Obama	• $16,200 to Hillary Clinton • $4,150 to Barack Obama • $100 to John S McCain
Total Contributions	**$37,129**	**$6,520**	**$20,450**
Grand Total Contribution – All Years	**$64,099**		
Source:	http://www.fec.gov/		

Table 7.3: Family Members' Contributions to Presidential Campaigns (2016, 2012 and 2008)			
Year	**2016 Presidential Elections**	**2012 Presidential Elections**	**2008 Presidential Elections**
Whether Marc Lasry Family Members Contributed Individually and/or to PACs Related to Presidential Candidates	• Lasry Fleisher, Samantha $2,700 to Hillary Clinton • Lasry, Cathy $2,700 to Hillary Clinton • Lasry, Cathy $2,700 to Hillary Clinton • Lasry, Alexander Jacob $2,525 to	• Nil	• Nil

Table 7.3: Family Members' Contributions to Presidential Campaigns (2016, 2012 and 2008)			
Year	**2016 Presidential Elections**	**2012 Presidential Elections**	**2008 Presidential Elections**
	Hillary Clinton • Lasry, Cathy $33,400 to Hillary Victory Fund • Lasry, Alexander Jacob $471 to Hillary Victory Fund		
Total Contributions	**$44,496**	**-**	**-**
Grand Total Contribution – All Years	**$44,496**		
Source:	http://www.fec.gov/		

Table 7.4: Contributions to Foundations Related to 'Presidential Candidates'	
Whether Marc Lasry and/or his Companies/ Foundations/ Family Members Contributed to Foundations Related to Presidential Candidates	• Marc Lasry has also donated between $100,001 to $250,000 to the Clinton Foundation • Avenue Capital Management II, L.P. (operates as a subsidiary of Avenue Capital Group.) has also donated between $50,000 to $100,000 to the Clinton Foundation

Table 7.5: Contributions Via Paid Speeches/Assignments to 'Presidential Candidates', Within Three Years of Candidacy Announcement	
Whether Marc Lasry and/or his Companies/ Foundations/ Family Members Gave Speaking and Advisory Assignments to Presidential candidates	• Nil

About the Author

Ramesh S Arunachalam wears many hats. In the last two decades, he has been a columnist (with the *Hindu Business Line* and *Moneylife*), an entrepreneur, a filmmaker and also a development practitioner working on issues pertaining to financial inclusion and livelihood security. His clients include both state and national governments, bi-lateral and multi-lateral agencies, and the private sector in countries across Asia, Africa, North America and Europe.

Title – **Where Angels Prey**
Author – Ramesh S Arunachalam
Size – 5.5 inches × 8.5 inches
No of Pages – 204
Binding – Paperback
ISBN – 978-9384439378

While the rest of the world reels under a severe financial crisis, India's microfinance sector enjoys an unprecedented boom. Why on earth are people investing such huge amounts of money in an obscure industry, especially at the time of global recession? And why is Wall Street suddenly so interested in India's poor?

That is exactly what Robert Bradlee, senior correspondent with *The New York Post*, sets off to investigate, along with his journalist friend, Chandresh. Little does he know that his search for a scoop would lead him through a complex multi-pronged web of deceit, fraud, manipulation and financial crime, remote controlled from distant lands by an entire chain of financial sector stakeholders.

Gripping, racy and meticulously researched, this financial thriller weaves in and out of the affluent world of high-powered boardrooms and the gruelling poverty of the remotest villages of India, to reveal the devastating truths that often lurk behind "good intentions".

www.ingramcontent.com/pod-product-compliance
Lightning Source LLC
Chambersburg PA
CBHW050435290526
45786CB00006B/2041

* 9 7 8 1 5 3 7 6 8 0 0 9 5 *